Accounting
for
Business

SECOND CANADIAN EDITION

Jack Sands

What the numbers mean and how to use them

ARENA BOOKS
Toronto

Accounting for Business

Copyright © 1999, 2002 by John E. Sands

Published by
Arena Books Inc.
Toronto, Canada

National Library of Canada Cataloguing in Publication

Sands, Jack, 1930-
    Accounting for business : what the numbers mean and how to use them/
Jack Sands. — 2nd Canadian ed.

Includes index.
ISBN 0-9685621-2-4

    1. Accounting.   I. Title.

HF5635.S175 2002   657'.042   C2002-901763-7

Printed and bound in Canada.

For
Parvin and Ian

Acknowledgements

I want to acknowledge the help of two people in producing this work, my daughter Nancy and my wife Parvin.

Nancy was an English major at university who, until she read my drafts, knew virtually nothing about accounting. Nancy cleaned up my language in places but most important, she was able to show me where I failed to explain things adequately.

I am grateful to Parvin for listening long and patiently while I agonized and for supporting my efforts throughout.

For the rest, I am to blame.

Contents

Introduction

Accounting is a process. It is a process of recording, measuring, interpreting and communicating information about economic wealth and income.

The accounting process can be applied to virtually any entity, a person, a group of people, a business corporation, a not-for-profit corporation, a government, anything to which economic wealth can be attributed. The focus of this book is on accounting for business. In accounting for business, income is a key element. It is not always an important factor in accounting for not-for-profit entities.

Everyone is affected by accounting. Business managers rely on it to plan and control their operations. Owners, investors, and creditors use it to assess management performance and the merits of alternative investments and loans. Governments use it for purposes of taxation and regulation. People who might never use it directly are affected by the decisions of those who do. It is useful, therefore, for everyone to have an understanding of the meaning and uses of accounting information. For people involved with business as investors, managers, administrators or creditors, it is essential.

Accountants are people who perform the accounting process. To be an accountant, one must learn the appropriate methods and techniques of recording and processing economic data. Most people don't want to be accountants, some do. This book is directed mainly towards those who don't want to be accountants; investors, managers and students who take a single course in the subject; who want to know what accounting data mean but don't want to be part of the process of producing the data. For them, it contains probably everything they need to know about the subject, with a minimum of technical detail. For those who think they do want to be accountants, the book is an appropriate place to start. It is an introductory overview, covering a wide range of business accounting topics and providing a broad foundation for additional study.

Most business managers and accountants are men, but large and increasing proportions of both are women. At some places in the book, it is necessary to refer to a manager or accountant as he or she. Unfortunately, there is no pronoun in the English language meaning either. Constantly repeating the phrase "he or she" to describe a person of either sex is tedious and redundant. Instead, in most places, the single pronoun he is used, as in calling the human race mankind.

Although the range of subject matter covered is extensive, the book is relatively short. There is no filler, so don't attempt to skim it. Like most social intercourse, it is best when taken slowly. Relax and enjoy it.

PART

I

—

BASICS

CHAPTER 1

Business Organization

As a preliminary to understanding accounting for business, one should understand the legal forms a business can take. Almost all businesses take one of the following forms:

- Proprietorship
- Partnership
- Corporation

The following are brief descriptions of the distinctions between them and the advantages and disadvantages of each.

PROPRIETORSHIP

A proprietorship is simply an individual in business for himself. He usually manages the business and takes whatever profits are made from it. A proprietorship is characterized by its lack of legal form. The law makes no distinction between a proprietorship and the proprietor. The business creditors of a proprietorship have an equal right to demand payment from the proprietor's personal wealth as from the business, and the personal creditors can demand payment from business resources as well as personal. Many proprietors do not distinguish clearly themselves between those things that are business and those that are personal. For example, a proprietor might use part of a residence for business purposes at times, or use a car for both business and pleasure.

Many businesses are operated as proprietorships. Since they are not legally distinct from the proprietors, they have the advantage of being able to do anything an individual can do. On the other hand, they have the disadvantage of being dependent on the continued existence of a single individual for their own continuity. They are not subject to income taxes separately from their proprietors, which can be an advantage or a disadvantage, depending on the circumstances. Proprietorships are found mainly in businesses that can be carried on without large investments, such as retailing, small scale farming and the professions.

PARTNERSHIP

A partnership is two or more individuals in business for their common advantage. It is formed simply by the agreement of the parties to carry on business together. Agreements should be in writing to avoid misunderstandings between partners, but unwritten agreements can be legally binding.

In most partnerships, all partners take some part in the management of the business. In the absence of agreement among them to the contrary, they all have an equal right to do so. Outsiders dealing with a partnership are entitled to assume that all partners have the authority to act on its behalf in any capacity, unless the outsiders are informed of restrictions to the contrary.

Partners can agree to any form of compensation or profit sharing among themselves that they wish. Profits and losses are usually shared by partners on the basis of predetermined ratios. Fixed salaries and interest on investment are often paid to partners before the determination of profits to be shared in the agreed ratios. In the absence of agreement as to the distribution of profits and losses, no salaries or interest are payable, and the profits are equally divisible among the partners.

In a partnership, a greater distinction is made between those things that belong to the business and those that belong to the partners, than in a proprietorship. Those that belong to a partnership are owned jointly, not severally, by the partners; that is, they are owned by the partners as a group, not as individuals. It is important therefore, that the partners understand and agree clearly among themselves what things belong to the business and how they may be withdrawn by the partners.

The business creditors of a partnership are entitled to claim payment from the personal wealth of the partners, just as the creditors of a proprietorship can from the personal wealth of the proprietor; their personal creditors however, have a prior claim to payment from their personal resources. In the same way, the business creditors of a partnership have a prior claim to payment from the resources of the business, over the personal creditors of the partners.

Legally, a partnership ends whenever a partner withdraws from, or a new partner joins the partnership. The business might carry on virtually unchanged after a change in partners, but it is a new partnership. Since a partnership is formed by agreement among the partners, no new partner can enter without the agreement of all.

Partnerships have the advantages of proprietorships, of being able to do anything an individual can do, via one of the partners. In addition, they have the advantage of being able to draw on the wealth, borrowing power and management abilities of more than one person. As a practical matter, most partnerships consist of relatively few partners. Too many can make the management of a business top-heavy and unwieldy. In addition, since any partner can deal with, and commit the business to outsiders on behalf of the group, in the absence of specific instructions to those outsiders to the contrary, the larger the number of partners, the more hazardous is the arrangement for an individual partner.

Besides having the disadvantages that any partner can usually commit the whole group to others, and personal wealth is risked along with business resources, partnerships suffer from the fact that they are legally terminated whenever a partner leaves, and all partners must agree to the admission of a new one. This can make it very difficult for a partner to sell his interest in a business to anyone else. Many profitable partnership businesses have to be terminated because the partners cannot agree, and no one has sufficient wealth of his own, nor can he find prospective new partners with it, to purchase the interests of the others. It can also impose serious financial difficulties on a partnership business when a partner dies, and the value of his interest must be paid to his heirs, either because the heirs do not want to become partners or because the other partners do not want them. To overcome this latter problem, partnerships often purchase insurance policies on the lives of the individual partners, so that funds will be available in the event of a death to repay the ownership interest of the deceased partner.

When partnership interests are sold or repaid, the selling partner or partners continue to be liable for the debts of the partnership existing at the date of sale.

Like proprietors, partners are subject to income taxes directly on their share of partnership earnings.

Limited Partnership

A variation of the general partnership form of organization is the limited partnership. In a limited partnership, one or more partners are limited in their rights to make decisions regarding the operation of the partnership, and in their obligations to creditors. Limited partners retain the right to vote on basic matters such as a change in the nature of the business, but give up any right to participate in the management. In return, their liability to creditors is limited to the amount of their investment in the partnership. Unlike general partners, their personal wealth is not at risk.

Limited partnerships must have at least one general partner responsible for management and fully liable to creditors. In the absence of other provisions, profits and losses are shared by limited partners in proportion to their investment, not equally as in the case of general partnerships.

CORPORATION

A corporation is an entity separate and distinct from the people who own it and manage it. It can be described as an artificial person. Corporations are created by law. Canada and each of the provinces have corporations or companies statutes. A corporation is formed by the grant of a licence to operate, known as a charter or as articles of incorporation, to applicants, under a companies statute.

Ownership of a corporation is represented by shares issued to investors. Management is delegated to a board of directors, elected by some or all of the shareholders, depending on the nature of their shares. Some kinds of shares include the right to vote for directors and others do not, some carry the right to multiple votes, others to only a single vote. The directors usually concern themselves only with matters of overall policy and direction. The day to day management of a corporation is conducted by a group of officers, a president, vice-presidents, treasurer, and others appointed by the board of directors. The shareholders as such have no authority to enter into the management or operations of the business, except through the election of directors.

Unlike proprietors and partners, shareholders are not personally liable to creditors for the debts of a corporation. Their risk is limited to the cost of their share investment. Similarly, creditors of shareholders cannot demand payment from the corporation, although they might be able to seize the shares owned by a debtor in some circumstances. Because the liability of shareholders is limited, statutes usually require corporations to identify themselves by including in their names words, or abbreviations of words, such as Limited or Incorporated.

A corporation usually has an unlimited lifetime. The death of one or all of its shareholders does not terminate it, the shares simply pass to their heirs. Shareholders cannot demand the return of their investment from a corporation, unless the shares they hold were issued with that provision.

Most large businesses are public corporations. Public corporations offer their shares for sale to the general public. Once issued, the shares are freely transferable. In most cases, the shares are traded regularly in organized stock markets.

The right to go to the public for funding carries with it the responsibility to keep shareholders and others adequately informed about a corporation. Public corporations are required to make regular reports in specified forms. Detailed annual financial reports and summarized quarterly reports are published, and additional data are provided to regulatory bodies and to stock exchanges.

Public corporations have the advantage that they are able to obtain funding from large numbers of investors through the issue of shares to the public, without having to extend the right to manage to those investors, except to the extent that some can vote for directors. The investors do not risk any more than the cost of their shares because they have no personal liability to creditors of the business, unlike proprietors and partners.

This arrangement is essential for the financing of businesses that require a large amount of money to operate. From the standpoint of the business, it means that management can be turned over to a small, able group of professionals, while funds are drawn from any who wish to invest. From the standpoint of individual investors, it means that they can put their money to work without having a large amount, without becoming involved in the management of a business, and without risking any more than they choose. In addition, the fact that shares in public corporations are actively traded means investors can buy shares in a variety of businesses with a relatively small amount of money, so their investment is not dependent on the success or failure of a single enterprise, and they can invest for as short or long a period of time as they wish.

The separation of management from investment in a corporation can be a disadvantage to shareholders. The interests of the managing group do not always coincide with the interests of other shareholders. In public corporations, control is often maintained by an individual or group owning a relatively small proportion of the total shares issued, when the remainder are widely scattered. Dissatisfied shareholders can sell their shares, but if other potential buyers do not have the same interests as the control group, the market price of the shares will be depressed.

Corporations are subject to tax on their income separately from their shareholders, and at rates different from those applicable to shareholders. When they distribute their income to shareholders in the form of dividends, the shareholders are taxed again on the dividends. This usually results in more tax in total to shareholders than to proprietors and partners in similar businesses, but not always. Depending on the amount of dividends paid, available tax deductions, and the taxable status of shareholders, some can have lower taxes.

Private Corporation

Many smaller businesses are private corporations. In private corporations, the number of shareholders is limited and the transfer of shares between owners is restricted.

Private corporations are usually incorporated for tax reasons or to limit business risk. Shareholders in private corporations can arrange their affairs so that payments they receive from the corporations are in the form of salary, or interest on loans to the corporation, or dividends out of corporate earnings. By choosing the right combination, they can minimize the total taxes payable.

Business risk is reduced by private corporation shareholders, because their personal wealth cannot be claimed by business creditors, except to the extent they might owe money to the corporation. Recognizing this limitation, some creditors, notably banks and other lenders, require shareholders in private corporations to guarantee the payment of corporate debts.

CHAPTER 2

The Balance Sheet

ASSETS

For an individual, wealth can mean many things. It can mean money in the bank, a good home, good health, a safe environment, and so on. For accounting purposes, not all of those things are included. Accounting is a process of measurement and communication. The value of wealth must be measurable and the measurement must be objective. For accounting purposes, wealth is defined as those things that can be and are exchanged for money. The amount of money paid for something is the objective measure of its value. Things that cannot be exchanged, such as good health, are excluded. Things their owners might think have much greater value, patents for example, are recorded at their cost.

In accounting terminology, wealth is described as assets. There is a wide variety of assets. Cash, productive equipment, stock in trade, and the debts owed to a business by its customers are some of the more common forms. Assets can be divided into the following three categories, according to their basic characteristics:

- Tangibles
- Claims and Currency
- Intangibles

Tangibles

Tangibles are those assets that exist in solid form, that is, those that can be seen and touched. They are things that can be consumed. The tangible assets of any business can be divided into two types, those that are used up or consumed physically, and those that provide services to the business. Tangible assets that are used up physically are generally described as **inventories**. Assets that provide services are usually described as **property, plant and equipment**, or simply **plant and equipment**, or sometimes as **fixed assets** or **capital assets**.

Inventories   Inventories are used up physically either by being sold or by being used in production. A business such as an advertising agency, that sells services rather than goods, will not have inventories. A trading business, that is, a wholesaler or retailer, will have only inventories of merchandise for sale. A manufacturer will have inventories of **raw materials**, **work in process**, that is, partly manufactured goods, and **finished goods** available for sale. The term raw materials is used to describe those materials a manufacturer starts with to create his product, it is not a term for natural resources. Whether something is described as raw material or finished good depends on the nature of the business, not on the characteristics of the asset itself. Lumber is a finished good for a lumber producer but raw material for a furniture manufacturer.

Occasionally miscellaneous goods such as office supplies are segregated from the inventory category and described as **prepaid expenses**, particularly by businesses that sell services not goods.

Natural resources, things such as mining properties and oil wells, are a specialized form of inventory, segregated from other forms and described generally as **wasting assets** or **depletable assets**. As the value of the resources is extracted, they are said to be depleted.

Property, Plant and Equipment   Property, plant and equipment consists of **land**, **buildings** and various kinds of **equipment**. Some of the more common classes of equipment are **machinery**, **furniture and fixtures**, and **automotive equipment**.

Whether an asset is described as property, plant and equipment, inventory, or depletable asset, depends on how it is used. The same automobile could be equipment to a cab company and inventory to a car maker. The same plot of land could be property to a resort owner, inventory to a real estate developer and depletable asset to a mining company.

Some land has more than one use. A mining property, for example, could be the site for a smelter as well as a source of extractable material. In that case it might be considered property for part of its value and depletable asset for the remainder.

Land used as a site or location for a business does not wear out, but all other forms of plant and equipment eventually do. As their capacity to render services is gradually used up, buildings and equipment are said to depreciate. For that reason, they are often described as **depreciable assets**.

Claims and Currency

Claims are rights to receive payment or service from someone else, from another business or a person or a government. Most claims arise from the day to day trading operations of a business. They include claims against banks and others for money deposited, claims against customers for payment for goods and services provided, and claims against suppliers for advance payments made.

Some claims arise from lending to or investing in someone or something else. Government bonds and corporation shares for example, represent claims for amounts lent or invested.

Currency consists of coins and bills issued by central banks which represent national governments. Originally, it consisted of precious metals and claims against precious metals held by governments. Today, governments no longer hold precious metals equivalent to the currency they issue. The value of currency depends on the taxing and borrowing abilities of the country.

Claims and currency are grouped in three main categories, cash, receivables and investments.

Cash Cash consists of **currency** and **bank deposits**, provided they are freely available for withdrawal. Restricted deposits, such as those for fixed time periods are classified as investments, not as cash.

Receivables   Most receivables arise from credit sales to customers. They can be either **accounts receivable** or **notes receivable**. Most businesses that sell on credit do so on what is called open book account, that is, their claim for payment is substantiated only by evidence of having provided the goods or services. These claims are simply accounts receivable. Occasionally a business extending credit will require the debtor to sign a note promising to pay the amount, usually with interest, by a certain date. These are described as notes receivable. When notes are required, it is usually because the credit has been extended for a longer period of time and the creditor business wants to obtain cash in the meantime by selling or discounting the note to a bank or other financial institution.

Accounts receivable can arise from other sources as well as from sales to customers. A claim for damages from a supplier, a carrier, an insurance company, or some other individual or organization for example, can give rise to an account receivable. **Advances** are sometimes made to employees against salaries or commissions, or for the payment of business expenses. Some suppliers, such as utilities, require advance **deposits** as an assurance that their accounts will be paid.

Advance payments for rent, insurance and municipal taxes are commonly segregated and described as **prepaid expenses**.

Investments   Investments are made in many forms for a variety of reasons. Businesses often invest temporary excess funds in short term bank notes or other marketable securities for a better rate of return than that available on simple bank deposits. Shares of other companies can be held for the purpose of controlling those companies, and loans can be made to assist in their financing. Investments in other companies can be purchased over an extended period of time and accumulated in a special fund to be sold at a later date for some special purpose, such as the repayment of an obligation or the purchase of a new plant. Insurance policies with cash surrender values are sometimes purchased on the lives of company executives to soften the financial blow of the loss of an important member of management.

Intangibles

Intangibles represent the conditions and circumstances in which a business operates, that contribute to its profits. They are what economists describe as conditions of imperfect competition. Some conditions, notably those represented by legal rights, can be identified specifically, for example the right represented by a patent to be the only producer of a certain product or user of a certain process. Most conditions, things like consumer tastes, cannot.

Identifiable intangibles include such things as **patents**, **copyrights**, **trade marks**, **franchises**, and **licences**. All those intangibles taken together that are not specifically identified in accounting are called **goodwill**. Goodwill includes not only the favorable attitudes of customers and employees toward a business and its products, but such things as the absence of competitors in the immediate vicinity. Every business has goodwill, since every business operates at least to some degree in a competitive environment. If a business is able to show a profit, its goodwill has a positive value; if it suffers losses, its goodwill is negative. Goodwill is recorded in accounting only under certain circumstances, which are explained later.

The use of the term intangibles in accounting can be misleading. The word intangible means lacking physical substance. Intangible assets do lack physical substance but that is not their distinguishing characteristic. Claims also lack physical substance. The distinguishing feature of intangible assets is that they represent competitive advantages.

EQUITIES

Businesses have obligations as well as assets. The obligations of a business include such things as the amounts owing to suppliers for goods purchased on credit, amounts owing to lenders for loans taken, and amounts owing to owners. The obligations of a business are described as equities. Equities are the same sort of thing as asset claims. Every amount owing to somebody is an amount owing by somebody else. For every claim against assets, someone must have a claim for assets.

In the final analysis all equities are similar, in that they all represent sources from which the assets of a business have been financed. Assets are financed by the purchase of goods on credit for example, just as they are by the investment of cash by an owner for the purpose of making purchases, and the assets of a business can be expanded through the use of more supplier credit just as they can through more owner investment. There are important economic and legal distinctions however, between the claims of creditors, suppliers and lenders, and those of owners. Creditors have a prior claim over owners against the assets of a business, but the amount of their claim is fixed, or will be fixed by reference to a contract. Owners rank last in priority for payment, but they are entitled to everything left after the creditors have been paid.

Equities can be divided into the following three categories:

- Operating Liabilities
- Borrowing Liabilities
- Ownership

Operating Liabilities

Operating liabilities are debts that arise out of the day to day operations of a business. They include amounts owing on the purchase of goods and services, tax liabilities, advance receipts and deposits from customers, and product liabilities.

Debts that arise out of individual transactions, such as the purchase of inventories, are described as **accounts payable**. Those that accumulate over time, such as for wages, are called **accrued liabilities**. Accounts payable and accrued liabilities are common to most businesses. Other forms of operating liabilities may or may not arise, depending on the nature of the business. They can include taxes, unearned revenues, deposit liabilities and product liabilities.

Unearned Revenues, sometimes called **deferred credits**, are amounts received in advance from customers for goods and services. They include such things as the amounts received by airlines on the sale of future flight accommodation, and the amounts received by magazine publishers on the sale of subscriptions for future issues.

Deposit Liabilities include such things as amounts put up by customers and suppliers as assurance that they will make payments and fulfil commitments according to contract, and amounts payable on the return of containers currently in customers' hands.

Product Liabilities are amounts that will have to be paid by a business in order to fulfil commitments with respect to goods and services it has sold. They include amounts payable under product guaranties and warranties.

Borrowing Liabilities

For accounting purposes, borrowing liabilities are divided into two categories, short term and long term.

Short term borrowings are loans repayable within one year. Businesses borrow short term for the purpose of increasing temporarily their investment in inventories and receivables. These are usually businesses that experience seasonal fluctuations in sales or production and therefore need to carry more inventory and advance more credit at some times of the year. Most current loans are made by banks, although some other financial institutions make them as well. Lenders often require special assurance that they will be repaid, in the form of a mortgage or lien or similar attachment to assets of the borrowing business.

Long term borrowings take one of the following four forms:

- Term Loans
- Instalment Purchases
- Lease Contracts
- Bonds and Debentures

Term Loans   Term loans are borrowings repayable over a period of years. They are taken most often by small to medium sized businesses that have opportunities for profitable expansion, but lack ownership money to take advantage of them. The loans are repaid and replaced by ownership investment out of future profits. Term loans are made by a variety of financial institutions. The lenders nearly always require a mortgage on some or all of the fixed assets of the business.

Instalment Purchases   Many businesses are able to purchase equipment by instalments payable over a period of years. Instalment purchases are usually made under arrangements by which the seller can repossess the equipment for non payment of his account. There is no difference in principle between this procedure and borrowing money on a term loan to buy the equipment.

Lease Contracts   In recent years it has become increasingly popular for businesses to lease fixed assets instead of buying them. It is now possible to lease a wide variety of machinery and equipment, as well as land and buildings. When businesses enter into extended lease contracts for the use of fixed assets, they are simply substituting one form of obligation for another, the lease contract for a loan contract. The treatment of lease obligations in accounting varies, depending on the terms of the lease. This subject is dealt with later.

Bonds and Debentures   Many public corporations and some other large businesses borrow from the public and from institutional investors such as pension and mutual funds, by issuing bonds and debentures. The issue of bonds and debentures to lenders is similar to the issue of shares to shareholders, except that the bonds and debentures are debt securities, not ownership. This form of borrowing is generally available to companies with substantial holdings of tangible assets and a proven record of profitability. For those companies, bond and debenture borrowings are usually a relatively permanent source of financing. As the borrowings come due, new bonds or debentures are issued to raise the money to repay them.

Bonds and debentures are usually secured by a mortgage on some or all of the fixed assets of a company, or by some other form of attachment on its assets that takes precedence over other creditors as well as over the owners. Bonds and debentures are described in more detail in Chapter 10.

Ownership

The description given to the ownership equity in a business depends on the form of business organization.

The equity of a **proprietor** is usually called either **proprietorship** or **capital**.

In a **partnership**, each partner's equity is called **capital**. In some partnerships a distinction is made between a portion of each partner's equity that is considered permanent and a portion that can be withdrawn. In that case, the permanent portion is called capital and the remainder is current account or loan.

In **corporations**, the equity of owners is divided into two parts, the amount paid in to the corporation by the owners and the amount of profits accumulated and retained by the corporation from its operations. Amounts paid in are described as **capital**. Accumulated profits are described as **retained earnings**. If the corporation has an accumulated loss instead of profits, it is described as **deficit**.

EQUITIES EQUAL ASSETS

The equities of every business or other entity always equal its assets. They both represent the same thing, the money invested. Assets show what the money bought; equities show where the money came from. Assets show the forms of an entity's wealth; equities show the sources of that wealth.

While assets equal equities in total, it is seldom possible to attribute specific assets to specific equities. A trade creditor for example, is entitled to payment of his claim from any or all of the assets of a business, not just from the existing cash or from the goods he supplied. Some creditors hold a lien or mortgage or other attachment against specific assets, but that does not mean that they have no claim to payment out of the other assets, nor that others cannot be paid out of the attached assets, as long as the lien- or mortgage-holders are paid first.

Owners hold the residual equity in assets, after all the liabilities to creditors have been satisfied. The proprietor holds the residual equity in a proprietorship, the partners in a partnership and the shareholders in a corporation. Ownership equals net assets, that is assets minus liabilities.

The fundamental identity of accounting, that assets equal equities, or that assets equal liabilities plus ownership, is the basis of the balance sheet. A balance sheet is a listing of the assets and equities of a business as at a given date. The name balance sheet comes from the fact that the statement balances, that is, that the assets and equities are equal. A balance sheet is a statement of financial position.

CURRENT POSITION

One of the most important factors in assessing the financial position of a business is the relationship between the amounts invested in **circulating**

assets, those that are acquired and disposed of constantly in the operation of the business, and the amounts that must be paid to creditors in the immediate future. If a business is to remain solvent, it must generate enough cash from its circulating assets to pay its liabilities as they come due. Assets that circulate are described as **current assets**. Liabilities coming due shortly are described as **current liabilities**. The relationship between them is the **current position** of the business. The excess of current assets over current liabilities is known as **working capital**.

Current assets are generally defined as those that are expected to be turned into cash within one year. In addition to **cash**, they include **short term investments**, **receivables**, **inventories** and **prepaid expenses**. Short term investments are normally temporary investments of excess cash. Receivables are constantly being acquired, mainly from credit sales, and eliminated by collection in cash. Inventories are constantly being purchased and sold or used up in production for sale. Prepayments are made for goods and services to be received and used in the near future. Prepaid expenses normally will not and often cannot be turned into cash, but their existence eliminates the need to make cash payments that would otherwise be required.

An exception to the one year rule is made for businesses whose normal operating cycle, that is the time required to purchase, process and sell its products, is more than a year. A distillery, for example, has inventory in process for more than a year in the normal course of its operations. That inventory is still considered a current asset. Receivables and prepayments not recoverable within one year, or the normal operating cycle if longer, are not considered current. For example, contributions to employee pension plans in excess of current requirements and applicable to future years are long term prepayments. Advance payments of this kind are often described as **deferred charges**.

Current liabilities are those payable within one year or the normal operating cycle if longer. They are those that will be paid out of existing current assets in the normal course of events. They include most operating liabilities, that is, **accounts payable and accrued**, **taxes**, **product liabilities** and **deposit liabilities**, plus **short term borrowings**. Operating liabilities not payable currently, for example deferred payments on pension obligations, are considered long term. They are sometimes described as **deferred credits**. If amounts are payable on long term debt within the coming year, instalments or complete repayments, those amounts are current, unless they will be made from sources other than current assets, from new long term borrowings for example. In that case they are classified as long term.

Current assets are listed in balance sheets in order of liquidity, according to how fast they can or will be turned into cash. Cash comes first, followed by temporary investments, receivables, inventories and prepaid expenses, in that order. Current liabilities are usually listed short term loans first, followed by accounts payable and accrued liabilities, and then by the others, whose arrangement varies. In general, the approach is to list them in the chronological order they will be paid but this is sometimes difficult because payment dates can be uncertain and can vary among individual items within categories.

Current assets are listed and totalled first in the asset category of the balance sheet. Current liabilities are listed and totalled first among the equities.

Non current assets are usually listed in the order **long term investments**, **depletable assets**, **property, plant and equipment**, and **intangibles**. Property, plant and equipment are usually listed in the order **land**, **buildings** and **equipment**. If goodwill has been recorded, it is listed last among the intangibles. The grouping, order of listing and description of non current assets varies somewhat among companies, depending in part on the nature of their business and in part on the preferences of those who produce the balance sheet.

Among the **non current equities**, **long term debt** is listed first, followed by **ownership**. Long term debt items are usually listed in order according to the length of their terms. Bonds with a term of ten years for example are listed before bonds with a term of fifteen years.

Balance Sheet Illustrations

The following examples illustrate the appearance and some of the variations of balance sheets.

Leslie Brown, Dentist
Balance Sheet
as at December 31, 20X

Current Assets			Current Liabilities	
Cash on hand and in bank		$ 1,121.92	Accounts payable	$ 224.62
Accounts receivable		3,050.00	Accrued wages	585.46
Prepaid expenses		463.17		810.08
		4,635.09		
Office furniture and equipment	$15,157.12		Proprietorship	14,579.78
Less accumulated depreciation	4,402.35			
		10,754.77		
		$15,389.86		$15,389.86

Leslie Brown is a single proprietor with a dental practice. The heading of the statement is standard, showing first the name of the business, then the name of the statement, and finally the date of the statement. The assets are those that one might expect to find in a dental practice, a cash balance, accounts receivable from patients, some prepaid expenses, perhaps prepaid insurance and rent, and some office furniture and equipment. There are no inventories, Brown sells services rather than goods. There is no land or building, the office accommodation is rented.

The equities too are those that one would expect to find, accounts payable to suppliers, accrued wages of office help, and Brown's residual equity, proprietorship. It is customary to show two amounts for depreciable fixed asset categories, the original cost and the estimated amount of that cost used up to date, called **accumulated depreciation**. Sub-totals are shown for current assets and current liabilities.

Black, Green and White operate a trading business in partnership under the name National Wholesalers. Their balance sheet is prepared in an alternative format. The current liabilities are deducted from the current assets first to arrive at working capital. The other assets are then listed and added to working capital. Long term liabilities and ownership amounts are then listed and totalled. Because of the equality of total assets and total equities,

National Wholesalers
Statement of Financial Position
as of June 30, 20X

Current Assets		
Cash		$ 3,155
Temporary investments		9,964
Accounts receivable		20,293
Inventory		48,746
Prepaid expenses		921
		83,079
Current Liabilities		
Accounts payable and accrued		19,659
Container deposits		4,014
Current portion of instalment purchase contract		1,200
		24,873
Working Capital		58,206
Fixed Assets		
Land		4,971
Building	$26,663	
Less accumulated depreciation	6,112	
		20,551
Equipment	9,843	
Less accumulated depreciation	3,022	
		6,821
		32,343
		$90,549
Long Term Liabilities		
Instalment purchase contract		$ 5,000
Less current portion included above		1,200
		3,800
Loan payable to Green		10,000
7% mortgage payable March 31, 20Z		12,000
		25,800
Ownership		
Black		21,050
Green		29,096
White		14,603
		64,749
		$90,549

the two final totals in this form are also equal. A variation on this format is to deduct long term liabilities from the total of working capital and fixed assets to show a net amount equal to ownership.

The advantages claimed for this form of balance sheet are that it makes clearer the current position and working capital of the business, and it emphasizes the borrowings and ownership sources of financing. Despite the alleged advantages of this format, it is rarely used.

In this balance sheet, the heading Statement of Financial Position is used. This terminology is more descriptive than balance sheet but is not often used. Amounts have been rounded to the nearest dollar. Cents are eliminated from almost all financial statements as redundant.

This balance sheet reflects the nature of the business and its legal form of organization. Since it is a trading business, its assets include inventory of stock in trade. The firm has accounts receivable because it sells on credit. It has some prepaid expenses, insurance and property taxes. The business experiences seasonal fluctuations in sales volume. At the date of the balance sheet, sales are low and therefore the required investment in inventories and receivables is also low. The excess cash thus freed has been put into temporary investments. The partners own their warehouse and equipment.

The firm has the usual accounts payable and accrued, amounts owing to suppliers and employees. In addition it has an obligation to redeem containers charged to customers. The partners have financed the purchase of their warehouse partly by borrowing on the strength of a real estate mortgage. They have financed the purchase of equipment partly by an instalment purchase. The remainder of the funds required for the business have been supplied by the partners themselves, by capital investment and loan.

The Acme Manufacturing Limited balance sheet lists all the assets first and then all the equities. This form is the most commonly used for all types of business. Amounts have been rounded to the nearest thousand dollars. This is a common practice followed to simplify and clarify the statement. Some very large corporations round amounts to the nearest million.

In this statement two amounts are shown pertaining to accounts receivable, the amount actually owed by customers and an estimate of the amount

Acme Manufacturing Limited
Balance Sheet
at October 31, 20X
(dollar amounts in thousands)

Assets

Accounts receivable		$108
Less allowance for doubtful accounts		5
		103
Loans to directors		10
Inventories		
Raw materials	$ 66	
Work in process	20	
Finished goods	129	
		215
Total current assets		328
Investment-shares of Acme Parts Inc.		120
Property, Plant and Equipment		
Land		14
Buildings	51	
Less accumulated depreciation	15	
		36
Machinery and equipment	86	
Less accumulated depreciation	31	
		55
		105
Patents		25
Total assets		$578

Liabilities and Shareholders' Equity

Bank loan	$ 12
Accounts payable and accrued	54
Income taxes payable	14
Advance payments from customers	13
Estimated warranty liabilities	6
Total current liabilities	99
10% bonds payable April 15, 20Z	90
Total liabilities	189
Shareholders' Equity	
Capital stock	262
Retained earnings	127
	389
Total liabilities and shareholders' equity	$578

that will be uncollectable, called **allowance for doubtful accounts**. This procedure is alternative to showing only one figure for the estimated collectable amount as was done in the previous illustrations.

Loans to directors are segregated from trade accounts receivable, because they are very different in nature. Their inclusion in current assets indicates that collection is expected within the coming year, and the fact that they are not added to the trade receivables before applying the allowance for doubtful accounts indicates that no such allowance is considered necessary in respect of them.

The company, being a manufacturer, has inventories of raw materials and work in process, as well as of goods available for sale.

The company has made a long term investment in another company, Acme Parts Inc., by purchasing shares in that company.

Under the heading property, plant and equipment are shown the land, buildings and equipment employed by the company.

The intangible asset patents is shown separately.

Current liabilities include several items. The bank loan represents short term financing, to permit an expansion of inventories and accounts receivable to meet temporarily increased sales and production requirements. Accounts payable and accrued include the usual supplier accounts, accrued wages and so on. Estimated income taxes payable are shown separately from the accounts payable and accrued, as a different class of liability. The company has two other distinct types of current liability, both of them to its customers. One is for payments received in advance of the delivery of goods, the other is for making good the warranties it has attached to goods sold.

Long term financing has been raised by issuing bonds, by issuing shares and by retaining earnings within the corporation. These sources of funding are shown as bonds payable, capital stock and retained earnings.

In the published balance sheets of public companies, amounts in the major categories of assets and equities are usually summarized, with totals only shown on the face of the statement. Details are provided in notes to the financial statements.

Published statements also include comparative amounts for the corresponding preceding period. Some include comparative data for the preceding two periods. Comparative amounts were omitted from the previous illustrations for simplicity. In practice, they are usually included in the financial statements of all types of businesses. The following is an illustration of how a published balance sheet for Acme Manufacturing Limited might appear.

Acme Manufacturing Limited
Balance Sheet
at October 31, 20X and 20W
(dollar amounts in thousands)

	20X	20W
Accounts receivable (note 1)	$113	$89
Inventories (note 2)	215	192
Total current assets	328	281
Investment in Acme Parts Inc. (note 3)	120	120
Property, plant and equipment (note 4)	105	108
Patents	25	28
	$578	$537
Bank loan	$ 12	$ 10
Accounts payable and accrued	54	53
Income taxes payable	14	13
Advance payments from customers	13	11
Estimated warranty liabilities	6	5
Total current liabilities	99	92
Bonds payable (note 5)	90	90
Total liabilities	189	182
Capital stock (note 6)	262	250
Retained earnings	127	105
Total shareholders' equity	389	355
	$578	$537

Summary of Key Concepts

- Equities equal Assets
- Assets show the forms of an entity's wealth; equities show the sources of that wealth.
- Ownership equals net assets, assets minus liabilities.
- A balance sheet (statement of financial position) is a listing of assets and equities as at a given date.
- Working capital is the excess of current (circulating) assets over current liabilities.

CHAPTER 3

Income and Ownership

INCOME

Income, like wealth, can mean different things to different people. Economists have produced a variety of definitions. In accounting, income is defined as an increase in ownership equity, with one exception. An increase resulting from investment by owners does not constitute income.

Accounting income is mainly the result of revenues and expenses. Revenues increase income, expenses decrease it. Most revenues are generated by sales of goods and services. A few, such as interest on investments, are generated by allowing someone else to use assets belonging to the business, in this case cash. Expenses are the costs of goods and services used in operating the business.

INCOME STATEMENTS

A statement of income is a listing of the revenues and expenses of a business for a given period of time. The period can be anything chosen by those who prepare and use the information. Statements for management are usually produced for monthly periods. Statements for shareholders of public companies are produced for quarterly periods and for yearly periods, called **financial years**. Financial years need not coincide with calendar years. It is generally considered better if they reflect the natural business year of the firm, beginning and ending at the annual month-end date of lowest business activity. Many retailers, for example, have financial years ending January 31.

Revenue from the main activity of a business is listed first in the statement of income, followed by expenses. The kinds of revenues and expenses described reflect the nature and methods of operation of the business. Most businesses have only one main activity and source of revenue, sales. When a business has additional revenues, such as royalties or interest, they are sometimes listed immediately after the main source of revenue and sometimes after expenses. Expenses are usually listed in the order, cost of goods sold, if any, selling and administrative expenses, and interest. Expenses are deducted from revenues to arrive at operating income. If the business is a corporation, corporate taxes on income are also deducted in arriving at income from operations.

Income Statement Illustrations

The following examples illustrate the appearance and some of the variations of statements of income.

Leslie Brown, Dentist
Income Statement
for the month of December 20X

Fees revenue		$7,100.00
Expenses		
Wages	$1,011.34	
Rent	450.00	
Supplies	112.50	
Telephone	91.65	
Insurance	111.78	
Depreciation of furniture & equipment	319.29	
		2,096.56
Income for the month		$5,003.44

The heading of Leslie Brown's statement shows the name of the business, the name of the statement and the period of time covered by the statement. It is similar in form to the heading of a balance sheet, except that the statement of income is prepared for a period of time while a balance sheet is prepared as of a given date.

In this statement the only revenue is fees from professional services. Expenses consist of wages, rent, supplies, telephone, insurance and depreciation. Depreciation is a measure of the cost of the furniture and equipment used up during the period.

National Wholesalers
Statement of Earnings
for the three months ended June 30, 20X

Sales		$81,242
Less returns and allowances		3,162
Net sales		78,080
Cost of goods sold		40,228
Gross margin		37,852
Selling and administrative expenses		
Salaries and wages	$10,225	
Freight out on sales	7,483	
Supplies	2,006	
Insurance	312	
Bad debts	1,484	
Property taxes	226	
Depreciation — building	333	
— equipment	492	
		22,561
		15,291
Financial revenue and expense		
Interest expense	335	
Less interest revenue	106	
		229
Net earnings		$15,062

The statement for National Wholesalers is headed Statement of Earnings. The word earnings is used interchangeably with income. The period of time covered is three months.

The statement is prepared in a form often used by businesses that deal in goods rather than services. The cost of the goods sold is deducted from net sales to arrive at what is called **gross margin** or **gross profit** on sales. The other expenses are then classified and deducted to arrive at the earnings for the period. In this statement there are several steps or sub-totals shown before the final figure for net earnings. The number of steps and the descriptions applied to the sub-totals vary. Most statements combine selling and administrative expenses, as was done above, but some list them separately. Some combine interest with selling and administrative expenses under the general heading expenses. Some businesses report only a net sales amount, eliminating the step of deducting returns and allowances from gross sales. Some list interest and other miscellaneous revenue immediately after sales.

Acme Manufacturing Limited
Statement of Income
for the year ended October 31, 20X
(dollar amounts in thousands)

Sales		$1442
Cost of goods sold		
Finished goods, beginning inventory	$119	
Cost of goods manufactured	878	
Goods available for sale	997	
Finished goods, ending inventory	129	
		868
Selling expenses		
Advertising	48	
Salaries and commissions	229	
Travelling expenses	24	
Sundry	12	
		313
General and administrative expenses		
Salaries	98	
Directors' fees	30	
Office supplies	12	
Depreciation - office equipment	2	
Bad debts	13	
Sundry	11	
		166
Interest		12
		1,359
Income before income taxes		83
Income taxes		42
Net income		$ 41

In the Acme Manufacturing example, cost of goods sold is not deducted from sales to show an amount for gross margin. Instead, it is added to the totals of the other main categories of expense, and the grand total is deducted from revenues to arrive at income before taxes. Income taxes are deducted separately. This method of deducting expenses is frequently used, especially by public companies.

As in the case of balance sheets, amounts shown on the face of published statements of income are usually summarized. Little additional detail is provided in notes however. For competitive reasons, most corporations prefer not to disclose any more information concerning their operations than is reasonably necessary to keep shareholders adequately informed. The following illustration shows how a published statement of earnings for Acme Manufacturing Limited might appear.

Acme Manufacturing Limited
Statement of Income
for the years ended October 31, 20X and 20W
(dollar amounts in thousands)

	20X	20W
Sales	$1,442	$1,308
Cost of goods sold	868	794
Selling and administrative expenses	479	423
Interest	12	12
	1,359	1,229
Income before income taxes	83	79
Income taxes (note 7)	42	40
Net income	$ 41	$ 39

GAINS AND LOSSES

In addition to revenues and expenses, income is affected by gains and losses. Revenues and expenses are the result of the usual activities of a business. The terms gains and losses are used to describe the effects on income of transactions and events outside the usual course of business. The cost of a fire, for example, would be called a loss, not an expense. Gains and losses are reported net, that is, as single amounts. The fire loss would be shown in a statement of income as one figure, not as the cost of assets destroyed less the insurance and salvage recoveries.

The method of reporting gains and losses in statements of income depends on their nature. If they are "extraordinary gains and losses" or if they result from "discontinued operations", they are given special treatment.

Discontinued Operations

Some companies operate in more than one distinct line of business. If they sell or close down or otherwise dispose of an entire line, it is a discontinued operation. A company might operate both breweries and sports franchises for example. If it disposed of all the franchises, that would be a discontinued operation. Disposing of only part of the group would not.

An operation is considered discontinued once a formal decision and plan of disposal has been adopted by management, even though the disposal might not happen until a later date. The results of discontinued operations are divided into two parts. One is the operating results for the period up to the date of decision. The other is the operating results after the date of decision plus the results of asset and liability disposals. Any related income tax effects are included in calculating the amounts for each part. Each part is reported separately in the statement of income in the year the decision is made. They are listed below income from continuing operations after taxes.

The final disposal of assets and liabilities can occur in a year after the one the decision is made. In that case, the calculation of gain or loss on disposal requires estimates of future revenues and expenses, as well as of asset and liability disposal values, for inclusion in the income statement in the year of decision. A final adjustment is recorded in the year the disposals are completed.

Extraordinary Gains and Losses

An extraordinary gain or loss has three characteristics. First, it is not a recurring event. Costs incurred as a result of severe winter storms for example, are not extraordinary if they recur every few years. They might be unusual but they are not extraordinary. Secondly, they do not result from the normal activities of a business. A loss on the sale of a company's office building for example, is not extraordinary. It is unusual, because companies do not often sell their office buildings; but it is not extraordinary, because buying and ultimately disposing of assets is a normal activity of a business. Thirdly, the gain or loss is outside the control of management and owners. If a trucker elects not to carry collision insurance on his vehicle because the potential repair costs are judged to be less than the cost of insurance for example, a collision loss is not extraordinary. It is the result of a management decision not to carry insurance.

A loss resulting from a tornado is extraordinary, because it is non-recurring, outside the normal activities of a business and outside the control of management.

Extraordinary gains and losses are calculated taking into account any related income tax effects. They are shown in income statements below income from continuing operations after taxes, and after any gain or loss from discontinued operations.

Other

Gains and losses other than those from discontinued operations and extraordinary items are reported in statements of income after operating income but before income taxes, and are included in the tax calculation.

Gains and Losses Illustration

The treatment of gains and losses is illustrated on page 38, using the income statement of Acme Manufacturing Limited. For the purpose of this illustration, the following additional circumstances are assumed.

1. Gain on the sale of land and office building, $16,000 (before tax).

2. Losses from discontinued operations of Foundry Division.
   Loss on operations to date of decision, $3,000 (after tax recovery of $2,000).
   Loss on disposal, including operating losses during phase-out period, $6,000 (after tax recovery of $4,000).

3. Loss resulting from tornado, $5,000 (after tax recovery of $3,000).

Acme Manufacturing Limited
Statement of Income
for the year ended October 31, 20X
(dollar amounts in thousands)

Sales		$1,442
Cost of goods sold		868
Selling and administrative expenses		479
Interest		12
		1,359
Income before unusual items and income taxes		83
Gain on the sale of land and building		16
Income from continuing operations before taxes		99
Income taxes		51
Income from continuing operations		48
Discontinued operations		
Loss from operations of discontinued Foundry Division (less tax recovery of $2)	$3	
Loss on disposal of Foundry Division including operating losses during phase-out period (less tax recovery of $4)	6	
		9
Income before extraordinary loss		39
Loss resulting from tornado (less tax recovery of $3)		5
Net income		$ 34

OWNERSHIP

A complete description of the change in ownership equity during the period requires a report of owner investment or disinvestment as well as of income. This can be done in one of two ways. If changes in investment are few and simple, they can be shown on the face of either the balance sheet or the statement of income. If not, a separate statement is prepared.

The investment activity of Leslie Brown, Dentist, could be shown on the balance sheet by expanding the proprietorship section as shown below:

Proprietorship	
Investment November 30, 20X	15,076.34
Income for the month of December	5,003.44
	20,079.78
Withdrawals	5,500.00
Investment December 31, 20X	14,579.78

Alternatively it could be shown at the bottom of the income statement as shown below:

Income for the month	5,003.44
Investment November 30, 20X	15,076.34
	20,079.78
Withdrawals	5,500.00
Investment December 31, 20X	14,579.78

In this case the statement would likely be called a **statement of income and investment**.

A separate statement showing details of changes to the ownership of National Wholesalers might appear as shown below:

National Wholesalers
Statement of Partners' Capital
for the three months ended June 30, 20X

	Black	Green	White	Total
Capital March 31, 20X	$15,067	$29,941	$13,679	$58,687
Additional investment	5,000	—	—	5,000
Salaries	—	4,000	8,000	12,000
Interest on capital	271	443	212	926
Remainder of profit for the period	712	712	712	2,136
	21,050	35,096	22,603	78,749
Withdrawals	—	6,000	8,000	14,000
Capital June 30, 20X	$21,050	$29,096	$14,603	$64,749

The net profit for the period was divided among Black, Green and White in accordance with the terms of their partnership agreement. Green received a salary of $4,000 in return for devoting half time to the business and White received $8,000 for full time services. Black did not work for the business. The partners received 6% interest on their average capital investment during the quarter. The remainder of the profit for the quarter, after salaries and interest on capital, was divided equally among the partners. During the period Black put an additional $5,000 into the business, while Green and White withdrew $6,000 and $8,000 respectively.

In both the Leslie Brown and National Wholesalers reports, the amounts received and withdrawn by the owners were treated as distributions of profit rather than expenses. The practice of ignoring the value of owners' services in calculating the expenses of a business is followed almost invariably in proprietorships, and usually in partnerships. It is somewhat misleading, because if the owners did not manage their business themselves, they would have to hire someone else to do it for them and the business profits would be less to the extent of the management salaries.

A description of ownership reporting for corporations is provided in chapter 10, Corporate Debt and Ownership.

Summary of Key Concepts

- Income (earnings) is an increase in ownership equity.
- Income is increased by revenues and gains; it is decreased by expenses and losses.
- Revenues and expenses result from the usual activities of a business; gains and losses result from events outside the usual course of business.
- A statement of income is a listing of revenues, gains, expenses and losses for a given period of time.

CHAPTER 4

Double Entry Bookkeeping

DEBITS AND CREDITS

The foundation of accounting is double entry bookkeeping. In double entry bookkeeping, assets are called debits (abbreviated Dr.) and equities are called credits (abbreviated Cr.). The words debit and credit correspond with the words debtor and creditor. A debtor of a business is someone against whom the business has a claim, which is an asset; a creditor is someone who has a claim against the business, which is an equity. It is sometimes confusing at first to find that an asset is a debit, because banks describe the accounts of their depositors as credits. They do that because to them, customer deposits are liabilities. They owe the amounts deposited to their customers.

The terms debit and credit are used not only as nouns to describe existing assets and equities, but also as verbs to describe changes in assets and equities. An asset is increased by debiting it and decreased by crediting it. An equity is increased by crediting it and decreased by debiting it. In this respect, the use of the terms debit and credit in accounting is comparable to the use of the terms plus and minus in mathematics. An asset of a business, or debit, can be thought of as a plus quantity, and an equity claim against a business, or credit, as a minus quantity. In mathematics, a plus quantity is increased by a plus and decreased by a minus. In accounting, an asset, or debit quantity, is increased by a debit and decreased by a credit. In mathematics, a minus quantity is increased by a minus and decreased by a plus. In accounting, an equity, or credit quantity, is increased by a credit and decreased by a debit.

Revenues increase ownership equity and expenses decrease it. Since an increase in equity is a credit and a decrease is a debit, revenues are credits and expenses are debits. Carrying the process one step further, an increase in revenue is a credit and a decrease a debit, while an increase in an expense is a debit and a decrease a credit. It is sometimes difficult to understand why expenses are debits when assets are debits, and why revenues are credits when liabilities are credits. The answer is that debits show what the business bought with its money and credits show where the money came from. When a business pays wages or other expenses, it is buying something of value just as if it were buying a piece of machinery. Revenues are a source of money for investment just as liabilities are a source.

To summarize, accounting categories of data are debits or credits for bookkeeping purposes as follows:

Debits	**Credits**
(what the money bought)	(where the money came from)
Assets	Liabilities
Expenses	Ownership
	Revenues

In practice, the word charge is sometimes used in place of debit. An asset or expense is increased by a charge. An equity or revenue is reduced by a charge.

EXCHANGES

Double entry bookkeeping is based on recording exchanges. Every exchange, every transaction, has two equal sides, something is received and something equal is given in return. When an asset is purchased, either cash or an agreement to pay cash in future, equal to the price of the asset, is given in return. When an asset is sold, either cash is received or an agreement to receive cash in the future, equal to the price of the asset, is accepted in return. If an investment of money is received in a business, an equal equity interest in that business is given in return.

In the process of bookkeeping, those things that are received in exchanges are recorded as debits and the things given in return are recorded as credits. Thus an investment of $5,000.00 received in the National Whole-salers bank account from Black is recorded as follows:

| Bank | 5,000.00 | |
| Black, capital | | 5,000.00 |

The money received, the asset, is recorded as the debit and the equivalent equity given in return is recorded as the credit. The debit is shown above and to the left and the credit below and to the right. This corresponds to the balance sheet presentation of assets on the left or above, and equities on the right or below.

A purchase of equipment for $2,000.00, paid by cheque, is recorded as follows:

| Equipment | 2,000.00 | |
| Bank | | 2,000.00 |

The equipment received is an asset and therefore a debit. The payment is a reduction of an asset, the bank account, which is a credit.

A sale of merchandise for $1,000.00 on credit, is recorded as follows:

| Accounts receivable | 1,000.00 | |
| Sales | | 1,000.00 |

The account receivable or claim for payment received from the customer is an asset and a debit. The sale represents what was given in return. It is a revenue and a credit. Note that when goods are sold, the credit is made to a sales account, not to an inventory account. The cost of goods sold and the corresponding reduction in inventory are recorded separately. The cost of the merchandise will not be the same as the selling price.

Whatever the effect of any happening on the assets, equities, expenses, and revenues of a business, the debit/credit mechanism can be used to describe that happening. At first it may seem difficult to translate all business transactions into debits and credits, but with practice it becomes automatic.

The equities of an entity are always equal to its assets. Assets are represented by debits and equities by credits. The double entry process maintains the identity by recording equal debits and credits for all transactions.

BOOKS OF ACCOUNT

Accounting data, in the form of debits and credits, are recorded in books of account. Originally these were hand written records; today they are more likely produced mechanically or electronically. Regardless of the methods used to record, process and store the data, the basic "books" are the same.

The master book is known as the **general ledger**. It contains an **account** (in written records a page) for each category of asset, equity, expense, and revenue to be included in the financial statements. All debits and credits are summarized in these accounts. At the end of each accounting period, financial statements are prepared using the net debit or credit amount, called the **balance**, remaining in each account.

The amounts shown in the general ledger accounts are the totals for each account category, for example, total accounts receivable. For most enterprises, effective management requires more detailed information concerning some of these accounts. For example, management needs to know the amount receivable from each customer. For this purpose, **subsidiary ledgers** are kept when required to show the details of general ledger accounts. The total of the individual balances in a subsidiary ledger will equal the overall total balance in the corresponding general ledger account.

In addition to a general ledger and subsidiary ledgers, virtually all enterprises keep what is called a **general journal**. A general journal is a **book of original entry**. That means it is a book in which transactions are recorded first, before being recorded in the general ledger. It may seem at first sight, that recording transactions first in a journal and then again in the ledger is an unnecessary duplication of effort, but there is good reason for it. A journal provides a complete record, debit and credit, of each transaction. A single general ledger account shows only one debit or credit from each transaction. If an error is made in debiting or crediting a ledger account, it is much easier to find and correct it by tracing back to the journal where the corresponding debits and credits are recorded together, than it would be to search through the ledger accounts trying to match them. The debit and credit illustrations given earlier to record investment in a business, purchase of equipment and sale of merchandise, are in the form that would be found in a general journal kept manually.

Most businesses keep other books of original entry, in addition to a general journal. They do this because most transactions fall into relatively few categories and the process of recording them can be shortened and simplified by using specialized books to summarize them, instead of recording them item by item in a general journal. Most transactions are either cash collections, cash payments, sales or purchases, or some combination of these, with wages being a specialized form of purchase. For most enterprises therefore, the other books of original entry are some or all of the following.

- Cash receipts journal
- Cash payments or disbursements journal
- Sales journal
- Purchase journal
- Payroll journal

Not all businesses require all of these books. A business that does not extend credit can combine the cash receipts journal and sales journal in a single book for example.

The specific format of the ledgers and journals used in a particular enterprise depends on the nature of the enterprise and the methods employed to process data.

BOOKKEEPING CYCLE

Day by day the transactions of a business — purchases, sales, payments and collections — are recorded in the books of original entry. When the date arrives that financial statements are wanted, usually the end of the month, the debits and credits in these books are totalled by account category and the amounts are recorded in the accounts of the general ledger, a process called **posting**. The general ledger then shows the net results of all the exchanges between the business and other parties that have been recorded during the period.

It does not however, show all of the information needed to produce the financial statements. For one thing, exchanges are not always recorded in the period in which they occur. This is frequently the case when services are provided continuously over a period of time and paid for at discrete intervals. For example, if employees are paid for their services at the end of each week and the month end falls mid-week, the payroll journal will not contain all of the wages for the month on the month end date. An **adjusting entry** to the accounts is required to correct for these timing differences. A typical adjustment for wages earned but unrecorded at the month end is the following.

Wages expense	1,500.00	
Accrued wages		1,500.00

Wages expense is increased by the amount of wages earned but unpaid (debit) and a liability is recorded for the amount owing (credit). Similar adjustments are frequently required for such things as interest on debt and taxes.

Adjusting entries are also required because assets can change in value and liabilities in amount without any exchange taking place. For example productive equipment depreciates independently of any exchange. Similarly a warranty claim can arise without an exchange. A typical adjustment to record depreciation is the following.

Depreciation expense	500.00	
Accumulated depreciation		500.00

Depreciation expense is recorded (debit) and the value of the asset is reduced (credit). As noted earlier, accumulated depreciation is deducted from the original cost of depreciable assets. Adjustments might also be required to the value of accounts receivable to allow for bad debts, to prepaid expenses and depletable assets for amounts used, and to intangibles.

In businesses that sell goods, an adjustment is required to the inventory account to record the cost of goods sold. A typical adjustment is the following.

Cost of goods sold	35,000.00	
Inventory		35,000.00

Cost of goods sold expense is recorded (debit) and the value of the inventory is reduced by an equivalent amount (credit).

It is the responsibility of the accountant to review all account categories at the end of each accounting period, to determine what adjusting entries need to be made. After all these adjustments have been determined, the financial statements can be prepared.

Although most businesses prepare monthly financial statements from adjusted account balances, they do not usually record the month end adjustments in the accounts themselves. Instead they list the unadjusted account balances and make the necessary adjustments on a **worksheet**. The complete bookkeeping cycle is almost always a year. At the end of the business year, the appropriate adjustments are recorded in the accounts, usually via the general journal.

The bookkeeping cycle is finished by **closing the books**. The books are closed by a general journal entry that returns all of the revenue and expense accounts, called **nominal accounts**, to zero, and transfers the net difference between the credit and debit amounts, the net income or loss, to ownership equity. The general ledger then shows only asset, liability and ownership account balances, called **real accounts**, and is ready for the next bookkeeping cycle.

Bookkeeping Illustration

The double entry bookkeeping process can be illustrated by reference to the National Wholesalers financial statements presented in the previous two chapters. A listing of the amounts shown in its general ledger accounts, known as a **trial balance**, at the end of its last fiscal year, March 31, 20X appeared as shown below: (Cents are omitted to simplify the illustration.)

National Wholesalers
General Ledger Trial Balance
March 31, 20X

	Debit	Credit
Bank	2,828	
Temporary investments	9,858	
Accounts receivable	18,676	
Inventory	43,765	
Prepaid expenses	1,459	
Land	4,971	
Building	26,663	
Accumulated depreciation building		5,779
Equipment	9,540	
Accumulated depreciation equipment		2,530
Accounts payable		18,724
Accrued liabilities (wages)		507
Container deposits		4,233
Instalment purchase liability		5,300
Mortgage payable		12,000
Loan, Green		10,000
Capital, Black		15,067
Green		29,941
White		13,679
Totals	117,760	117,760

The following things happened during the three months ended June 30, 20X.

(1) The company sold goods to customers on credit at prices totalling 81,242, and in addition billed them 11,245 for returnable container deposits. These transactions were recorded daily in the sales journal. At the end of the three month period, the sales journal showed the following totals.

Accounts receivable	92,487	
Sales		81,242
Container deposits		11,245

Accounts receivable were increased by 92,487 as a result of charges to customers (debit), sales revenue of 81,242 was recorded (credit) and a liability to repay 11,245 on the return of containers was incurred (credit). These totals were posted from the sales journal to the general ledger at the end of June. Amounts receivable from individual customers were posted daily to the accounts receivable subsidiary ledger.

(2) The company received payments from customers of 74,760 and additional investment from Black of 5,000. These receipts were deposited in the bank and recorded in the cash receipts journal daily. At the end of the period, the cash receipts journal showed

Bank	79,760	
Accounts receivable		74,760
Black, capital		5,000

The bank account had been increased by 79,760 (debit), accounts receivable had been decreased by 74,760 as a result of customer payments (credit) and the capital investment equity of Black had been increased by 5,000 (credit). These amounts were also posted to the general ledger accounts at the end of June. Amounts received from individual customers were posted daily to the accounts receivable subsidiary ledger.

(3) Customers returned goods for credit having selling prices of 3,162 and returned containers billed at 11,464. Because of the frequency of these transactions, the company records them daily in a special journal designed for the purpose. At the end of the period, the journal showed the following totals.

Sales returns and allowances	3,162	
Container deposits	11,464	
Accounts receivable		14,626

Sales returns and allowances, a revenue deduction, amounted to 3,162 (debit), the liability to customers to repay their deposits was reduced by 11,464 (debit) and amounts receivable from customers were reduced by 14,626 (credit). Again, the totals were posted to the general ledger at the end of the period and to individual customer accounts in the subsidiary ledger daily.

(4) Salaries and wages were paid of 10,520. These were recorded in the payroll journal, whose totals were posted at the end of the period as follows:

Salaries and wages	10,520	
Bank		10,520

Salary and wage expense was 10,520 (debit) and the payments reduced the bank account by 10,520 (credit). (For simplicity it is assumed that tax and other deductions were paid at the same time as the net salaries and wages.)

(5) Purchases of inventory were made from suppliers totalling 45,209, freight costs on sales were incurred of 7,483, sundry supplies of 2,006 were purchased and consumed, and new equipment costing 303 was purchased, all on credit. These were recorded daily in the purchases journal. Totals were posted to the general ledger at the end of the period as follows:

Inventory	45,209	
Freight out on sales	7,483	
Supplies expense	2,006	
Equipment	303	
Accounts payable		55,001

The assets, inventory and equipment, were increased by 45,209 and 303 respectively (debits), freight out and supplies expense were incurred of 7,483 and 2,006 respectively (debits), and liabilities to trade creditors in the form of accounts payable were incurred of 55,001 (credit). Amounts owing to individual suppliers were posted daily to the accounts payable subsidiary ledger.

(6) Payments were made from the bank to trade creditors totalling 54,488, payments of 300 and 125 were made on the instalment contract for principal and interest respectively and withdrawals were made of 6,000 by Green and 8,000 by White. These were recorded in the cash payments journal daily and the totals posted to the general ledger at the end of the period as follows:

Accounts payable	54,488	
Instalment contract payable	300	
Interest expense	125	
Green, capital	6,000	
White, capital	8,000	
Bank		68,913

Accounts payable were reduced by the payments of 54,488 (debit), the instalment contract liability was reduced by 300 (debit), interest expense of 125 was recorded (debit), the capital accounts of Green and White were reduced by their withdrawals of 6,000 and 8,000 respectively (debits), and the bank account was reduced by 68,913 (credit). Amounts paid to individual suppliers were posted daily to the accounts payable subsidiary ledger.

The worksheet shown on the next page summarizes all of the transactions recorded in the books of original entry and posted to the ledgers during the three months ended June 30, 20X.

On reviewing the accounts at the end of June, the accountant determined the following additional information.

(A) Interest receivable of 106 had accumulated (accrued) on the temporary investments.

(B) Accounts receivable of 1,484 were uncollectable.

(C) Inventory on hand at June 30 was worth 48,746.

(D) Prepaid insurance worth 312 and prepaid property taxes of 226 had been absorbed into expenses during the period.

(E) The building had depreciated by an estimated 333 and the equipment by an estimated 492.

National Wholesalers
General Ledger Accounts

	March 31, 20X Dr.	March 31, 20X Cr.	Postings Dr.	Postings Cr.	June 30, 20X Dr.	June 30, 20X Cr.
Bank	2,828		79,760(2)	10,520(4) 68,913(6)	3,155	
Temporary investments	9,858				9,858	
Accounts receivable	18,676		92,487(1)	74,760(2) 14,626(3)	21,777	
Inventory	43,765		45,209(5)		88,974	
Prepaid expenses	1,459				1,459	
Land	4,971				4,971	
Building	26,663				26,663	
Accumulated depreciation building		5,779				5,779
Equipment	9,540		303(5)		9,843	
Accumulated depreciation equipment		2,530				2,530
Accounts payable		18,724	54,488(6)	55,001(5)		19,237
Accrued liabilities		507				507
Container deposits		4,233	11,464(3)	11,245(1)		4,014
Instalment purchase		5,300	300(6)			5,000
Mortgage		12,000				12,000
Loan, Green		10,000				10,000
Capital, Black		15,067		5,000(2)		20,067
Green		29,941	6,000(6)			23,941
White		13,679	8,000(6)			5,679
Sales				81,242(1)		81,242
Sales returns and allowances			3,162(3)		3,162	
Salaries and wages			10,520(4)		10,520	
Freight on sales			7,483(5)		7,483	
Supplies expense			2,006(5)		2,006	
Interest expense			125(6)		125	
Totals	117,760	117,760	321,307	321,307	189,996	189,996

(F)   Wages accrued and unpaid at June 30 amounted to 212, and interest of 210 had accrued and was unpaid since March 31 on the mortgage payable, for total accrued liabilities of 422.

The accountant therefore made the following adjustments. Since the accountant was preparing quarterly statements, the adjustments were made on a worksheet, not in the general ledger accounts. The worksheet is shown on page 54.

(A) Temporary investments   106
     Interest revenue   106

The investments had increased in value by the accrued interest (debit) which represented interest revenue (credit).

(B) Bad debts   1,484
     Accounts receivable   1,484

Bad debts expense of 1,484 had been incurred (debit) and the accounts receivable were reduced by that amount (credit).

(C) Cost of goods sold   40,228
     Inventory   40,228

This adjustment was calculated as follows:

Inventory at March 31	43,765
Plus inventory purchased	45,209
Total available	88,974
Inventory at June 30	48,746
Cost of goods sold	40,228

The cost of goods sold was recorded 40,228 (debit) and the inventory was reduced 40,228 (credit).

(D) Insurance   312
    Property taxes   226
     Prepaid expenses   538

Insurance and property taxes expenses of 312 and 226 respectively were incurred (debits) and the prepaid portion of those expenses, an asset, declined by 538 (credit).

(E) Depreciation-building   333
     Accumulated depreciation —building   333
    Depreciation-equipment   492
     Accumulated depreciation —equipment   492

Depreciation expense on the building of 333 and on the equipment of 492 were recorded (debits), and the corresponding reductions in the asset values were recorded in the accumulated depreciation accounts for deduction from the assets (credits).

(F) Accrued liabilities   85
    Interest expense   210
        Salaries and wages   295

This is a combined adjustment for wages and interest. Accrued wages decreased by 295, from 507 at March 31 to 212 at June 30. Wage expense for the period was also less by 295 than the amount paid, since 507 was paid for the preceding period, while 212 remained to be paid for the current period. Accrued liabilities were reduced 295 (debit) and wages were reduced 295 (credit).

Accrued liabilities   295
    Salaries and wages   295

Interest had accrued and was unpaid in the amount of 210. Interest expense was increased 210 (debit) and accrued liabilities were increased 210 (credit).

Interest expense   210
    Accrued liabilities   210

Combined, accrued liabilities decreased 85 (debit), interest expense increased 210 (debit) and wages decreased 295 (credit).

Using the amounts shown in the final debit and credit columns of the worksheet, the accountant then prepared the balance sheet and income statement illustrated in chapters 2 and 3 and reproduced on pages 55 and 56. (For simplicity, the details of individual partners' accounts have been omitted.)

National Wholesalers
General Ledger Worksheet
June 30, 20X

	Preliminary Dr.	Preliminary Cr.	Adjustments Dr.	Adjustments Cr.	Final Dr.	Final Cr.
Bank	3,155				3,155	
Temporary investments	9,858		106(A)		9,964	
Accounts receivable	21,777			1,484(B)	20,293	
Inventory	88,974			40,228(C)	48,746	
Prepaid expenses	1,459			538(D)	921	
Land	4,971				4,971	
Building	26,663				26,663	
Accumulated depreciation building		5,779		333(E)		6,112
Equipment	9,843				9,843	
Accumulated depreciation equipment		2,530		492(E)		3,022
Accounts payable		19,237				19,237
Accrued liabilities		507	85(F)			422
Container deposits		4,014				4,014
Instalment purchase		5,000				5,000
Mortgage		12,000				12,000
Loan, Green		10,000				10,000
Capital, Black		20,067				20,067
Green		23,941				23,941
White		5,679				5,679
Sales		81,242				81,242
Sales returns and allowances	3,162				3,162	
Cost of goods sold			40,228(C)		40,228	
Salaries and wages	10,520			295(F)	10,225	
Freight on sales	7,483				7,483	
Supplies	2,006				2,006	
Insurance			312(D)		312	
Bad debts			1,484(B)		1,484	
Property taxes			226(D)		226	
Depreciation building			333(E)		333	
Depreciation equipment			492(E)		492	
Interest expense	125		210(F)		335	
Interest revenue				106(A)		106
	189,996	189,996	43,476	43,476	190,842	190,842

National Wholesalers
Statement of Financial Position
as of June 30, 20X

Current assets		
Cash		$ 3,155
Temporary investments		9,964
Accounts receivable		20,293
Inventory		48,746
Prepaid expenses		921
		83,079
Current liabilities		
Accounts payable and accrued		19,659
Container deposits		4,014
Current portion of instalment purchase contract		1,200
		24,873
Working capital		58,206
Fixed assets		
Land		4,971
Building	$26,663	
Less accumulated depreciation	6,112	
		20,551
Equipment	9,843	
Less accumulated depreciation	3,022	
		6,821
		32,343
		$90,549
Long term liabilities		
Instalment purchase contract		$5,000
Less current portion included above		1,200
		3,800
Loan payable to Green		10,000
7% mortgage payable March 31, 20Z		12,000
		25,800
Ownership		
Black		21,050
Green		29,096
White		14,603
		64,749
		$90,549

National Wholesalers
Statement of Earnings
for the three months ended June 30, 20X

Sales		$81,242
Less returns and allowances		3,162
Net sales		78,080
Cost of goods sold		40,228
Gross margin		37,852
Selling and administrative expenses		
Salaries and wages	$10,225	
Freight out on sales	7,483	
Supplies	2,006	
Insurance	312	
Bad debts	1,484	
Property taxes	226	
Depreciation —building	333	
—equipment	492	
		22,561
		15,291
Financial revenue and expense		
Interest expense	335	
Less interest revenue	106	
		229
Net earnings		$15,062

If June 30, 20X had been the company's financial year end, the accountant would have recorded the adjustments in the general ledger accounts via the general journal. The nominal, or income statement accounts for the year would then have been closed out to ownership, by means of the following general journal entry.

Sales	81,242	
Interest revenue	106	
Sales returns and allowances		3,162
Cost of goods sold		40,228
Salaries and wages		10,225
Freight on sales		7,483
Supplies		2,006
Insurance		312
Bad debts		1,484
Property taxes		226
Depreciation—building		333
—equipment		492
Interest expense		335
Ownership accounts (in detail)		15,062

Summary of Key Concepts

-

Debits (what the money bought)	**Credits** (where the money came from)
Assets Expenses	Liabilities Ownership Revenues

- Debit amounts are increased by debits and decreased by credits; credit amounts are increased by credits and decreased by debits.

- Double entry bookkeeping is based on recording exchanges. Every exchange has two sides, something is received and something equal is given in return.

- Things received in exchanges are recorded as debits, things given are credits.

- Equities always equal assets. The identity of assets and equities is maintained by recording equal debits and credits for all transactions.

NET ASSETS AND INCOME

It is important to appreciate the direct relationship between the value of net assets, that is assets minus liabilities, and the calculation of accounting income, revenues minus expenses. Every adjustment to the estimated value of an asset or the amount of a liability has an equal effect on income. This can be seen by reference to the illustration in this chapter. The adjustments to the value of temporary investments and the amount of accrued liabilities had equivalent effects in increasing the amount of income. The adjustments to the value of accounts receivable, prepaid expenses and buildings and equipment had equivalent effects in reducing income. The estimate of inventory on hand at June 30 was reflected directly in cost of goods sold.

In some cases, the values attached to assets and liabilities can be determined with reasonable precision, the amount of interest accrued on an investment or a debt for example, or the amount of wages accrued. In others, the value of assets or amount of liabilities can only be estimated. Allowances for depreciation of productive assets for example, can only be estimated, as can provisions for future payments on product warranties. In the final analysis therefore, the calculation of accounting income can depend very much on the judgment of those who make the estimates.

PART

II

—

MEASUREMENT

CHAPTER 5

Concepts, Conventions and Principles

ACCOUNTING ENTITIES

Accounting measurements are based on a few fundamental concepts and conventions. One is the accounting entity. The accounting entity is the economic unit, the business, that is being accounted for. It is not necessarily a legal entity. A proprietorship is not a legal entity. A corporation is a legal entity but sometimes a single corporation operates more than one business and at other times two or more corporations act together as a single business.

For accounting purposes a business is defined by its assets. The sum of the assets is the accounting entity. Since a business is not necessarily a legal entity, its assets cannot be defined simply by reference to legal ownership. A proprietor might own all of his business assets but he would own many other things as well. Even when a corporation and a business are essentially the same, things legally owned by others are sometimes considered assets of the business and things owned by the corporation not. Land, buildings and equipment leased by one company to another for example, are considered assets of the lessee and not the lessor under certain circumstances. Accounting for leases is discussed in chapter 6.

In general, assets are attributed to a business if the economic benefits and risks of ownership accrue to that business. A truck owned by the proprietor of a delivery service is an asset of that business. A truck leased for a period of years might or might not be, depending on the terms of the lease. A truck rented for a week is not.

Sometimes the existence of an asset is uncertain. For example, one business could make a claim for damages against another and the other deny it. It cannot be known whether the claim is an asset of the first business until such time as a court judgment is obtained or the two businesses come to an agreement. Assets whose existence is in question are called **contingent assets**. They are not recorded formally in accounts. They are described in notes to financial statements, if they are considered probable.

Goodwill is never recorded as an asset, unless a business or a controlling interest in a business is purchased from another owner. When a business is purchased and the price paid exceeds the value of all the other identifiable assets, it is assumed that the excess was paid for goodwill, and goodwill is then recorded. It is not recorded otherwise because there is no objective measure of its value without a purchase by an independent party. The accounting treatment of goodwill and other intangibles is discussed in more detail in chapter 6.

The equities of an accounting entity are determined in the process of defining its assets. They are those amounts that will ultimately have to be paid in respect of its assets. If property being leased is considered an asset of the lessee, all the payments that will have to be made under the lease are a liability. If the property is not considered an asset of the lessee, not all payments to be made in respect of it are a liability, only the amount that is currently due.

Liabilities are not always legal debts. When goods are sold under guaranty or warranty for example, a legal debt is not created until a valid claim is made. For accounting purposes however, a liability can be established simply by recording as assets the cash or accounts receivable obtained on the sale. If it is reasonably certain that amounts will have to be paid to make good the assets, a liability exists for accounting purposes and an estimate of the amount is made.

Amounts payable in respect of assets must be beyond the discretion of management to constitute liabilities. Many businesses employ collection agencies to assist them in collecting accounts receivable. The anticipated cost of a collection agency is not a liability in respect of accounts receivable however. It is within the discretion of management to employ a collection agency or not as it sees fit. Any cost anticipated from doing so simply reduces the estimated collectable value of the receivables.

Equities may not have to be paid for a long or indefinite period of time. So long as a corporation continues in existence it does not repay its shareholders in full, and there is seldom any limit imposed by its charter on the lifetime of a corporation.

The existence of an equity, like the existence of an asset, can be questionable. When a disputed claim is made against a business for example, a liability might or might not exist. Liabilities that are doubtful are called **contingent liabilities**. Whether a liability is real or contingent depends on the degree of certainty about it. If it is probable that the amount will have to be paid, the liability is real; if it is possible but subject to reasonable doubt, the liability is contingent. Contingent liabilities, like contingent assets, are described in notes to financial statements, not in the accounts.

A liability can be probable, and therefore real, but the amount not reasonably determinable. For example, it might be fairly certain that some amount will have to be paid as a result of a lawsuit, but the amount cannot be reasonably estimated. In that case, the lower limit of the probability will be recorded in the accounts if it is determinable, and the range of possible liability will be reported in a note to the financial statements.

The fact that something might or might not be considered an asset, and a related item a liability, depending on the circumstances, means that financial statements can be prepared for two very similar businesses showing very dissimilar information. For example, if National Wholesalers, described in chapters 2 and 3, leased its land and building on certain conditions, instead of owning them and borrowing on a mortgage, its reported fixed assets would be almost 80% less, its total assets almost 30% less and its long term debt more than 45% less. Financial statements for the same business can be very different from one year to the next, if ownership control changes and goodwill is recorded for the first time. The effects of alternative practices of recording and measuring assets and liabilities is described in more detail in later chapters dealing with the measurement of specific items.

REVENUES

Revenue is generally deemed to be created when goods and services are provided in return for payment or a promise of payment, in other words, when an exchange transaction occurs. In accounting terminology, it is said to be **realized** at that point. Realization is based on recording exchanges, because exchanges provide an objective measure of the revenue. In an economic sense of value added, revenue is generated by all the activities of a business leading up to, and in some cases following, an exchange. If management did not believe an activity contributed to generating revenue, they would discontinue it. Until there is an exchange with an independent party however, the revenue is not usually objectively measurable.

The time of realization is usually taken to be the time services are performed or legal title to goods passes. No revenue is realized on goods shipped to an agent on consignment, for example, nor on goods shipped to a customer on approval until approval is given.

In some situations, realization based on a strict legal interpretation of when title passes does not reflect the economic substance of a transaction. In these situations, realization is deemed to occur at the time the significant benefits and risks of ownership are transferred, regardless of legal ownership. Whether the benefits and risks of ownership have been transferred depends on the circumstances. If goods are sold in return for instalment payments that amount to little more than rent and there is substantial risk of default by buyers before payment in full, the benefits and risks have not been effectively transferred. Depending on the extent of the risk retained by the selling business, it will either record partial realization as each instalment is paid, or defer realization until all costs related to the sale have been recovered.

In some other situations, realization can be subject to substantial uncertainty regarding other future events besides collection. This is often the case for businesses that provide goods or services under long term contracts. For example, a construction company could contract to build a long stretch of highway, for a fixed price, over a period of two or three or more years. As each section was completed, it could be turned over to the appropriate authority and a proportional amount of the total price billed and recorded as realized revenue. The related costs and expenses of that section would also have to be recorded in the calculation of income. If the costs of all sections were comparable or at least reasonably predictable, a satisfactory estimate of income, section by section, could be made. If the costs of future sections were uncertain because of unknown soil conditions or possible bad weather or potential work stoppages however, income from the contract as a whole could be very different from that indicated by the beginning sections. It could be a loss. In situations such as this, some businesses elect to defer recording revenue as realized until the contract is substantially completed. In the meantime, progress billings received are recorded as advance payments from customers and costs are recorded as a form of inventory.

In a few situations, when costs are difficult to allocate and products are easily marketable, meat packing and some mining for example, revenue is recognized at the time production is completed.

Application of the realization concept can convey somewhat misleading impressions of profitability, when sales are not recorded at the same rate as the overall activity of the business. An extreme example would be a construction company working on a single long term contract and recording no revenue until its completion. It could show no revenue and no income for one or more years, and much revenue and income in a later year, all based on the same work. To a lesser extent, a similar result will be produced for any business whose recorded sales fluctuate out of phase with its operations as a whole. Higher income will be reported in periods of higher sales and lower income in periods of lower sales.

COSTS

Costs, like revenues, are determined by exchange transactions, in this case by purchases. The price paid to purchase something is usually an objective measure of its value. There are however, exceptions. If the purchase is not made in an "arms length" transaction, the price will not necessarily reflect an objective valuation. If a corporation purchases something from its controlling shareholder, for example, the price can be very different from what it would pay to an independent third party. In that case it is not a satisfactory valuation. The asset should be recorded at fair market value and the difference between that and the price paid should be reflected as part of shareholders' investment.

Sometimes things are acquired in whole or in part by gift or subsidy. Governments sometimes provide financial assistance to companies for the purchase of fixed assets, for example, or for the payment of certain expenses. An objective market value for these things would be the amount the company would pay in an unsubsidized transaction. In practice, the amount of subsidy received is deducted from the recorded cost of the asset or expense.

The reported cost does not reflect the fair market value. This is discussed further in chapter 6.

The cost of an asset includes all outlays needed to put that asset into service. For example, the cost of freight paid by a company to bring inventory to its plant is part of the cost of the inventory. Similarly, the amount paid to a mechanic to set up a new machine is part of the cost of that machine. On the other hand, cost does not include outlays that do not contribute to the ongoing value of an asset, what can be described as excess costs. For example, if the mechanic paid to set up a machine botched the job and it had to be redone, the additional payment would not properly be included in the cost of the asset.

The cost of something is dependent in part on who makes the purchase and how. The cost of auto parts is less to a car manufacturer than to a car dealer, and less still than to a business that pays to have its vehicle repaired. The cost of the same thing would be different in the books of each business. Sometimes a purchaser can reduce his cost by making something in his own plant instead of buying it from an outsider. Cost savings, regardless of how they are achieved, reduce the amounts recorded in the books of the purchaser. The fact that one business can buy something for less than another does not allow it to record a profit on a purchase. Revenue and profit are not generated until something is sold.

Valuation problems sometimes arise when the price paid for something is not paid in cash or a claim for cash. In a barter transaction, an estimate must be made of the cash equivalent of the values exchanged. Sometimes for example, corporations acquire assets in exchange for some of their shares. If the shares are being actively traded, a reference value is available. If not, the value must be estimated. In some cases, several assets are acquired together in this manner. A corporation might purchase a complete business in return for some of its shares. Even if the share value is readily determinable, an allocation of that value must be made among the various assets acquired.

EXPENSES

Some purchases are recorded initially as expenses and some as assets. Over time, most purchased assets become expenses; inventory becomes cost of goods sold, fixed assets become depreciation. Decisions as to when purchases are, or become, expenses are based on when the economic benefits are consumed. Since the purpose of all purchases is to produce revenues, the economic benefits of purchases are usually deemed to be consumed as revenues are generated. The attempt is made to match expenses with revenues.

The need for matching arises from the fact that revenues are usually recorded only when goods or services are sold, the realization concept. Goods may be produced in one accounting period and sold in another. No revenue is recorded in the production period, even though much value may have been added. Revenue is recorded only in the selling period. If a meaningful measure of income is to be produced, expenses must be recognized in the same accounting period as the revenue they generate. Expenses must be matched with the corresponding revenues.

For many purchases it is difficult to know or estimate when the benefits are consumed. The purchase of salesmen's services, for example, contributes not only to current sales but to future sales, as the salesmen develop favorable customer relationships. Administrative services are devoted partly to current sales effort and partly to the manufacture of products for future sale.

Whenever doubt exists as to whether a purchase will contribute future benefits and therefore be considered an asset, it is treated as an expense. This practice is based on **conservatism**. It is considered better to err on the side of reporting asset values and income too low than too high. Users of accounting information are less likely to suffer from believing underestimates of wealth and income than from overestimates. Based on conservatism, spending on selling and administrative activities is nearly always considered expense.

Conservatism as applied to expenses can have a significant effect on the assets and income reported by companies that spend large amounts to produce intangible value, because the existence of intangible value is hard to prove and in most cases impossible to quantify. Companies such as pharmaceutical manufacturers, for example, spend large sums over long periods of time on research and development to create new products. Almost all research and development costs are treated as expenses. The value created by research and development however, can be very great. In some businesses, the value of unrecorded intangibles is by far the most important. The effect of not recording this intangible value as an asset is to show much less income, possibly losses during the time the money is spent, and potentially very high income when the product is sold.

MARKET VALUES

Cost is a measure of the market value of an asset to a business at the time of purchase, but it is not the only measure of market. It represents market value to the business as a buyer, not as a seller. If a business attempted to resell an asset immediately after purchase, it would likely find the asset had a different market value. As a simple example, if a company bought a new car and then tried to resell it immediately, it is doubtful the company could get as much as it paid. The market value to buy is different from the market value to sell, because the company operates under different market conditions as a buyer and a seller. It does not have the same advantages in selling a car as the car dealer from whom it bought.

The fact that many assets have resale values less than their cost is ignored in accounting, provided there is no immediate intention to resell. If the intention is to continue to use an asset in the operation of a business, the relevant measure is the purchase price, not the resale value. This is described as the **going concern** concept in accounting. As long as a business is a going concern, that is, as long as it continues to operate actively, it will not be selling its productive assets and therefore the selling value is not relevant.

For some businesses, some assets have immediate resale values greater than their cost. This is true of most inventory items purchased by retailers, the car dealer for example. For these too, the relevant measure is the purchase market, based on the realization convention. No revenue or increase in value is recognized until an asset is sold.

The going concern concept of valuation has important implications for business lenders such as banks. The values reported for assets are premised on the assumption that the business will continue to operate. If the business ceases to operate, the assets will be worth much less. Fixed assets are often virtually worthless, inventories that might be worth more in a going concern will almost certainly be worth less in a distress sale, and accounts receivable will be harder to collect. In assessing the value of his security, a lender must be guided by the selling values.

The market value of assets changes over time. The cost of buying some assets increases, the cost of others decreases. Based on the realization concept and conservatism, increases in market values are never recorded without some form of exchange transaction. Decreases are treated differently, depending on whether an asset is current or non current. When the value of a current asset declines, the decrease is usually recorded and the reduction included as an expense of the current period. This is true for receivables and most short term investments, as well as for tangible inventories. The practice is based on conservatism and the fact that by definition, current assets will be sold or collected in the near future. Non current assets are generally not reduced in value unless a significant decline can be identified and the decline is judged permanent. This practice is based on the going concern concept and the fact that non current assets are retained for long term use in the business. Once an asset, current or non current, has been reduced in value, it is never subsequently increased, regardless of what happens to market values.

Asset valuation conventions bring anticipated losses into the calculation of current income, while deferring anticipated gains to future periods. This produces consistently lower asset valuations and a conservative balance sheet but it does not always have the same effect on reported income. If more of the cost of an asset is charged against income in the current period, there is less of it left to charge against income in future periods. The lower, conservative estimate of income in the current period will be offset by a higher, unconservative estimate in the future.

INTEREST

Many assets and most liabilities are monetary in nature; that is, they require cash settlements, payments either to or from the business. Accounts receivable are claims for payment to the business, accounts payable and borrowings are claims for payment from the business. Monetary items involve interest, because cash a year from now is not worth as much as the same amount of cash today.

When interest is part of an exchange transaction, it is recognized and recorded in accounting. If interest is charged on an account or note receivable, it is recorded as revenue. If it is paid on a debt, it is an expense. When it is not made explicit in an exchange, it is usually ignored. Interest is not recorded on receivables and payables, if it is not specifically referred to in the selling or purchase agreements, unless the debts are expected to be outstanding for at least a year. It does still exist, however. An amount collectable or payable one or two months from now is not worth as much as the same amount collectable or payable today. A company that sells for cash but is able to buy on credit is better off than one that sells on credit but has to pay cash for purchases, because it can operate with less borrowings and owner investment.

Interest that is not specifically recorded becomes part of the calculation of income indirectly. The business that buys on credit and sells for cash pays less interest to borrow and earns a higher return for its owners on a smaller investment, than the one that sells on credit and buys for cash. Although unrecorded interest becomes a factor of income in this way, it does not become a factor in the valuation of assets and liabilities. Current receivables and payables are shown in the balance sheet at their face amounts, the amounts that will ultimately be received or paid, not at their present value.

CONSTANT DOLLAR ACCOUNTING

Accounting data are recorded in money values, in this country in dollars. Money itself however, changes in value in terms of what it will buy, due to inflation or less often to deflation. As money changes in value, the current dollar value of data recorded in the accounts also changes. This change is independent of any change in the relative market values of the other assets and liabilities themselves.

The significance of changing money values to accounting measurements depends on the rate of inflation and the period of time involved. If the rate of inflation is moderate, the effect on current revenues and expenses recorded over the course of a year will not be significant. Neither will the effect on current assets and liabilities recorded during the year. Over a period of several years however, the cumulative effect on the current dollar value of long term assets and liabilities can be substantial. Recorded values of long term assets and liabilities can be much lower than current dollar values. To the extent that long term asset costs are amortized, as in recording depreciation over the lifetime of an asset, the expense will also be much lower and reported income higher.

In general, the effect of ignoring changes in dollar values during periods of inflation is to understate investment in assets and to overstate income. The magnitude of that effect depends on the extent to which a business invests in long term assets. A steel producer, with heavy investment in plant and equipment, will be relatively much more affected than a moving picture producer, with little long term investment.

In recent years proposals have been made to adjust accounting measurements for changing dollar values, described as constant dollar accounting. A general price index is used to translate historical costs recorded in the books into current dollar values. In Canada, either the Consumer Price Index or the Gross National Expenditure Implicit Price Deflator is used. Both are published by Statistics Canada. Some accountants are attracted to this kind of adjustment because of its relative simplicity, but it is subject to the criticism that it ignores all changes in value other than changes in the dollar. Adjusting for dollar changes but not other changes can give the impression but not the reality of current values. In practice, constant dollar data are seldom calculated.

CURRENT COST ACCOUNTING

Most accountants who favor making value adjustments prefer a system, described as current cost accounting, that adjusts recorded data for all value changes, not just dollar value changes. This is much more difficult than adjusting for dollars only, both conceptually and practically. The value of tangible assets to a business is in their capacity to provide services and to generate income. This is not necessarily reflected in the current cost of similar assets, because technology changes, products change and businesses generally change. Attempting to calculate asset value changes by reference to their service and income generating capacity can be a formidable and costly undertaking for a large company.

Accountants have experimented with value adjustments in the form of supplementary information to financial statements prepared in the traditional way, but not by making changes directly to the original data. Today, even this limited attempt at adjustment has been largely abandoned. The difficulties and costs involved have been judged excessive for the value of the additional information provided. General comments on changing price levels are sometimes included in the annual reports of public corporations but little more.

PRINCIPLES

The term accounting principles is used to describe the basic concepts and conventions of accounting, plus a wide range of measurement and reporting methods. **Generally accepted accounting principles**, often referred to as **GAAP**, are those concepts, conventions and methods considered acceptable by accountants and by those who use accounting information. GAAP result from the findings, decisions and pronouncements of many official and semi-official bodies: accounting standards boards, professional accounting associations, governmental authorities, securities commissions and stock exchanges, among others.

What is acceptable depends on where in the world the information is to be used and when it is produced. Practices considered acceptable in one country are not always acceptable in another. GAAP in Canada are not precisely the same as in the United States or Britain or Mexico, for example. GAAP also change over time. Financial statements prepared in accordance with GAAP twenty years ago might not be acceptable today. In Canada, GAAP are defined in Recommendations and Guidelines issued by the Accounting Standards Board (AcSB) of the Canadian Institute of Chartered Accountants (CICA). The CICA is one of three main associations of professional accountants in Canada. The others are the Certified General Accountants' Association of Canada and the Society of Management Accountants of Canada. The AcSB includes members of all three associations as well as representatives of accounting user groups. A compilation of current Recommendations and Guidelines is published in what is called the **CICA Handbook**. Similar compilations are produced in other countries. These compilations are constantly revised and updated to reflect current practice.

Not all accounting data are produced in accordance with GAAP. People can keep records and produce reports any way they choose. Accounting information that is produced in accordance with GAAP however, meets defined standards and therefore has a level of credibility it would not otherwise have for those who wish to use it. A business applying for a bank loan, for example, would have an easier time if it could provide financial statements prepared in accordance with GAAP, than if not. As part of their responsibility to shareholders, public corporations are expected to provide them with regular financial reports prepared in accordance with GAAP. Requirements to this effect are included in federal and provincial corporations and securities legislation.

The basic concepts and conventions embodied in GAAP are virtually universal. Within the basic framework however, there is much diversity of method, both within and among countries. Depreciation, for example, is calculated in several different ways by different companies in Canada, sometimes in two or more ways for different kinds of assets by the same company. The same is true in the United States, but the mix of methods there is different as well. Some differences in method are based on perceived differences between businesses but others reflect nothing more than a preference on the part of those responsible for producing the measurements. Those preferences in turn can depend on the meanings the producers want to convey to the users of their measurements. Companies in different lines of business could calculate depreciation differently because they use assets in different ways, an electric power producer for example, as compared with a chain of food stores. On the other hand, two food chains might calculate depreciation differently because one wanted to show more income in the current year and the other in later years.

The discussion of concepts, conventions and methods earlier in this chapter and descriptions of financial statements and double entry bookkeeping in the preceding chapters are based on GAAP in Canada. Financial statement requirements in general are elaborated in the following section of this chapter. GAAP methods and requirements as they pertain to specific assets, liabilities and ownership are discussed in the remaining chapters of this part of the book.

FINANCIAL REPORTING

The basic financial statements of a business consist of a **balance sheet**, an **income statement**, a **statement of retained earnings** and a **cash flow statement**, also known as a **statement of changes in financial position**.

Balance sheets were discussed in chapter 2 and income statements in chapter 3. Statements of ownership including retained earnings for unincorporated businesses were discussed in chapter 3 as well. Ownership reporting for corporations is discussed in chapter 10. Cash flow statements are prepared from the same data as balance sheets and statements of income. They are discussed in chapter 13. The basic statements are produced annually.

The basic statements should meet the needs of external users, in particular shareholders and creditors, for financial information concerning a business. To meet these needs, financial statements should be **understandable**, **relevant**, **reliable** and **comparable**. These requirements raise three issues. The first is the question of **cost**, the cost of producing and reporting the information. Management must decide at what point the cost of providing additional information is no longer justified by the added **benefit** for users. This cost versus benefit issue was noted earlier in connection with reporting the effects of changing prices.

The second issue is the significance of the information provided. It might not cost any more to report a small advance to an officer of a large corporation separately from other accounts receivable, but if the amount is not significant, it would detract from the understandability and relevance of a balance sheet, not enhance it. Information that is significant in accounting is said to be **material**. Something is material if the knowledge of it would influence a report user's decision concerning the business. Information that is not material is not reported.

The third issue is that of **comparability**. As noted earlier, there is much diversity in measurement methods among different businesses. Two very similar companies could produce very different financial statements and still satisfy GAAP. The requirement for comparability relates to different statements prepared by the same business, in particular to statements for successive years, not to statements of different businesses. A business is expected to apply the same methods consistently year after year. On those rare occasions when a change in method is necessary, the effect of that change on the current financial statements, and the effect it would have had if applied to any previous financial statements presented for comparative purposes, must be reported so far as it is possible to do so.

Occasionally an **error** is discovered in financial reports after they have been issued. When that happens and a correction is made, the effect of the correction on the current and on any previous statements presented for comparative purposes must be reported as well.

Many accounting measurements are based on estimates and sometimes estimates are revised in the light of new information. The estimated useful lifetime and therefore the depreciation of a factory building for example, might be changed after several years in use. **Changes in estimates** are not considered corrections of errors. The effect of a change in estimate is restricted to the current financial statements and to future statements, if applicable. No change is made to the amounts reported in prior periods. The result is that current and future charges for an element of expense can be higher or lower than past charges for the same element.

Full disclosure of the relevant financial information about a business requires more than reports of the amounts shown in its accounting records. **Notes to the financial statements** are required to provide additional information on a variety of matters. One such note is a description of the significant accounting policies of the business. This is a description of the **measurement methods** used, when alternative methods are acceptable. The note for public corporations is usually extensive, referring to several categories of assets and liabilities. It is usually the first note, if there is more than one, or is reported in the form of a summary, cross-referenced to the statements.

Reference was made earlier to the need for notes concerning contingent assets and liabilities. Similar notes are required to disclose certain **commitments**. Many businesses enter into contracts involving future obligations, purchase contracts for future deliveries of raw materials for example. If these commitments are significant in relation to the size of the business, they are reported.

Sometimes **subsequent events** that have a significant effect on the affairs of a business occur after the company's year end but before its financial statements are issued. A decision to discontinue the operations of a line of business for example, might be made shortly after the year end. The decision would not affect the amounts shown in the financial statements for the year, but would be significant for the future of the company. Events of this nature are also reported by note.

Most public corporations report much more in their annual reports than the basic financial statements. Almost all published reports include summaries of financial information for the past five years or more, and highlight important information concerning the past two or three years.

Public corporations publish **quarterly financial reports** as well as annual reports. The same basic measurement practices are followed but the extent of the information provided is less. Some additional measurement problems are encountered in producing quarterly statements. Estimates have to be made of such things as taxes and bonuses that will be determined after the year is complete.

CHAPTER 6

Property, Plant and Equipment; Intangibles

Property, Plant and Equipment

COST

Property, plant and equipment are recorded initially at their cost to the acquiring business. That cost includes all outlays required to put the assets into the place and condition they can be used for the intended purpose of the acquirer. For example it can include freight, installation, assembly and testing costs, construction permit fees, real estate commissions and legal and architectural fees. If land has to be cleared or drained or levelled to make it usable, the costs involved are part of the cost of the land.

Sometimes taxes have to be paid for the construction of roads or the installation of services such as water service to a property. If these are one time charges, they are considered part of the cost of the property. If they are recurring, they are treated as expense of the period when levied. Other costs, such as landscaping, can also be considered either an asset cost or a current expense, depending on whether they represent permanent improvements or are temporary and recurring.

If land is purchased with a building on it but the intention is to demolish the building and construct something new, the cost of demolition less any recovery from the sale of scrap is part of the cost of the land. When land and building are purchased together and the intention is to use the combination, it must be decided how much of the cost should be allocated to each. It is often the case that the total of the estimated value of each independently is different from the cost of the two together. The decision as to how the cost is allocated will affect future calculations of income, because the building will depreciate but the land will not. The accepted practice is to allocate the cost in proportion to the estimated values of the land and building separately.

Sometimes a company will undertake to build a depreciable asset for itself, instead of buying it from a supplier. A construction company, for example, might opt to build its own head office, rather than to buy an existing property. When that happens, all costs directly attributable to the construction, such as building materials, plus a fair share of other, indirect costs such as general business administration are allocated to the asset. Any cost savings, such as discounts on purchases, are reductions of cost. Similarly, any miscellaneous earnings, such as fees from leasing parking space on a building site during construction, are reductions of cost, not revenues.

Sometimes a company will end up paying more than anticipated for an asset, due to unforseen circumstances. For example, a company constructing its own building could suffer cost overruns as a result of a work stoppage. In that case, the excess costs are charged to expense, not added to the cost of the asset, based on conservatism. What can appear to be excess costs are not always that however. A company might find it necessary to purchase options on two or more properties in the course of acquiring one suitable site. The cost of all options could be considered part of the cost of the final location.

When an asset is acquired over an extended period of time, as in the case of a building being constructed, the interest cost of the funds required during the period of acquisition can be included in the cost of the asset. If money is borrowed specifically for the purpose, the interest on that debt is the appropriate amount. If not, interest calculated at the weighted average rate of interest on company borrowings is used.

Government assistance is sometimes provided to businesses to assist in the purchase of assets. This assistance can take the form of grants or forgivable loans or tax reductions. In some cases, the benefit can only be secured by satisfying certain conditions in future years. A forgivable loan, for example, requires conditions to be fulfilled for forgiveness. In other cases, the benefit is secured immediately upon a business completing a single transaction, a subsidy in aid of the purchase of a factory building in a depressed area, for example. Regardless of the terms of government assistance, it is always considered applicable to the time the relevant assets are used. An outright gift towards the purchase of an asset is not considered an immediate benefit to the owners of a business, even though it involves no future commitment from them.

Government assistance towards the purchase of assets can be recorded in one of two ways, the choice is optional. It can be deducted from the cost of the asset purchased, or it can be recorded as a form of unrealized benefit, similar to amounts received on the sale of tickets for future services. If it is deducted from cost, the recorded asset value will not reflect market value. In either case, the benefit is amortized to income over the lifetime of the asset, either as a reduction in the amount of depreciation charged or as a realization of the deferred benefit.

DEPRECIATION

With the exception of land as a location, all fixed assets lose their value, or depreciate, over time. They depreciate for two reasons, physical deterioration and economic obsolescence. Physical deterioration results in part from the usage of an asset, wear and tear, and in part from the passage of time, the effect of the elements. Economic obsolescence can result from changes in technology and from changes in market demands. Some assets are more affected by one factor than another. A drill press is more likely to depreciate for physical reasons and a computer for economic reasons. It is usually easier to forecast the rate of physical depreciation than that of economic depreciation.

Depreciation expense for a period is recorded by transferring an amount to an expense account and reducing the asset value. The reduction in value is recorded in what is called an asset valuation allowance account. When financial statements are prepared, the total amount accumulated to date in the asset valuation allowance is deducted from the original cost and both amounts are shown in the balance sheet. This is more informative than simply showing the remaining undepreciated amount of the asset, because it shows how much an asset cost and how much of the original value remains to be used.

In calculating depreciation expense, the first thing to be determined is what the depreciable unit is going to be. This involves two decisions. One is to decide what different types of fixed assets should be distinguished. For example, should automotive equipment be separated from other forms of equipment and if so, should cars be separated from trucks? The answer to this question is usually based on the relative rates at which the assets depreciate and the amounts invested in each category. If automotive equipment depreciates at a significantly different rate from other equipment and if the amounts invested are significant, they should be segregated.

The other question is how many units of a given category should be grouped together? Should all cars purchased in a year be regarded as a single unit for depreciation purposes, or should each one be depreciated individually? The answer to this question determines the frequency with which errors of estimate are corrected. If each car is treated individually, an error in depreciating that car will be corrected at the latest when the car is retired from service. If all cars are grouped together, errors might not become apparent until they were all retired. Again, the amount invested will influence the decision.

The total amount to be charged to expense over the useful lifetime of a depreciable unit is original cost less the residual value, if any. That amount can be apportioned to years of service in one of several ways. The most common methods of apportionment can be described as **straight line**, **decreasing charge** and **usage**. Other methods are possible, for example increasing charge, but they are rarely used.

Straight Line

The straight line method is the simplest. The total amount to be charged to expense is divided by the estimated number of years of use, and the resulting amount is charged each year to depreciation. For example:

Asset cost	$5,000	100%
Estimated residual value	1,000	20
Amount to be charged to expense	4,000	80
Years of expected use	4	4
Annual depreciation	$1,000	20%

Decreasing Charge

The decreasing charge method generally used in Canada is described as the **declining balance** method. Depreciation each year is calculated as a percentage of the asset value remaining undepreciated at the end of the previous year, that is, on the cost less accumulated depreciation. The percentage used most often is twice the straight line percentage. For example:

Asset cost	$5,000	
Depreciation year 1: 40% of 5,000	2,000	$2,000
Remainder undepreciated	3,000	
Depreciation year 2: 40% of 3,000	1,200	1,200
Remainder undepreciated	1,800	
Depreciation year 3: 40% of 1,800	720	720
Remainder undepreciated	1,080	
Depreciation year 4: 40% of 1,080	432	432
	$ 648	$4,352

The total charged to depreciation and the residual value remaining are not the same using the percentage calculations as in the other calculations. Which is more correct can only be known after the asset is finally taken out of service.

Usage

Usage methods are based on estimates of the amount of service that can be expected from an asset. For example, a machine might be expected to run for 10,000 hours, or to produce 10,000 units of product before it is retired. Based on the following assumed units of usage year by year, the depreciation calculations would be as follows:

Asset cost	$ 5,000
Estimated residual value	1,000
Amount to be charged to expense	4,000
Units of service	10,000
Depreciation per unit	$ .40
Depreciation	
year 1: 2,800 units × .40	$ 1,120
year 2: 2,400 units × .40	960
year 3: 2,600 units × .40	1,040
year 4: 2,200 units × .40	880
Total 10,000	$ 4,000

A comparison of the effects of using different methods of calculating depreciation in the previous examples shows the following.

Year	Straight Line	Declining Balance	Usage
1	$1,000	$2,000	$1,120
2	1,000	1,200	960
3	1,000	720	1,040
4	1,000	432	880
	$4,000	$4,352	$4,000

Using straight line, depreciation is the same each year. With declining balance, it is much higher in the earlier years and much lower in the later years. Based on usage, it can be either higher or lower, depending on the level of activity.

The various methods of calculating depreciation can be rationalized in different ways, depending on the emphasis put on the factors that cause the value of assets to decline. Straight line puts the emphasis on time. Declining balance recognizes the probable need for the additional cost of increasing maintenance as assets age, and possible growing obsolescence and decreasing utility. Usage places the emphasis on physical wear and tear. Whatever method is chosen, it is, in the final analysis, arbitrary. Accounting depreciation is only a systematic allocation of cost, it is not a process of valuation.

In Canada, the straight line method is by far the most often used. Almost all public companies apply it to some of their depreciable assets, most apply it to all. The next most popular is the declining balance method. This method is required to be used in calculating depreciation (described in tax language as capital cost allowance) for Canadian income tax purposes. Although it is not required to be used in calculating accounting income, many businesses find it easier to use the same method for both purposes. Tax law prescribes the percentage depreciation rates to be used and the categories in which assets must be grouped. Usage methods are used most commonly by companies using plant and equipment in conjunction with depletable assets, such as mines. The plant is depreciated at a rate consistent with the use of the available resource.

GAAP require the methods of calculating depreciation and the amount of depreciation charged to income to be reported in financial statements.

Some businesses are obliged to remove assets or to rehabilitate sites after they have finished using them. When that is the case, a provision is made for the estimated costs. Each year an amount is recorded as an expense of removal or restoration and a corresponding amount recorded as a liability. The procedure is similar to that of recording depreciation expense, except that the credit is to a liability, not a reduction of the asset.

As a practical alternative to depreciation accounting, most businesses follow the practice of charging the cost of small items of equipment directly to expense. This can be done in a variety of ways. Items can be expensed at the time of purchase, at the time of issue to employees, or at the time of retirement or disposal. An inventory of small items can be taken at the end of each year and an amount charged to expense equal to what was on hand at the beginning plus purchases minus what is left. The cost of replacing small items can be charged to expense whenever they are replaced. Containers are usually expensed if they fail to return within a given period of time.

Depreciation is directly related to repairs and maintenance expense. Within limits, more spent on maintenance will result in less physical deterioration and prolong the life of an asset. In fact, much maintenance consists of the replacement of part of a depreciable asset. As a practical matter, most small costs of replacement are charged to expense when incurred.

ADJUSTMENTS

Sometimes adjustments are required to the recorded cost or accumulated depreciation of assets. If costs are incurred that go beyond the maintenance of an asset and increase its productive capacity or its useful lifetime, they are added to the original cost of the asset. The cost and accumulated depreciation of parts replaced in the course of improving assets are removed from the accounts to the extent they can be estimated. All adjustments to cost and accumulated depreciation require new calculations of depreciation expense for future years.

Adjustments are also required when it becomes apparent that the value of an asset has been impaired. New developments in technology could significantly impair the value of computer assets, for example. In that case, a lump sum increase in accumulated depreciation and a corresponding loss are recorded, and a new calculation of depreciation for the current and future years is made. Adjustments are not made to accumulated depreciation for changes in estimates of an asset's expected lifetime or salvage value. Corrections of estimates are reflected in revised charges for depreciation over an asset's remaining lifetime, as described in Chapter 5. In practice, corrections of estimates are seldom made, particularly when a lifetime is underestimated. As a result, some companies have assets still in use that have been fully depreciated and have no value in the accounts.

When an asset is retired from service, the original cost and the related accumulated depreciation are eliminated from the accounts. If the cost less the accumulated depreciation exceeds the proceeds of disposal, the difference is usually described as a loss on disposal. If the opposite is the case, it is a gain on disposal. They are seldom really gains or losses however. Unless an asset is retired from service prematurely as a result of some unusual circumstance such as accidental damage, what are commonly called gains and losses on disposal are really corrections of the depreciation estimates recorded over the lives of the assets. When the amounts are not large, they are usually recorded as adjustments to depreciation expense in the year of disposal.

The nominal amount received for an asset on retirement is not always the appropriate amount to use in calculating the adjustment on disposal. Trade in allowances on the purchase of replacements are often inflated to effect a reduction in the price of the new asset. In that case, an adjustment to reflect estimated market values is appropriate.

For management purposes, appraisals of specific asset values are often made. They are made for a variety of reasons: deciding whether to sell or replace an asset, using assets as collateral for borrowings, determining the amount of insurance coverage to carry, and so on. In accordance with GAAP, it is not acceptable to record appraised values in the accounts unless they indicate an impairment of value.

LEASES

Many companies lease long term assets instead of buying them. Not only land and buildings, but many kinds of equipment are leased. For accounting purposes, a lease is either a **capital lease** or an **operating lease** depending on the terms of the leasing agreement. If the agreement transfers substantially all of the benefits and risks of ownership to the lessee, it is a capital lease. An effective transfer of the benefits and risks is indicated by any of the following criteria:

1. It is reasonably certain that legal ownership will pass by the end of the lease term, either because the lease provides for that or because it provides for a purchase by the lessee at a bargain price.

2. The lease term is for substantially all of the economically valuable life span of the asset. 75% or more is usually considered substantially all.

3. The present value of the minimum lease payments is substantially equal to the fair market value of the asset. 90% or more is usually considered substantially equal.

Capital leases are recorded by **lessees** in a manner similar to depreciable assets. The lower of the present discounted value of payments required under the lease and the fair value of the property, is recorded as an asset, and a corresponding amount is recorded as a long term liability. The asset value of the lease is transferred to expense year by year in the same manner as owned assets are depreciated, with two exceptions. One is that the time period over which the asset is written off is limited to the term of the lease, not the lifetime of the asset, unless the lease provides for a transfer of ownership to the lessee at some point, or allows the lessee to purchase the asset at a future time for a bargain price. The other is that the current and accumulated expenses are described as amortization, not depreciation. Amortization is almost always calculated using the straight line method. Because the long term liability to the lessor has been recorded at the discounted value of the payments required, the actual payments, when made, will exceed the recorded liability. The excess of each payment over the amount of the liability discharged is interest expense. GAAP requirements for reporting information concerning assets and expenses under capital leases are essentially the same as for owned assets. In addition they require disclosure of the particulars of the lease obligations.

Operating leases are treated as simple rental contracts. Payments are recorded as made, either as rental expense or as a prepayment. Disclosure of the lease obligations is also required, although they are not recorded as a liability in the accounts.

In the books of **lessors**, what is considered a capital lease to a lessee is usually recorded as an investment in the nature of a long term account receivable bearing interest. As payments are received over the term of the lease, the amount of the investment is reduced and the interest element of the payments is taken into income. An exception to this practice is made when a lease involves significant ongoing risk associated with ownership to the lessor. If there is significant risk of lease payments being uncollectable or from potentially costly commitments such as guaranties, the lease is treated as an operating lease. The asset is recorded and depreciated in the books of the lessor and rental revenue is recorded as earned.

In most cases, the lessor under a capital lease is a financing agent that provides the money to finance the asset purchase. In some, the lessor is also the producer or seller of the asset. In the latter case there is usually an initial profit on the selling transaction as well as the ongoing interest revenue in the lease payments. This profit is recorded at the time the lease is initiated. When there is a profit element, the lease is described as a **sales-type lease**; when there is not, it is called a **direct financing lease**.

Sometimes a capital lease is created as a result of a **sale and lease-back transaction**. A company sells a productive asset, a building for example, to an investor, and agrees to lease it back. If the asset is sold for a fair market value less than its recorded book value, the difference is recorded as a loss at the time of sale. If it is sold for a fair market value in excess of its book value, the difference is deferred and amortized over the term of the lease as an adjustment to the rental cost.

When companies enter into long term leases, capital and operating, they often spend money to improve or add to the leased assets. A company leasing office space, for example, might add interior walls and doors to adapt the space to its specific requirements. These additions are described as

leasehold improvements. If a lease is a capital lease, the cost of leasehold improvements will be amortized in the same manner as the cost of the leased assets, unless they have more limited lifetimes, in which case they will be amortized over a shorter period. If it is an operating lease, they will be amortized over the shorter of their estimated lifetimes and the term of the lease. If the term of the lease can be extended by a renewal provision, the amortization period can be extended as well.

Depending on whether a company owns or leases assets under capital leases, or it leases them under operating leases, it can show very different figures in its financial statements. In an ownership or capital lease situation, a company will show the acquisition cost of the assets and any continuing liability in respect of them in its balance sheet. Under an operating lease, no asset or liability will be reflected in the body of the statement. The disclosure will be in a reference to future lease commitments in the notes. In assessing the financial strength of a business and comparing it with others therefore, a reader must consider the implications of possibly significant obligations not shown in the body of the balance sheet and of the corresponding commitment to assets. In the income statement, depending on the method of acquiring fixed assets, the expense will be shown as depreciation or amortization or rent. If assets are acquired by lease and the lease term is long, the amounts shown as amortization are likely to be similar to those that would have been reported as depreciation had the assets been purchased. If assets are acquired on short term leases however, current rental expenses can diverge substantially over time from the depreciation or amortization expenses that would have been recorded had those same assets been purchased or leased long term.

Intangibles

Intangibles, like other assets, are recorded at cost. With the exception of goodwill however, they are recorded only when a cost can be assigned to a legal right or transferable form of intangible asset. As a result, little intangible value is recorded in accounts, other than that represented by legal rights such as **patents**, **trade marks**, **franchises**, **licences** and **copyrights**, and that represented by transferable trade secrets, such as **customer lists** and **product formulas**. Competitive advantages occurring freely, such as a lack of competing businesses, are not recorded because they have no cost. Many advantages purchased, such as favorable customer attitudes in response to advertising, are not recorded because the costs cannot be assigned to specific legal or transferable intangible assets. Those advantages that are recorded, such as patents, are only assigned the costs incurred directly in acquiring them and occasionally in defending them. If a patent as such is purchased, the amount paid is an asset. If it is acquired after research, the costs of research are an expense, not a cost of the patent.

Goodwill is a special case. When a business as a whole is purchased, the amount paid is for all of the perceived value of that business, intangible as well as tangible. To the extent the price exceeds the estimated value of the tangible assets and the legal or transferable intangibles, it is paid for other intangibles, described as goodwill. In this case, the intangible asset goodwill is recorded in the amount of the excess. It is not acceptable practice to write off the cost of goodwill at the time of acquisition.

Occasionally, a business in financial difficulty will be purchased for less than the value of its tangibles and identified intangibles, indicating negative goodwill. Negative goodwill is applied to reduce the values assigned to other assets purchased.

For the purpose of calculating income, intangibles are divided into two categories, those with limited lifetimes, such as patents and copyrights, and those with unlimited or indeterminate lifetimes, such as trade marks and goodwill. The cost of those with limited lifetimes is amortized to expense over the shorter of their economic and legal lifetimes, usually by the straight line method. The cost of those with unlimited or indeterminate lifetimes is only charged to expense when and to the extent their value becomes impaired. This is determined each year, or more often if circumstances warrant, by estimating their current value and comparing it with recorded cost.

Accounting practices for goodwill result in inconsistencies in both the balance sheet and in calculations of income because it is virtually always recorded when a business changes hands but never otherwise. When a business is purchased, goodwill can suddenly appear in the balance sheet, sometimes in significant amount, where none existed before. If the goodwill is negative, the reduced value is applied to other assets and they are undervalued. When goodwill is charged to expense, total expense increases and income decreases. When the goodwill is negative, future income increases because the cost of other assets, which becomes expense in future, is reduced. The rate at which it becomes recorded as future income depends on which assets are undervalued and how quickly they are consumed.

CHAPTER 7

Inventories

COST

The cost of inventories, like that of other assets, includes all those outlays necessary to put them in the place and condition for them to be used, in this case to be sold.

Depending on the nature of a business, those outlays can be few or many in number and variety. In a merchandising business, a retailer or wholesaler, they are relatively few, consisting only of the invoiced prices of goods purchased and such additional outlays as transportation costs and customs duties. In a manufacturing concern, they include labor and many other factory costs as well. Discounts on purchases are reductions of costs. Theoretically, lost discounts should be treated as current expenses and deducted from the amounts paid in recording inventory purchases, but as a practical matter they are frequently ignored. Buying and receiving costs are usually written off as current expenses by merchandisers, although not by manufacturers. Many small items, such as some packaging materials, are frequently written off to expense at the time of purchase. Excess costs or losses of any kind are charged to expense. For example, the cost to a retailer of moving goods from one store to another to correct an inventory imbalance would be written off.

For a manufacturer, the process of determining the costs of inventory can be much more complex than for a retailer or wholesaler. To begin with, there are many more factors of costs than just the price of the materials purchased and perhaps some freight or customs duties or other incidental charges. Manufacturing costs include wages of labor, salaries of supervision and administration, depreciation of productive facilities, power to operate equipment and so on. The first question to be answered in measuring the cost of inventory is what costs should be included? As a practical matter, the answer is usually to include all the costs of operating the factory but nothing else. If the factory includes a purchasing department or a production control department, the costs of operating those departments are usually considered part of the cost of producing the inventory. Costs incurred outside the factory, such as the salary of a general manager are usually excluded even though they might contribute in part to production. In some cases an arbitrary allocation of part or all of a cost factor is made, for example the depreciation of a building used for both production and sales purposes. Costs included in the valuation of inventory are described as **product costs**. Costs not included are described as **period costs**, since they are charged against income in the period they are incurred.

The decision as to whether something is a product cost or a period cost will obviously affect the value attached to inventory, the more product costs, the higher the inventory value. It also affects the calculation of income by accounting periods when sales volumes fluctuate. If more costs are allocated to product, the cost per unit of goods sold will be higher, gross margin per unit will be lower, and an increase in the number of units sold will have less effect in increasing income. Similarly, a decrease in sales volume will have less effect in decreasing income. In general, the more costs that are product costs, the less the effect of sales fluctuations on the calculation of income. Conversely, the more costs that are period costs, the greater the effect of sales fluctuations on the calculation of income.

DIRECT AND INDIRECT PRODUCT COSTS

For accounting purposes, product costs are divided into direct costs and indirect costs, or overhead. Direct costs are those that can be attributed directly to the product, for example raw materials that become part of the finished product and labor that is applied directly to the product. Indirect costs are those that must be allocated in some arbitrary way, for example depreciation on a factory building. In most cases, product costs include both direct materials and direct labor, but in some, notably automated processes, only materials are direct.

Direct costs are variable, that is they vary in proportion to the volume of production. If twice as much product is produced, the cost of direct materials should be twice as great. Indirect costs are almost always semi-variable or fixed, at least in the short run. The fact that indirect costs are not variable means that the amount of indirect cost incurred per unit of product will vary with the level of production. If fewer units are produced, the cost per unit will be higher, because semi-variable and fixed costs will be spread over the smaller number. In the absence of any adjustment, the lower the level of production, the more valuable the inventory will become, per unit, at cost.

NORMAL OVERHEADS

To overcome the problem of fluctuating indirect costs per unit, most manufacturers use what is called a "normal overhead rate" to apply indirect costs to product. They determine what they consider to be a normal volume of production and what the total of indirect costs should be at that level, and on that basis they determine what the normal indirect cost per unit should be, the normal overhead rate. Production is valued at direct material and labor costs and normal overhead, producing consistent amounts per unit. The difference between the total indirect costs incurred and the amounts applied to production is considered a period cost of the production period.

The use of a normal overhead rate means that the gross margin per unit of sales remains constant, regardless of the level of production, while the cost effects of high or low production volumes are taken into the calculation of income in the production period. Using an actual overhead rate, the cost effects of production variations are taken into the valuation of inventory and reflected as higher or lower costs of goods sold in the periods the inventories are sold.

Using a normal overhead rate can mean that inventories are valued at more than their actual cost, if the level of production is high and the actual overhead per unit is lower than the calculated normal as a result. This violates the conventional accounting practices of not valuing assets in excess of cost and not taking up a gain in advance of a sale. If the amounts involved are small, they are usually ignored, but if they are significant, most accountants will make an adjustment to inventory value and to cost of sales to reduce the cost of units produced to actual; in effect, they revert back from normal to actual overhead costs.

STANDARD COSTS

Some manufacturers apply the concept of normal cost to direct material and labor costs as well as to overheads, using what are described as standard costs. They determine in advance how much direct material and labor cost should be incurred to produce a unit of product, and they value production by applying those predetermined amounts to the number of units produced. The differences between actual and standard material and labor costs are written off in the production period, in the same manner as differences between actual and normal overhead. Standard costs are used primarily as a device for controlling costs. They are discussed in more detail in chapter 20.

DEPARTMENTAL OVERHEADS

In most production, the product moves through a series of stages or production departments. Most manufacturers calculate individual overhead rates for different departments, instead of using one overall rate for the factory as a whole. The costs of operating one department can be very different from those of another. If different products require differing amounts of processing in each department, departmental rates produce a more realistic allocation of costs.

Departmental costs, like product costs, can be either direct or indirect. Direct departmental costs are those that can be assigned to departments without using any arbitrary basis of allocation. Examples are the wages of employees and salaries of supervisors working in one specific department only. Indirect costs are those that must be apportioned to departments on some basis. Examples are the cost of building space and the cost of overall plant management.

Indirect costs are allocated on the basis of factors that can be easily identified and that have some causal or proportional relationship to those costs. The cost of building space might be allocated on the basis of floor space occupied, or of cubic content, for example. Plant management costs might be allocated on the basis of labor costs, labor hours, or number of employees. In the final analysis, the basis chosen is arbitrary.

SERVICE DEPARTMENTS

As a first step in allocating indirect costs to production departments, some of them can be allocated to service departments. Purchasing and production control are examples of organizational service groups to which costs can be assigned initially, for further assignment to production departments. Other cost departments, having no organizational basis, can be set up as well. For example, the costs of providing building space — depreciation, heat, light, insurance, taxes, and so on — can be accumulated as a building services department for allocation to production departments, without there being any building services group as such within the organization. The same procedures are followed in allocating costs to service departments, and from service departments to production departments, as in allocating the costs directly to the production departments.

MULTIPLE SERVICE DEPARTMENTS

When two or more service departments are distinguished, they usually render service to each other as well as to the production departments. For example, a building services department, a maintenance department and a purchasing department would each provide services to the others. Ultimately, all their costs must be allocated to units of product via production departments. The question is how to deal with the costs of servicing each other as well as the production departments?

The easiest and most popular method of allocating the costs of multiple service departments is simply to ignore the fact that they serve each other and to allocate the cost of each directly to the production departments. The next most common method is to rank the service departments in reverse order according to how much service value each receives from the others, and to allocate their costs in that order. For example, it might be decided that maintenance receives the least value from the others, purchasing receives less than building services, and building services receives the most from the other two. In that case, maintenance would be allocated first to the other service departments and the production departments. Purchasing, including the amount allocated from maintenance would be allocated next to building services and the production departments. Building services, including the amounts allocated from maintenance and from purchasing, would then be allocated to the production departments. A few manufacturers use more sophisticated mathematical techniques to deal with interallocations. Whatever the method used, the differences in the ultimate calculated product valuations are unlikely to be significant, and in the final analysis the allocations are arbitrary in any case.

PROCESS COSTS

The cost per unit of product produced is calculated in different ways depending on the nature of the production process. The simplest situation from an accounting standpoint, is one in which only one product is produced and only one process is used to do it. The cost per unit produced during a period is then the total cost of direct materials, direct labor and overhead for the period divided by the number of units produced. The only complication is that the number of units in process at the beginning of the period might be different from the number in process at the end. If there are more units in process at the end of the period than there were at the beginning, then some of the costs added pertain to the increase in work in process. A decrease in units in process would indicate that some of the initial cost of work in process became finished goods at the end. In calculating the cost per unit of goods produced therefore, any change in the quantity of goods in process between the beginning and end of a period must be taken into account. This is done by measuring work in process at beginning and end in terms of equivalent completed units. Production for the period consists of the number of units completed, plus the number of equivalent units in process at the end, minus the number of equivalent units in process at the beginning.

What constitutes an equivalent unit will depend on the nature of the process and can be different for different elements of cost. Direct materials, for example, might all be committed to the process at the beginning, or alternatively they might be committed gradually during the process. Labor might be applied continuously or at intervals during the process. Overhead is usually considered to be incurred continuously over time. If costs are incurred continuously, the amount applicable to units in process can be taken on average as one half that applicable to completed units. If they are committed at the beginning, the amount applicable to units in process will be equal to that of completed units. If some other situation prevails, an appropriate corresponding calculation is made. The following example illustrates the calculation of equivalent units for a product when the materials are all committed at the beginning and the labor and overhead, referred to as **conversion costs**, are applied continuously.

Units in process, beginning	1,000
Units completed	10,000
Units in process, ending	500

Equivalent material units

Units completed	10,000
+ Units in process, ending	500
	10,500
– Units in process beginning	1,000
	9,500

Since material is all committed at the beginning, the equivalent amount of material committed during the period was that for the units completed, plus that for the units still in process at the end, minus that for the units in process at the beginning. The material for those in process at the beginning was committed in the previous period.

Equivalent conversion units

Units completed	10,000
+ Units in process, ending ($1/2 \times 500$)	250
	10,250
– Units in process beginning ($1/2 \times 1,000$)	500
	9,750

Since conversion is applied continuously, the equivalent amount of conversion applied during the period was that for the units completed, plus on average one half that for the units still in process at the end, minus on average one half that for the units in process at the beginning.

Material costs for the period are divided by the equivalent material units, and conversion costs by the equivalent conversion units, to determine the material and conversion costs per unit.

When a single product is produced using more than one process, units of product typically proceed through a process or department, pause, and then enter the next department. The quantities at rest between departments can vary. In these circumstances, a separate calculation of unit costs is required for each department. The same procedures are followed in accounting for each department as for a single process, except that all product costs must first be allocated to the production departments.

JOB COSTS

In most kinds of manufacturing, goods are produced in batches or jobs, not in continuous processes. Batches can be different products made in the same production facilities or they can be separate quantities of the same product. A factory making furniture, for example, will produce batches of different styles. A brewery might simply make different batches of the same beer. Batches, or jobs, are costed by setting up a separate job account for each one in a subsidiary work in process ledger. Product costs — direct materials, direct labor and overhead — are allocated to these job accounts. When a job is completed, the total accumulated cost is transferred to finished goods inventory. The total, divided by the number of units completed, is the cost per unit.

Direct materials are assigned to specific jobs when they are drawn from raw materials inventory. Direct labor is assigned to specific jobs by workers or supervisors on the production floor. Overhead can be allocated to jobs on the basis of any factor that is common to all jobs and that can be measured directly and independently. Since most overhead costs, depreciation, supervision, insurance and so on, accumulate over time and are incurred to provide factory time for production, the factor usually chosen is either direct labor hours, or direct labor dollars if they produce essentially the same result, or machine hours. If production is labor intensive, direct labor hours is appropriate. When production is essentially a machine process and labor consists of attending the machines, machine hours is more appropriate. In that case, labor is included with overhead costs and the total, conversion costs, is applied to jobs on the basis of machine hours.

When overheads are allocated to jobs based on labor or machine hours, it is not always important for valuation purposes that they be allocated to different departments first. If individual departmental overhead rates do not differ from each other significantly, an overall factory overhead rate will produce essentially the same result as departmental rates. If all jobs spend proportionately the same amount of time in each department, an overall factory rate will produce the same result regardless of differences in departmental rates.

JOINT PRODUCTS

In some industries, two or more products result from the same production process or processes. Oil refining, for example, produces several end products. For product costing purposes, common costs must be allocated among joint products.

There are two basic approaches to the allocation of joint costs, one is to apportion them on the basis of some physical factor such as weight or volume, the other is to allocate them on the basis of the selling prices of the products produced. The use of a physical factor does not usually produce a very satisfactory result from an accounting standpoint. The end products can differ widely in their selling prices per kilogram or litre. If they are valued equally, sales of one might show a very large profit and of another a large loss. Since they both result from the same productive process, this is not a logical result. In fact, the cost of raw materials usually reflects the relative quantity of each end product that can be extracted. The cost per barrel of crude oil, for example, depends in part on the quantities of various grades of gasoline, oil and other products it contains. In some cases, the use of a physical factor for allocation is not feasible, because the end products have widely different physical characteristics, meat and hides from meat packing for example.

Allocating joint costs on the basis of selling prices produces a more logical result. If joint products can be sold in the form they take at the point of split-off from the others, joint costs are allocated in proportion to the selling values at that point. If additional production costs are required to make a joint product marketable, those costs must also be taken into consideration in calculating the allocation. This is usually done by deducting the additional costs from the ultimate selling prices, and dividing the joint cost in proportion to the resulting net amounts. The following example illustrates the procedure.

	A	B	Total
Joint cost for one unit of each of A and B			$18
Selling prices after additional processing	$21	$15	$36
Costs of additional processing	1	5	6
Net selling value	$20	$10	$30
Allocation of joint cost	(20÷30)×$18 = $12	(10÷30)×$18 = $ 6	$18

Selling prices, costs and margins are the following:

	A	B	Total
Selling prices	$21	$15	$36
Joint costs	12	6	18
Additional costs	1	5	6
	13	11	24
Gross margin	$ 8	$ 4	$12
Gross margin percentage	38%	27%	33%

A criticism of this method is that it attributes all of the value added, the gross margin, to the joint processing and none to the additional processing. The gross margins are proportional to the joint costs (two thirds of joint costs in this case), not the selling prices, producing different gross profit percentages for the two products.

Consistent gross margin percentages can be produced by allocating total costs in proportion to selling prices, and deducting additional costs from the totals to arrive at the joint cost allocation. Using the data from the example:

Joint cost for one unit of each of A and B			$18
	A	**B**	**Total**
Selling prices	$21	$15	$36
Allocation of total costs	(21÷36)×$24 = $14	(15÷36)×$24 = $10	$24
Additional costs	1	5	6
Allocation of joint costs	$13	$5	$18

Selling prices, costs and margins are then the following:

	A	**B**	**Total**
Selling prices	$21	$15	$36
Joint costs	13	5	18
Additional costs	1	5	6
	14	10	24
Gross margin	$ 7	$ 5	$12
Gross margin percentage	33%	33%	33%

Although this is a logically better result, the method is seldom used in practice.

A weakness inherent in all selling price allocations is that they produce variable product valuations when selling prices fluctuate. When price changes are small and infrequent, this is not a serious drawback. If price changes are large and happen often, an estimate can be made of the long run relationship of selling prices between joint products, for purposes of cost allocation. Price fluctuations are then reflected in the profitability of the individual products, not in their costs.

BY PRODUCTS, SCRAP AND WASTE

Joint products that have relatively little sales value are usually described as by products, or in some cases as scrap. Because they have little value, by products do not have costs allocated to them unless they require additional processing before sale, in which case they are charged with the additional costs only. By products are usually accounted for in one of two ways. The estimated selling value, net of additional costs, is applied as a reduction of the cost of the main product or products; or the net revenue from sales, after additional costs, is recorded as miscellaneous income. Reducing the value of the main product is a more conservative practice than taking up income from the sale of products that bear no share of common costs.

Waste is material that has no value and usually involves costs of disposal. Those costs are part of the cost of production.

MANUFACTURING STATEMENTS

In manufacturing businesses it is common practice to produce for management what is called a manufacturing statement, or cost of goods manufactured statement, as a supplement to the income statement. The manufacturing statement, as its name indicates, is a summary of the costs incurred during the period in producing inventories of finished goods for sale. The following is a manufacturing statement for Acme Manufacturing Limited.

Acme Manufacturing Limited
Statement of Cost of Goods Manufactured
for the year ended October 31, 20X
(dollar amounts in thousands)

Raw materials			
Inventory October 31, 20W			$ 55
Purchases	$320		
Less returns and allowances	3		
			317
Freight in			9
			381
Inventory, October 31, 20X			66
Cost of raw materials used			315
Direct labor			366
Manufacturing overhead			
Indirect labor	132		
Factory supplies	20		
Light, heat and power	15		
Insurance	2		
Depreciation — building	2		
machinery and equipment	9		
Amortization of patents	3		
Repairs and maintenance	7		
Property taxes	5		
Sundry	4		
			199
Total manufacturing cost			880
Plus work in process, October 31, 20W			18
			898
Less work in process, October 31, 20X			20
Cost of goods manufactured			$878

CHAPTER 8

Inventories; Natural Resources

Inventories

COST FLOW

When identical items of inventory are acquired at different costs, as they frequently are over a period of time, it must be decided which costs should be used to value inventory and which to value cost of goods manufactured or sold. This decision is made on the basis of assumptions about the order in which the items are used. Are the first ones acquired the first to be used, or are the last ones acquired the first to be used, or are the items used a random group of all those in the inventory? Depending on the assumption, one or other of the following methods is used to determine cost.

- First in, first out; or FIFO
- Last in, first out; or LIFO
- Weighted average

Each of these methods is illustrated with an example based on the following data.

Units in beginning inventory	1,000	at	$1.00 each	$1,000
Purchases 1	2,000		1.12	2,240
Purchases 2	2,000		1.22	2,440
	5,000			$5,680
Units in ending inventory	2,000			
Units sold	3,000			

First In, First Out

Units sold	1,000	at	$1.00 each	$1,000
	2,000		1.12	2,240
Cost of units sold				$3,240
Cost of units remaining in inventory	2,000		1.22	$2,440

Last In, First Out

Units sold	2,000	at	$1.22	$2,440
	1,000		1.12	1,120
Cost of units sold				$3,560
Cost of units remaining in inventory	1,000		$1.12	$1,120
	1,000		1.00	1,000
				$2,120

Weighted Average

Total cost of 5,000 units				$5,680
Weighted average cost per unit	$5,680			
	5,000	=	$1.136	
Cost of units sold	3,000	at	1.136	3,408
Cost of units remaining in inventory	2,000		1.136	$2,272

From an accounting standpoint, it is not important whether the method used conforms to the physical flow of items through inventory. What is important is the effect it has on reported asset value and on income, via cost of goods sold. If costs remain constant, all three methods will produce the same result. When costs are generally rising, as they have been for many years, the results can diverge widely.

The first in, first out method produces an inventory valuation close to current market cost because it includes the most recent purchase costs. In terms of current values, it slightly underestimates cost of goods sold, because it uses earlier costs incurred at a lower price level. In a sense it includes an element of inflation in the calculation of income.

The last in, first out method does the opposite. It values cost of goods sold close to current market and thereby eliminates most of the inflation element in calculating income. Over an extended period of time however, it can result in an inventory figure much below current market, since it will be based on purchases made many years earlier. It can also create unusual variations in inventory and cost of goods sold calculations, if the number of items in inventory fluctuates significantly, because at some times very old costs will be drawn on in costing goods sold and at other times they will not.

The weighted average method produces a result somewhere between FIFO and LIFO in the calculation of cost of goods sold, usually approximately mid-way. In the valuation of inventory, it produces a result much closer to FIFO, because it continues to include the effect of the most recent purchases.

The extent to which the results will vary from the use of each method is affected by the rate of turnover of the inventory. If inventory turns over rapidly, meaning a large volume of sales and therefore cost of sales is generated from a small investment in inventory, the method of valuing that inventory will have much less significance than if a large investment in inventory is maintained to generate a relatively small volume of sales.

PERIODIC AND PERPETUAL INVENTORIES

A business can record inventory transactions in one of two ways, described as periodic inventory and perpetual inventory. Using the periodic inventory method, the cost of goods used in manufacture or sale is calculated and recorded at the end of each accounting period, by adding the cost of goods purchased to the value of inventory at the beginning and deducting the value of inventory at the end. With the perpetual inventory method, the cost of goods used is calculated and recorded constantly as they are used. The periodic method does not require detailed records of inventory items to be kept. All that is needed is a record of purchases and values for inventory at the beginning and end of the period. The perpetual inventory method requires a separate account to be kept for each category of stock. When units are acquired, the quantities and costs are added to the account. When units are used or sold, the quantities and costs are deducted.

When perpetual inventory records are kept, the calculation of inventory and cost of goods sold amounts can be different from those with periodic inventories using the same cost flow assumptions. The differences can be illustrated by assuming that purchase number one (2,000 units at $1.12 = $2,240) was made at the beginning of the period and purchase number two (2,000 units at $1.22 = $2,440) was made half way through the period, and that the sales of 3,000 units were made uniformly throughout the period (1,500 in the first half and 1,500 in the second half). The calculations based on a periodic inventory are those described in the preceding pages. Since the calculations are made at the end of the period, the timing of purchases and sales within the period has no effect. The calculations based on a perpetual inventory are the following.

First In, First Out

Units in beginning inventory	1,000 at	$1.00	$1,000	
Purchase number 1	2,000	1.12	2,240	
	3,000		3,240	
Units sold, first half	1,000	1.00	1,000	$1,000
	500	1.12	560	560
	1,500		1,560	
Units remaining	1,500		1,680	
Purchase number 2	2,000	1.22	2,440	
	3,500		4,120	
Units sold, second half	1,500	1.12	1,680	1,680
Units in ending inventory	2,000		$2,440	
Cost of units sold				$3,240

Last In, First Out

Units in beginning inventory	1,000	at $1.00	$1,000	
Purchase number 1	2,000	1.12	2,240	
	3,000		3,240	
Units sold, first half	1,500	1.12	1,680	$1,680
Units remaining	1,500		1,560	
Purchase number 2	2,000	1.22	2,440	
	3,500		4,000	
Units sold, second half	1,500	1.22	1,830	1,830
Units in ending inventory	2,000		$2,170	
Cost of units sold				$3,510

Weighted Average

Units in beginning inventory	1,000	at $1.00	$1,000	
Purchase number 1	2,000	1.12	2,240	
	3,000		3,240	

Weighted average cost per unit
$$\frac{\$3,240}{3,000} = \$1.08$$

Units sold, first half	1,500	1.08	1,620	$1,620
Units remaining	1,500		1,620	
Purchase number 2	2,000	1.22	2,440	
	3,500		4,060	

Weighted average cost per unit
$$\frac{\$4,060}{3,500} = \$1.16$$

Units sold, second half	1,500	1.16	1,740	1,740
Units in ending inventory	2,000		$2,320	
Cost of units sold				$3,360

In summary, the results produced using different cost flow assumptions with each of periodic and perpetual inventory methods are shown in the following table.

	Cost of Sales	Inventory Value
FIFO,		
periodic inventory	$3,240	$2,440
perpetual inventory	3,240	2,440
LIFO,		
periodic inventory	3,560	2,120
perpetual inventory	3,510	2,170
Weighted average,		
periodic inventory	3,408	2,272
perpetual inventory	3,360	2,320

Using FIFO there is no difference in the result from using either periodic or perpetual inventory methods. In either case, units are charged to cost of goods sold in the order they were acquired.

Using LIFO and weighted average, the effect on inventory value of the most recent purchase prices is greater with the perpetual inventory method than with periodic. In both cases this is because earlier costs are assigned to cost of goods sold sooner, throughout the period, leaving more of the later costs in inventory.

Perpetual inventories, by recording individual units purchased and sold, facilitate another alternative to the cost flow assumptions, known as **specific identification**. Some items, such as new cars in a dealer's inventory, can be and are identified specifically. This basis of assigning cost is appropriate for unique items. It is not appropriate for identical items however, because inventory and cost of goods sold calculations depend on which items are chosen to be sold. Values can be changed by an arbitrary selection of items, allowing cost and income figures to be manipulated. One of the cost flow assumptions should be used for consistency in costing identical items.

FIFO is the most commonly used method of measuring cost flow in Canada, with weighted average a close second. Many companies use both for different categories of inventory. LIFO is seldom used, probably because it is not acceptable for calculating taxable income and the cost of maintaining separate inventory records for tax and other purposes can seldom be justified. In the United States, where LIFO is acceptable for tax purposes provided it is used for other reporting as well, it is the second most popular method after FIFO. It produces the highest cost of sales calculation and therefore the lowest taxable income. Specific identification has very limited applicability.

MARKET

Inventories are generally valued at cost or market, whichever is lower. Market value can be less than cost for a variety of reasons. Units of product can be defective in some way, as a result of production flaws or spoilage. They can be used products accepted as returns from customers or used as demonstrators. They can be obsolescent. When the loss of value is the result of one of these factors, market is measured by reference to selling price. It is either net realizable value, defined as selling price less the costs required to sell, or net realizable value less a normal profit margin.

In most cases, a loss of market value is the result of supply and demand forces affecting the cost of acquiring inventory or the price at which it can be sold. In these circumstances, market can be measured either by reference to selling price or by reference to cost. Market can be net realizable value, net realizable value less a normal profit margin, or replacement or reproduction cost. Depending on how market is measured, a decline in market value will have different effects on inventory valuations and income calculations. These effects are described using the following assumed data for a unit of product.

Product cost	$ 50
Selling costs	40
	90
Profit margin	10
Selling price	$100

Net Realizable Value Less Profit Margin

Any decline in selling price will reduce the value of inventory. In the example, any selling price below $100 will fail to cover the selling costs ($40) and profit margin ($10) and recover the product cost ($50). The reduction in inventory value will reduce income by an equivalent amount in the current period. It will permit the business to cover its selling costs and show a normal margin when the inventory is sold in future.

Net Realizable Value

A decline in selling price in excess of the profit margin will reduce the value of inventory, a decline of less than the profit margin will not. In the example, a selling price of $90 or more will cover the selling costs ($40) and recover the product cost ($50). Below $90 it will not. Any loss in profit margin will be a loss of the future, when the inventory is sold. Only to the extent that selling price fails to cover costs, product and selling, is there a reduction of inventory value and income in the current period.

Replacement or Reproduction Cost

Any decline in replacement or reproduction cost will reduce the value of inventory and the income of the current period. Future income will be increased by an equivalent amount as the lower valued inventory is sold, but the effect on future profit margin will vary. It could be normal, higher than normal, lower, or negative. Profit margin is dependent on selling price and selling price is not included in the measurement.

In Canada, there is not general agreement as to which method of measuring market value should be used. Most companies use net realizable value but many use replacement cost. Some use both for different categories of inventory. Manufacturers often use replacement cost for raw materials and net realizable value for finished goods. Relatively few use net realizable value less normal profit margin. In published financial statements, the method of measuring market is described.

It is often the case that while the market value of some items or groups of items in inventory has decreased, that of other items or groups has increased. The possibilities are illustrated in the table on page 113.

If lower of cost and market is measured taking each item individually, it is $1,470. If it is measured by inventory groups, it is $1,490. If it is measured in total, it is $1,500, market exceeds cost. This pattern is reflected whenever some items decline in value while others increase. If lower of cost and market is applied item by item, a maximum write-down will be required. If it is applied to the whole, there will be a minimum or

		Cost	Market	Lower Item	Lower Group
Group A	Item 1	$ 250	$ 240	$ 240	
	Item 2	150	150	150	
		400	390		$390
Group B	Item 3	200	190	190	
	Item 4	100	110	100	
		300	300		300
Group C	Item 5	500	530	500	
	Item 6	300	290	290	
		800	820		800
Total		$1,500	$1,510	$1,470	$1,490

no write-down. If it is applied to groups of inventory items, the result will be somewhere between the other two.

In practice the decision whether to write down the value of inventory in these circumstances is usually based on the similarity of the items and groups. If goods are similar, a decline in the market value of some can be offset by an increase in the market value of others. If they are significantly dissimilar, they will be valued individually. A department store chain selling both clothing and household appliances for example, might offset a decline in some appliance values against an increase in others, but would not offset a decline in clothing values against appliances.

In statements of income, inventory reductions to market are usually included in cost of goods sold unless they are substantial, in which case they are segregated and reported separately. After inventory has been reduced in value to market, that value becomes "cost" for subsequent accounting purposes.

RETAIL INVENTORY

Some businesses calculate the value of their inventories using what is called the retail inventory method. The use of this method allows them to estimate inventories and cost of goods sold without taking a physical count of stock on hand and without the need for perpetual inventory records. It is based on the application of percentages to selling prices.

When goods are purchased, a record is made of the total selling price assigned to the goods, as well as the total cost. The difference between selling price and cost is described as the markup. If prices are increased by additional markups or decreased by markdowns, a record is made of these totals as well. By adding and deducting markups and markdowns, an up to date record of the selling price of goods purchased is maintained. The markup and markdown percentages are also readily calculated. Using the appropriate percentages, the value of inventory and cost of goods sold can be calculated. The following example illustrates the procedure.

Purchases at cost	$240,000
Markups	160,000
Selling prices before markdowns	400,000
Markdowns	60,000
Selling prices after markdowns	320,000
Sales	280,000
Inventory at selling price	$ 40,000

The cost of goods purchased as a percentage of the final selling price (selling price after markdowns) was 75% (240/320 × 100%). Cost of sales and inventory therefore, were the following.

Cost of sales 75% of	$280,000	=	$210,000
Cost of inventory 75% of	40,000	=	30,000
Total	$320,000		$240,000

This calculation has to be adjusted for two reasons. One is that it makes no allowance for market declines in value. The fact that markdowns had to be made indicates that some loss in market value occurred during the period. The extent of the market decline is indicated by the percentage of markdowns to selling prices before markdowns, 15% (60/400 × 100%). Applying that percentage to the value of inventory at selling price produces a reduction from cost to market of $6,000 (15% of $40,000). The value of inventory at lower of cost and market therefore is $24,000 ($30,000 minus $6,000). The same result can be calculated directly using the percentage of cost to selling prices before markdowns, 60% (240/400 × 100%). 60% of the inventory value at selling price, $40,000, is $24,000.

The other adjustment that must be made is for inventory shrinkage. Almost invariably there are losses from theft and damage. The exact extent of these losses can only be confirmed by a physical count of stock on hand. In the absence of a count, a percentage allowance based on experience can be applied to approximate shrinkage losses. Using the example, if shrinkage is estimated to be 2% of sales, the amount of shrinkage at selling price is $5,600 (2% of $280,00). At lower of cost and market it is $3,360 (60% of $5,600). The inventory value is then $20,640 ($24,000 minus $3,360). This can be calculated directly as follows:

Inventory before shrinkage at selling price	$40,000
Shrinkage (2% of $280,000)	5,600
Inventory after shrinkage, at selling price	$34,400
Inventory value at lower of cost and market, 60% of $34,400	$20,640

All businesses count their inventories periodically, usually once a year. Using the retail inventory method, counts are recorded at selling prices. If a count at selling prices totalled $35,000, the value at lower of cost and market would be 60% of $35,000, or $21,000.

Inherent in the use of the retail inventory method is the assumption that the ending inventory is representative of all items purchased and sold. If it is not, a calculation of value based on the totals will not be valid. For example, the markup percentages in a department store can vary widely from one department to another. Markups in the same department can vary depending on the time of year or on special sales promotions. The effects of these variations can be minimized by dividing the inventory into categories or departments for purposes of calculation and by making calculations more frequently.

The retail inventory method is useful to many small businesses, but is less commonly used today than it was a few years ago. Virtually all large retailers and many smaller ones now find it valuable and feasible to keep perpetual inventory records by computer.

Natural Resources

Natural resources, minerals, oil and gas, can be acquired in one of two ways, they can be purchased or they can be discovered. If a resource property is purchased, it is recorded at the price paid. If it is discovered, it is recorded at the cost of finding and developing it. This includes exploration, land acquisition, drilling, testing and mine or well development.

A difficulty in recording the cost of discoveries is that much of the cost can be incurred before it is known whether a property has commercial value. If it has no value, costs are an expense. If it has value equal to or greater than the costs, they are an asset. If it has value less than the costs, they are part asset and part expense. Accounting practices vary. Some companies record costs as expense up to the point that value is confirmed and as asset after that point. Others record costs as assets and write them off to expense only if the value is not subsequently confirmed.

Another difficulty is in defining a resource property for purposes of cost allocation. In oil and gas exploration, some companies use what is called **successful efforts** accounting, while others use **full cost** accounting. In successful efforts accounting, only the costs of successful wells are considered applicable to reserves discovered. The costs of dry holes are written off to expense. In full cost accounting, the cost of all exploration and development in an area is considered applicable to the reserves discovered in that area.

As minerals are extracted, reserves are depleted. Depletion expense is the estimated cost of the minerals extracted during a period. It is recorded in the same manner as depreciation, by transferring an amount to an expense account and recording the reduction in asset value in an asset valuation allowance account as accumulated depletion.

Depletion expense is calculated on units of mineral extracted. The estimated total cost of a property is divided by the estimated total reserves to calculate the per unit cost. Estimated total cost includes future development costs anticipated to be required to extract the reserves. Reserves are measured in units that equate commercial value for deposits of differing mineral concentrations, dollar value of metal per ton of ore for example, or energy value per barrel of oil.

In many cases, future costs are anticipated to rehabilitate or close down a property after the resources have been exhausted. An estimate of the applicable amount of these costs is also recorded as expense each period and a corresponding amount recorded as a liability.

The asset and depletion amounts reported for natural resources frequently bear little relation to economic values and are often not comparable for different companies, or for the same company from one year to another. The economic value of discoveries can be much greater than the cost of making them. Deciding whether costs exceed commercial value involves estimates of future costs and selling prices. The practices followed in recording costs vary widely. Calculations of depletion require estimates of the extent of mineral deposits and of future costs. The estimates frequently change from year to year but are not adjusted retroactively. Public companies report the methods they use to account for exploration, development and depletion in their financial statements in general terms, but seldom provide significant details.

CHAPTER 9

Debtors and Creditors

SALES AND RECEIVABLES

The value of sales and receivables can be different from the amounts charged to customers, for several reasons. One reason is that prices can be subject to a variety of discounts and allowances. A seller might offer volume discounts or rebates for example. If the discount is given at the time of sale, the transaction is recorded at the net amount. If it is refunded after collection, for example a volume discount calculated and paid at the end of the year, a liability should be recorded at the time of sale for the amount estimated payable and a corresponding amount charged as an expense or revenue reduction.

A seller can give discount vouchers or coupons to customers when they make purchases, redeemable against future sales. These too call for a liability to be recorded for the coupons to be redeemed. Only the net amount is revenue on current sales. Since not all coupons will be redeemed, the liability for coupons outstanding must be estimated. When coupons are redeemed, the new sales are recorded at the gross amount and the difference between that and the amount received or receivable is charged against and reduces the liability.

Sometimes refundable charges are made for product containers. The liability for these too must be estimated, since not all of them will be returned. The cost of containers not returned is offset against the excess of refundable charges over the estimated liability.

Amounts charged to customers are excluded from revenues if they are made on behalf of third parties. Sales taxes are an example. The tax charged is a liability to the government. The seller is merely acting as a collection agent. Transportation costs charged to customers are excluded from revenues if the price and terms of sale do not include delivery. They are offset against the transportation costs paid.

Many businesses allow customers to return products for various reasons, or agree to compensate them for defects through guaranties or warranties. If the dollar amount of returns and allowances is significant, an estimated liability and an expense or revenue reduction is recorded at the time of sale. When the amounts are small, they are often not recorded until a payment or allowance is made.

Receivables arising from transactions outside the normal day to day operations of a business are reported separately in the balance sheet. Loans to directors for example, were shown separately in the balance sheet of Acme Manufacturing Limited described in chapter 2. When receivables are collectable by instalments due over more than one year, that fact is also disclosed in the financial statements.

INTEREST

Businesses frequently offer discounts for prompt payment. For example a company might allow its customers to deduct 2% from an invoice price if it is paid within 15 days. Discounts of this kind are usually treated as a form of financing cost, or interest. The company pays to get its money sooner and thereby reduce the amount of its borrowings or shareholder investment. In fact, there is some question whether cash discounts are more properly regarded as a form of price reduction than a discount. If a company pays 2% to collect its accounts even 30 days sooner than it otherwise would (15 days instead of 45 days), it is paying an effective annual rate of 24% interest. Few companies pay that much for financing.

Instead of allowing a discount for prompt payment, some companies charge interest for slow payment. Many record the interest revenue and the increase in the amount receivable monthly, as it accrues. Some record it only when it is collected.

Many businesses allow their customers to pay by credit card or debit card. The bank charges they incur to provide this service are also frequently treated as a form of financing cost. As in the case of cash payment discounts, there is some question whether they are more properly a selling cost than a financing cost, considering the effective annual rate of interest implied.

Some companies collect cash on their receivables immediately by selling them to a factor, a financial institution that buys and collects receivables. An interest and collection charge is made by the factor in the form of a discount on their face value. The discount is recorded as a financial expense by the seller. Factors usually require a guaranty from the seller that it will repurchase any receivables that cannot be collected within a given period of time. When a guaranty is given, it is a contingent liability.

When businesses grant extended payment terms to customers, some charge interest on the amount outstanding at market rates, others at reduced rates, and some charge no interest. When no interest or interest below market rates is charged, it is a form of price reduction. Revenue from sales should be recorded at selling price less the effective interest reduction. The interest charged should be taken into revenue as it accrues over the payment period. Interest paid by the business to lenders to finance the extended payments is also recorded over the payment period.

BAD DEBTS

Virtually all businesses that extend credit suffer some bad debt losses. Bad debt losses arise from an inability to collect from a debtor, not from a lack of performance by the creditor business. Bad debt losses are usually treated as selling expenses.

In valuing receivables, a reduction of the total amount recorded is needed to allow for those that will not be collected. This was referred to in chapter 2 on the balance sheet and a bad debt write off was included in the bookkeeping illustration in chapter 4. In practice, the procedure followed in accounting for doubtful accounts and bad debt write offs is not quite as simple as that used in the illustration. Since it cannot be known in advance which accounts will not be collected, a reduction to allow for the amount uncollectable cannot be made directly to individual accounts.

Instead an asset valuation allowance account is set up, in this case an allowance for doubtful accounts. An estimate of the amount that will not be collected is made at the end of each accounting period. That amount is charged to a bad debt expense account and credited to the allowance for doubtful accounts. In preparing the financial statements, the credit balance in the allowance account is deducted from the total debit balance in accounts receivable to show the net estimated value. When specific amounts are determined to be uncollectable, they are eliminated by an equal reduction of the receivable and the allowance accounts. If ever the amounts are recovered, the procedure is reversed.

In most businesses, estimates of uncollectable amounts are made by reviewing the individual accounts receivable outstanding at the end of each accounting period. This is usually done by first preparing a list of receivables, separated into those that are less than 30 days old, those between 30 and 60 days, those between 60 and 90 days and those over 90 days old. Based on the amounts in each category, knowledge of individual customers and their payment practices and current economic conditions, it is then usually possible to make a reasonably good estimate. In some businesses where there are large numbers of customers with relatively small amounts due from each, a review of individual accounts is not feasible. In these cases an estimate can be made as a percentage of receivables or sales, based on past experience and adjusted to the extent necessary for current conditions.

PREPAYMENTS

The value of prepayments to suppliers is their original cost less the amount used to date. That amount is usually calculated on the basis of time. For example, if the cost of an insurance policy is paid annually, after six months one half that value has been used. When financial statements are prepared, the prepaid asset account is reduced and an insurance expense account is charged with half the cost. The same practice is applied to rental payments and to property taxes. Property taxes that are levied part way through the year are an accrued liability before payment and a prepaid expense afterward. Prior to being levied, the accrued liability must be estimated.

PAYABLES

In most cases there is no difficulty in measuring precisely the amount of accounts payable. The liability is determined by the prices at which the corresponding purchases were made. This is also the case for most unearned revenue; the liability is the price received in advance for future delivery of goods and services. If the goods and services are provided gradually over an extended period of time, it might be necessary to estimate the amount remaining unearned at the end of an accounting period.

Some accrued liabilities can be established precisely, while others cannot. Interest and most wages owing accumulate over time and are easily calculated. Corporate income taxes have to be estimated when financial statements are prepared during a taxation year, since the amount ultimately payable will depend in part on future operations. The same can be true for bonuses payable and for royalties. Product liabilities under guaranties and warranties must be estimated.

If overpayments are made either on receivables or payables, those overpayments become the opposite form of obligation. An overpayment by a customer on an account receivable becomes an account payable and an overpayment on a payable becomes a receivable. If amounts are due to and from the same person or business, they are offset and only the net amount payable or receivable is reported.

PENSIONS

Many companies have pension plans for their employees. These plans involve costs and obligations for the employers. Pension plans are of two main types, defined contribution plans and defined benefit plans.

Defined Contribution Plans

Defined contribution plans require the company to pay specific amounts each year to a third party, a trustee or insurance company, for the purchase of employee annuities. The amounts can be based on a variety of factors, such as wage levels, years of service, age of employees and so on, but the contributions payable are determined absolutely each year. The amount of the pensions ultimately payable to employees depends on the terms of the annuities that can be purchased with the annual contributions. The amounts payable each year are an expense of that year and if any are unpaid at the end of the year, they are current liabilities.

Defined Benefit Plans

In defined benefit plans, the employer contracts to provide for future pension payments of specific amounts. Each year the company estimates the current cost of providing the future payments and each year it puts money into investments, usually with a trustee, to accumulate the funds needed to make them. Measuring the costs and liabilities for these plans involves several difficult issues and calculations.

Cost   The current cost of providing for defined benefit pensions depends on the terms of the pension agreement and how they relate to existing employees. Factors such as retirement age, present employee ages, mortality rates, staff turnover, disability provisions and compensation levels can all affect the future payments. Many require estimates and assumptions. Some pension plans base payments on length of service only, and pay a fixed amount for each year of employment. Most plans base payments on a combination of length of service and salary or wage levels. Some pay based on the average annual wage earned during the period of employment, others pay based on the highest wages earned, usually those of the last year or last few years. When the amounts payable are based on career averages or highest wages earned, the question arises whether the current cost should be calculated at the current wage level only or should anticipate probable higher wage levels in the future. Current GAAP require that probable future levels be taken into account. This involves further estimates and assumptions about inflation, promotion, incentive payments if any, and whether employees will remain with the company until retirement age. Calculations are made by actuaries using statistical and interest rate data.

Most pension payments will not be made until several years in the future. In calculating the current cost, future payments are discounted at an appropriate rate of interest to their present value. Each year interest is calculated on the accumulated costs and added to the current year's cost to bring the costs up to date. The rate of interest is an assumed long term market rate pertinent to retirement annuity investments.

Earnings on pension plan investments reduce the cost of pension payments to a company. Each year the earnings expected from investments are deducted from the current cost. The expected rate of return is an assumed long term market rate.

Gains and Losses   The actual results of operating a defined benefit pension plan are never the same as those forecast. Employee attributes differ, resulting in different pension obligations. Interest rates change and returns on investment vary. Differences between actual and expected results are described as gains and losses.

Sometimes a change is made in the assumptions used to forecast pension costs. The expected rate of return on plan investments could be changed for example. The effects on costs of changes in assumptions are also described as gains and losses.

In accordance with GAAP, if accumulated gains and losses are significant in amount, they must be amortized over the expected average remaining service life of the employee group. Anything in excess of 10% of the pension benefit obligation or the value of the pension plan investments is defined as significant. Lesser gains and losses can be amortized at the discretion of the corporation.

Past Service Costs   Often when a pension plan is started, the employer provides benefits for past services. Sometimes an existing plan is amended to provide increased benefits for past services. Whenever benefits are provided for past services, the cost is amortized to the future services of the employees. This practice can be rationalized by noting that the cost is incurred to promote favorable future relations with employees and would not be incurred unless some future benefit was anticipated.

Pension payments in respect of past services are sometimes provided in defined contribution plans as well as in defined benefit plans. When they are, the cost is amortized to future services in the same way, regardless of when it is paid.

Changes in GAAP   GAAP requirements for measuring pension costs and obligations have evolved extensively in recent years. For many companies this has meant that costs and obligations recorded in the past have had to be revised upward. These revisions are usually treated in the same way as past service costs. They are amortized to future employee services. As an alternative, Canadian GAAP permit revisions to be applied to prior years.

Terminations   If a pension plan is terminated or settled, the effect on costs, pension assets and obligations is recorded in the year of settlement, with one exception. The cost of providing benefits for past services continues to be amortized against future services.

Pension Liabilities   The employer contributions paid into pension funds for investment each year are not the same as the annual calculated costs. They are determined by the terms of the pension agreements. They could be more or less than the estimated costs. If they are more, the difference is recorded as a long term prepayment. If they are less, it is recorded as a long term liability.

Disclosure

The amounts recorded in accounts for pension costs and obligations are frequently not meaningful. Pension fund assets and the accumulated liability to pay benefits from those assets are not recorded. Past service costs, significant gains and losses and the effects of most GAAP revisions are amortized to future years, although in most cases the changes have already occurred.

As a supplement to recorded data, GAAP require additional information to be reported in the form of notes to the financial statements. For defined benefit plans, this includes the total current value of the pension fund assets, the present value of the obligations for pension payments accumulated to date, the amount of unrecorded and unamortized costs, the employer contributions for the year, and various data concerning estimating methods. For defined contribution plans, the present value of future contributions required in respect of past service is reported. The employer has no immediate obligation for other payments.

OTHER POST RETIREMENT BENEFITS

Many companies provide other benefits to retired employees in addition to pensions, things like dental care and life insurance. In general, similar practices are followed in accounting for these benefits as in accounting for pension benefits, with two exceptions. First, the costs are allocated to the years up to the time employees become fully eligible for benefits, regardless of whether services are expected after that time. Secondly, the costs and obligations are usually much less than for pensions, and investment funds are often not required.

DEFERRED INCOME TAXES

Corporations are subject to tax on their income. In general, accounting income is used as the basis for taxation, but there are exceptions. A few forms of revenue and expense recognized in calculating accounting income are not recognized in calculating taxable income. Fines and interest on unpaid taxes for example, are not allowable expenses for tax purposes. Accounting income is adjusted to eliminate these revenues and expenses in calculating the tax expense and liability for the current year.

Some forms of revenue and expense are recognized in calculating both accounting and taxable income but not in the same year. Most companies use the straight line method for calculating depreciation for example, but the law requires taxable income to be calculated using the declining balance method. This means that most companies have higher depreciation charges and therefore lower income for tax purposes in the early years of an asset's life, and lower depreciation and higher taxable income in the later years. As a result, taxes currently payable are less than they would be on the accounting income reported in the early years and more in the later years.

GAAP require accounting tax expense to be based on allowable accounting revenues and expenses. Tax expense is therefore different from taxes currently payable whenever revenues or expenses are recognized in accounting income in one year and in taxable income in another. The difference is known as deferred income taxes. If tax expense is more than taxes currently payable, the difference is a liability for taxes payable in the future. If taxes currently payable are more than tax expense, the difference is an asset, a prepayment of future tax expense. Future taxes are calculated using tax rates and tax law in effect at the year end date. If tax rates or laws change, the future taxes are recalculated at subsequent year end dates.

Deferred income taxes can arise from differences in recording a variety of revenues and expenses for accounting and tax purposes, but by far the most significant are differences in calculating depreciation. Since depreciation is calculated over the life of long term assets, the deferred tax differences are long term as well. Since the declining balance method produces higher expense and lower taxes payable in the early years, the resulting deferred taxes are liabilities. Companies that are growing and expanding their investment in new depreciable assets continue to have lower taxable income and an increasing accumulation of deferred tax liabilities. When companies are static in size, their deferred tax liabilities remain static as well, as tax differences on newer assets offset those on older assets. Only when a company diminishes its rate of investment in new assets does it reduce its accumulation of deferred tax liabilities.

Deferred tax liabilities accumulated from differences in depreciation calculations can become very large and continue for a long and indefinite period of time in the future, since they continue to grow as a company expands and diminish only when it begins to reduce its investment in depreciable assets. Unlike pension obligations, deferred taxes are not discounted to reflect future payment. As a result, many corporations in their balance sheets report large amounts that are grossly overstated in relation to present value.

In financial statements, the current income tax expense is reported separately from the deferred tax expense. Public companies provide a reconciliation of tax expense to tax levied showing the reasons for differences.

TAX LOSSES

Tax law permits corporations to use losses suffered as an offset to reduce taxable income in other years. Within limits, losses can be carried back to recover taxes paid in previous years or carried forward to reduce taxes payable in future years. If possible, a loss will usually be carried back to recover taxes already paid. Sometimes this is not possible, because the corporation has not previously had enough taxable income to be offset. In that case, the corporation must look to future income for a recovery.

If a loss is carried back to recover taxes paid, it is recorded in the loss year as a current receivable and a reduction of the loss. If it must be carried forward, it may or may not be recorded depending on the circumstances. If it is more likely than not (more than a 50% probability) that a future tax recovery will be obtained, it is recorded as an asset and a reduction of the current loss. If not, the loss is not reduced and no asset is reported. Part or all of a tax recovery could be improbable because the corporation is not expected to earn enough income in the years the tax allowance is available. Depending on when a recovery is expected, it is recorded either as a current or a long term asset.

CHAPTER 10

Corporate Debt and Ownership

Public corporations raise long term capital by selling bonds, debentures and shares to investors. Bonds and debentures represent debt, shares represent ownership.

BONDS AND DEBENTURES

The term **bond** is used to describe a debt instrument secured by a mortgage or other charge against specific assets of a corporation, while the term **debenture** is applied to those secured by a general pledge of the corporation. With that exception, they are the same and the following descriptions of bonds apply to both.

The typical bond entitles its holder to a fixed interest payment yearly or semi-yearly, and to a lump sum repayment of his investment at a future date. The amount of the lump sum repayment is called the redemption or **face value** of the bond. Bonds can be issued for their face value or not. If the interest rate payable on an issue of bonds is not enough to induce investors to buy them at face amount, they will be sold at a **discount**. If the interest rate is higher than necessary, a bond issue will be sold at a **premium**. Discounts and premiums represent adjustments of interest rates. Bonds are sometimes issued with no interest payable as such, the interest element being entirely in the form of a discount. Another variation sometimes found is the **income bond**, on which interest is payable only if the corporation earns sufficient income in the year of payment.

Bonds can be **registered** or **coupon**, sometimes called **bearer**. For registered bonds, an up to date list of the names of the bondholders is maintained by the corporation or its agent, and interest payments are made to those on the list. Coupon bonds are issued with interest coupons attached. As interest comes due, the appropriate coupon is detached by the bondholder and presented to the corporation or its agent for payment.

All bonds of an issue can be repayable on the same date, or they can be repayable on various dates. Bonds that are repayable, some each year for a number of years, are called **serial bonds**. Bonds can be issued **callable**. When they are, it means that the corporation can redeem them for a stated price at any time prior to the date otherwise set for their repayment. The call price is usually slightly higher than the face value, to compensate bondholders for the cost and inconvenience of having to reinvest their money elsewhere. Bonds can always be purchased by the issuing corporations on the market, but market values can change to the extent that it would cost more to do that than to call them and pay the call premium.

Some bonds, called **convertible bonds**, can be exchanged at specified rates for shares of the corporation, at the option of the bondholders.

Bondholders have a prior right to the payment of their claim against the assets of a corporation, over all shareholders. They usually have a prior claim over those of most other creditors as well. As further assurance that bonds will be repaid, a corporation is sometimes required to put a certain amount of money aside each year in what is called a sinking fund, to accumulate over the term of the bond for repayment at maturity. The money is usually turned over to a trustee, who invests it in the securities of other corporations and governments. Bonds carrying a sinking fund provision are called **sinking fund bonds**.

Bondholders do not normally enjoy the right to vote for corporation directors, except under special circumstances, such as the failure of a corporation to pay interest for a period of years.

SHARES

There are two basic kinds of shares, common and preferred. **Common shares** are residual equities, they represent claims to whatever is left of corporation assets after all other equities have been satisfied. In this respect they are similar to the equities of proprietors and partners. Common shareholders obtain the benefit of corporation profits in the form of increased values of their shares and in distributions of corporation profits, dividends. They suffer corporation losses in the form of decreased values of their shares.

When a corporation issues more than one class of shares, an order of precedence is established in respect of the claims of each against the corporation's assets. The class that ranks last is the common share issue, the other classes are usually called **preferred** or **preference share** issues. In some cases more than one class is called common. For example there could be a class A common and a class B common, with equal residual rights but some difference in other rights.

Preferred shareholders usually have a prior claim over common both to dividends and to the repayment of their investment. Their shares usually call for a fixed dividend rate similar to an interest rate. Unlike interest however, dividends do not become a liability of the corporation until they are declared by the directors. Because of this fact, dividends on preferred shares are often made **cumulative**, which means that if the directors do not declare the dividends called for by the terms of the shares, the dividends accumulate and they must be paid before any common dividends. Some preferred shares are **participating**, which means that they are entitled to dividends beyond the fixed rate, whenever common dividends in excess of a certain amount are paid.

On repayment of their investment, preferred shareholders are usually entitled to receive only a fixed amount, corresponding closely to the original amount of their investment. This means that preferred share values do not normally fluctuate significantly. If there are cumulative preferred dividends in arrears at the time preferred shares are repaid, the shareholders are entitled to those as well. A few preferred shares carry the right to participate in residual assets with the common shares after the payment of all other claims at the termination of a corporation's business. Participating preferred shares can fluctuate in value significantly.

Some preferred shares are issued **redeemable**, meaning that they can be called in and their holders repaid by the corporation, usually at an amount slightly higher than the price at which they were issued. In most jurisdictions, shares, both preferred and common, can also be purchased on the market by the issuing corporation. Corporations purchase their shares either because they have funds and ownership equity in excess of their foreseeable needs, or because the current market price of their shares is unduly low. In either case, the rate of return on their shares to the remaining shareholders is expected to be higher as a result of the purchase.

Some preferred shares are **convertible** at the option of the investors into other securities, usually common shares. Others are **retractable**, meaning that the holders can require them to be repaid by the corporation under specified circumstances.

Preferred shareholders sometimes have the right to vote for the directors of a corporation, but most often do not. Shares that do not carry the right to vote under ordinary circumstances, can have the right to do so under special conditions, such as non payment of preferred dividends for a period of years.

All shares, preferred and common, can have what is called a par value, or they can be no par value shares. The **par value** of par value shares is the amount that must be retained by the corporation as capital, unless the shares are redeemed or purchased. When **no par value** shares are issued, an amount called **stated value** is sometimes established in respect of them. This stated value for no par value shares corresponds to par value for par value shares. Par and stated values are set by company incorporators or directors. In some jurisdictions, the law determines the amounts that must be set.

The kinds of shares that can be issued by a corporation and the terms attaching to each class are authorized in the corporation's charter or in subsequent amendments to that charter. The amounts issued are determined by the directors. The directors decide how many shares to issue, when they should be issued, to whom, and at what price.

No par value shares can be issued at any price. Par value shares can be issued at any price in some jurisdictions but others require that they be issued for not less than their par value. When they are issued at a discount, some jurisdictions stipulate that the buyers remain liable for the discount, if that is required to meet the claims of creditors. Once they have been issued by a corporation, shares can be resold by the buyers for any price with no effect on the corporation. The market value of a share is entirely independent of its par or stated value.

Dividends are declared by the directors of a corporation and paid out of retained earnings. If a dividend is to be paid in cash, the directors must be satisfied that the corporation has adequate cash for the purpose, in addition to retained earnings. Otherwise, the payment of a dividend could jeopardize the life of the corporation and expose the directors to personal liability to creditors, who have claims to payment ahead of shareholders. If directors do not declare dividends called for by the terms of preferred shares, the preferred shareholders can pursue their rights against those of less preferred and common shareholders.

When directors declare a dividend, they declare a **record date** and a **payment date**. Corporations maintain a record, either directly or through an agent, of who are their shareholders. When shares are issued, the identity of the purchaser is registered. If the shares are resold, the new owner can have the registration changed. Those who are registered as shareholders on the record date are paid the dividend. The payment date is set a short time after the record date, to allow time for payments to be processed.

Sometimes corporations pay what are called **stock dividends**, instead of cash dividends. A stock dividend is a distribution of new shares to existing shareholders in proportion to their holdings. In fact, a stock dividend is not a dividend in the sense of it being a distribution of assets to shareholders. It has no effect whatsoever on the assets or liabilities of the corporation, or on the proportionate share of the corporation owned by each shareholder. It simply increases the total number of shares outstanding. It gives the appearance of a distribution to shareholders, without the need to pay out any cash. In spite of the fact that an increase in total shares outstanding dilutes the value of each share, a stock dividend seldom has a significant effect on the market value of a corporation's shares.

A stock dividend is a relatively small number of new shares issued to existing shareholders. If a large number is issued, it is described as a **stock split**. What is large is defined by the effect the additional shares have on the market price of the stock. If the price per share is reduced significantly, the transaction is considered a split, not a dividend. A stock split, like a stock dividend, has no effect on the assets, liabilities or relative position of share-holders in a corporation. It is usually undertaken to facilitate trading in the stock by reducing the market price per share.

The foregoing descriptions of shares and bonds include some of the more common variations of conditions and provisions, but not by any means all of them. The range of possibilities is virtually unlimited. Diversity in securities reflects in part the diversity of investment objectives of the millions of people who make up the market for securities. Share and bond varieties are designed to tap and satisfy all segments of the market. In this connection it is worth noting that all rights granted to any group of investors, bondholders or shareholders, affect the rights of the other groups in a corporation, and that the common shareholders are in the residual position in this regard.

In some cases, the conditions attaching to bonds and preferred shares are so similar as to make the two almost indistinguishable. Ultimately the distinction is based on whether repayment is mandatory. If it is, the security is debt, regardless of how it is described.

ACCOUNTING FOR DEBT

When bonds or debentures are issued, they are always recorded as debt at their face amount. If they are issued for more or less than the face amount, the difference is recorded separately as a premium or discount on issue. When financial statements are prepared, the premium or discount is shown separately as a deferred credit or a deferred charge (a long term credit or debit).

Over the lifetime of a bond, any premium or discount arising on issue is amortized as an adjustment of the interest paid. This has the effect of adjusting interest expense from the contract rate to the effective market rate. If the amount is significant, the premium or discount amortized each year should be calculated actuarially to give effect to the market rate of interest. If the cost of issuing bonds is significant, it is also deferred and amortized over the lifetime of the debt, using the straight line method.

When bonds are issued, their market value equals the issue price, the face value adjusted for premium or discount. At maturity the market value equals the face amount repaid. Between issue and repayment the market value will fluctuate, due to changes in interest rates generally and to changes in the fortunes of the company. If bonds are redeemed prior to maturity, either because they are called or are purchased in the market, the amount paid will almost invariably be different from the face amount adjusted by the unamortized premium or discount recorded in the accounts. The difference is a gain or loss in the calculation of income for the corporation.

ACCOUNTING FOR OWNERSHIP

The ownership equity of a corporation consists of two elements, capital invested and income. In accounting for ownership, a clear distinction is made between the two. Income consists of all revenues, expenses, gains and losses resulting from the operation of the business. These elements of income are reported in the statement of income each year and the net result is transferred to retained earnings at the end of the year. All income becomes part of retained earnings.

Capital investment results almost exclusively from transactions with shareholders, although on rare occasions a capital contribution is made by someone other than a shareholder, such as a government body. Capital investment transactions are never recorded as income. A corporation cannot generate profits or losses by dealing in its own shares.

Share Issues

Money or other assets invested in a corporation is recorded in one or both of two categories, capital stock and **contributed surplus**. The par value of par shares and the stated value of no par shares are capital stock. When shares are issued for more than their par or stated value, the excess is contributed surplus. If par value stock is issued at a discount, the discount is recorded separately and deducted from the par value. When no par shares are issued without a stated value, the full amount received is capital stock.

When shares are issued for assets other than cash or for services received, the directors must assign a value to those assets or services. If the same class of shares is being traded in the market, the value will be determined by reference to the price at which it is being traded. If not, the directors must estimate the value of the assets or services acquired and value the shares accordingly.

When assets are donated to a corporation, it represents an investment of capital but it does not involve the issue of shares. When the assets are recorded, the equity side of the transaction is contributed surplus.

When convertible securities, bonds or preferred shares, are converted to common shares, the amounts shown in the accounts for those securities are transferred to the common share category. Any unamortized discount or premium on bonds is transferred as well as the face amount. If the amounts transferred exceed the par or stated value of the common shares issued, the excess is recorded as contributed surplus.

Corporations often issue **rights** to purchase shares, sometimes described as **warrants**, and grant **options** to purchase. Rights and options entitle their holders to purchase shares at a fixed price for a given period of time. The price is either less than the market price of shares at the time the rights are issued, or less than a price anticipated during the time they can be exercised.

Share purchase rights are issued to existing shareholders and to investors purchasing new issues of shares and bonds. They are issued to existing shareholders as a means of raising new capital for the corporation. Since they allow the shareholders to purchase shares below the market price, they are a strong inducement for the sale of new shares. If the existing shareholders are unwilling or unable to buy more shares themselves, they can sell the rights to others who will. Share purchase rights are issued to new investors as a means of making new security issues more attractive, a sort of bonus.

No entry is required in the accounts to record rights issued to existing shareholders at the time they are issued, since no consideration is received at that time. As and when they are exercised, the issue of shares is recorded in the same way as any other issue would be; the amount received is credited to capital stock or to capital stock and contributed surplus. When rights are issued together with other securities to new investors, the consideration received should be allocated between rights and other securities based on their relative separate market values. Any amount allocated to the rights is recorded as contributed surplus. If and when the rights are exercised, the amount received at that time is recorded as capital stock, and as contributed surplus to the extent it exceeds par or stated value.

Share purchase options are granted for services, usually to management personnel. They are granted as incentives. If management performs well, the company and its shares can be expected to increase in value and options to purchase shares at fixed prices will increase in value as well. Options can be granted at market price at the time of granting, at prices above market, or at prices slightly below. If options are granted at market or above market prices, there is no immediate benefit to the recipient. The benefit will come if and when the market value of the shares increases. If they are granted at prices below current market, there is an immediate benefit to the recipient, because he could exercise the options and sell the shares for more than the option price immediately. The benefit to the recipient is a form of wage cost to the corporation. When options issued at or above market price are exercised, the cash received is recorded as capital stock, and as contributed surplus to the extent it exceeds par or stated value. When options issued below market price are exercised, the wage cost to the corporation is added to the amount of cash received to determine the total of capital stock and contributed surplus recorded.

Although stock dividends and stock splits are essentially the same, their accounting treatment is different. For a stock dividend, the procedure is to transfer an amount equal to the fair market value of the stock issued from retained earnings to capital stock for the par or stated value of the stock and to contributed surplus for any excess. For a stock split, there is usually no change made in the accounts.

Share Purchases

When shares are redeemed or purchased on the market, shareholders' equity is reduced by the amount paid. The usual procedure is to reduce the capital stock account by their par or stated value. If the amount paid to redeem or purchase the shares is more than their par or stated value, the difference is applied to reduce either or both of contributed surplus and retained earnings, depending on the circumstances. If contributed surplus was created by previous transactions in the same class of shares, it is reduced by the amount attributable to the shares redeemed. The remainder of the reduction if any, is applied to retained earnings. If no contributed surplus was created by previous transactions in the same class of shares, the reduction is applied in full to retained earnings. If the amount paid to redeem or purchase shares is less than their par or stated value, the difference is added to contributed surplus. Shares purchased are never recorded as assets of the corporation.

FINANCIAL STATEMENTS

The significant financial terms and conditions attaching to each class of its securities are described in a corporation's financial statements, either in the balance sheet, or in the notes. For bonds and debentures these include for each issue the amount outstanding, the interest rate, maturity date or dates, assets pledged, sinking fund requirements if any, and if they are convertible or callable, the relevant prices and terms. For shares, they include for each issue the number and amount authorized, number and amount issued, and par or stated values. For preferreds, they include dividend rates, whether they are cumulative or participating, arrears of dividend payments if any, and conversion, redemption and retraction provisions if any. In addition, details are provided of any warrants, rights or options outstanding for the purchase of shares.

Capital stock, contributed surplus and retained earnings are listed in that order in the balance sheet, with different classes of shares listed in decreasing order of preference. Any changes occurring during the year to capital stock or contributed surplus accounts are usually shown on the face of the balance sheet. Changes to retained earnings can also be shown on the balance sheet or combined with the statement of income, but are usually presented in a separate Statement of Retained Earnings.

Sometimes corporations segregate portions of retained earnings and describe them as **appropriations** or **reserves**. This is done to indicate that the amounts are not available for the payment of dividends. Some appropriations are compulsory. For example, the terms of a bond issue might call for appropriations to ensure that shareholders' equity is maintained at least equal to a minimum acceptable amount. Others are created voluntarily by the directors. For example, amounts might be reserved for a large future expenditure, such as a plant expansion. The reservation of retained earnings in itself however, does not ensure that the cash required will be available when needed. Appropriations made voluntarily by directors have little real significance, since all dividends must be declared by the directors in any case.

Illustration of Shareholders' Equity

In chapter 2 a balance sheet was illustrated for Acme Manufacturing Limited. Shareholders' Equity was shown simply as two amounts, capital and retained earnings, without further description or elaboration. In practice they would have been reported in detail, as in the illustration on this and the following page. (Comparative amounts for the preceding year have been omitted to simplify the illustration. Dollar amounts are in thousands.)

Shareholders' Equity
 Capital Stock
 Preferred 7% cumulative, par value $10
 Authorized and issued, 10,000 shares $100
 Common no par value, stated value $5
 Authorized 50,000 shares
 Issued, October 31, 20W, 28,000 shares   140
 Issued during the year, stock dividend,
   1,400 shares   7
                     247

 Contributed Surplus
 October 31, 20W   10
 Capitalized as part of stock dividend   5
                     15

 Retained earnings   127
 Total shareholders' equity $389

Acme Manufacturing Limited
Statement of Retained Earnings
for the year ended October 31, 20X
(dollar amounts in thousands)

Appropriated		
Provision for plant expansion, October 31, 20W		$ 20
Additional provision during the year		4
		24
Unappropriated		
October 31, 20W		85
Net income for the year		41
		126
Appropriation for plant expansion	4	
Preferred cash dividend	7	
Common stock dividend	12	
		23
		103
Total retained earnings		$127

CHAPTER 11

Investments and Combined Accounts

The asset category **investments** refers to holdings of obligations of other entities, usually other businesses or governments. Most investments consist of debt and ownership securities. They include corporate shares, bonds and debentures, government securities, investment certificates, and insurance policies with cash surrender values.

Investments are recorded at cost, which includes brokerage fees if any, plus any other transfer costs. Interest is accrued, cash dividends are recorded when received. Stock dividends and splits do not affect recorded cost or revenue. Dividends received on insurance policies are a reduction of insurance expense, not a revenue. When stock purchase rights or other forms of securities are issued to the holders of existing securities, the cost of the existing securities is reallocated to the existing and new securities based on their relative market prices.

Investments are divided into two categories: temporary investments and long-term investments.

TEMPORARY INVESTMENTS

Temporary investments are those that can be liquidated, that is turned into cash, reasonably quickly and that the management of a business intends to liquidate in the near term. In the balance sheet they are usually listed immediately after cash. In some cases, when they are highly liquid and there is no significant risk of a loss in value, they are combined with cash and the combination is described as **cash and cash equivalents**.

The accounting treatment of temporary investments is similar to that of inventories. When temporary investments are sold, or redeemed by the issuer, any profit or loss is recorded. If only part of a holding is sold and the securities were purchased at different times and prices, the cost is calculated at the average. When financial statements are prepared, temporary investments are valued at market if market is lower than recorded cost, and the anticipated loss up to that point is taken into the calculation of income. In calculating lower of cost and market, the investments can be considered individually or in total.

LONG-TERM INVESTMENTS

Long-term investments are those the management of a business does not intend to liquidate in the near future, regardless of whether it is possible to liquidate them reasonably quickly.

The accounting treatment of long-term investments depends on the degree of influence or control the investing company has in the company whose securities it holds. If a company has little or no influence, it accounts for the investment using what can be described as a **cost or market** method. If it has significant influence but not control, it accounts for the investment using an **equity** method. If it has control, it accounts for the investment as a **consolidation**. In deciding whether one company has significant influence or control over another, the presumption is based initially on the percentage of voting interest the investor holds in the shares of the other. If an investor holds less than 20% of the voting interest, it is presumed not to have significant influence. If it holds more than 50%, it is presumed to have control. Between 20% and 50%, the presumption is significant influence but not control. These presumptions can be overcome by other factors. Significant influence could be indicated by representation on the board of directors or participation in management for example, with a voting interest less than 20%. Control could be lacking with a voting interest in excess of 50%, if the company operated in a foreign country under strict regulation.

Cost or Market

The cost or market method can be applicable to both debt and ownership investments. Investments are recorded at cost. They may or may not be reduced to market if their market value declines. They are not reduced to market if a decline is considered temporary. Market value could decline temporarily because of general economic conditions for example. If the ultimate recovery of the investment is still reasonably assured, the value is not written down. Once an investment has been written down, it is not subsequently written up to record a recovery of market value.

When debt securities are purchased at a premium or discount, the premium or discount is amortized over the period to maturity as an adjustment to the effective interest rate.

Equity

The equity method is applicable only to ownership investments. Using this method, the investor records its investment initially at cost. Thereafter, the cost is adjusted to reflect the investor's share of any changes in the equity of the investee company. If an investor owns 25% of the shares of a company, it will record 25% of the income of that company each year as its income and as an increase in the value of its investment. If dividends are paid by the investee company, they reduce its equity and are recorded by the investor as a reduction in the value of the investment. Changes in the market value of the investment are not recorded.

Consolidation

In a consolidation, the investment account in the books of the controlling company is treated the same way as using the equity method. That is, it is adjusted to reflect the investor's share of any changes in the equity of the investee. When financial statements are prepared however, they are prepared as if the controlling, or parent company had purchased the assets and assumed the liabilities of the controlled, or subsidiary company, not the shares. The assets and liabilities of the subsidiary are added to those of the parent to produce a consolidated balance sheet. The revenues and expenses of the subsidiary are added to those of the parent to produce a consolidated statement of income. The following is a simple example of a balance sheet consolidation. P is the parent company, Q is the subsidiary.

P Company
Balance Sheet
December 31, 20X
(dollar amounts in thousands)

Accounts receivable	$ 50
Inventory	100
	150
Shares of Q Company	100
Plant and equipment	80
	$330
Accounts payable	$ 30
Ownership	300
	$330

Q Company
Balance Sheet
December 31, 20X
(dollar amounts in thousands)

Accounts receivable	$ 20
Inventory	50
	70
Plant and equipment	40
	$110
Accounts payable	$ 10
Ownership	100
	$110

P Company
Consolidated Balance Sheet
December 31, 20X
(dollar amounts in thousands)

Accounts receivable (50 + 20)	$ 70
Inventory (100 + 50)	150
	220
Plant and equipment (80 + 40)	120
	$340
Accounts payable (30 + 10)	$ 40
Ownership	300
	$340

The "investment in Q" account of company P was replaced by the assets and liabilities of Q. The corresponding equity in Q was eliminated since there is no shareholder ownership in the combination other than that of the parent company.

Implicit in this example are three assumptions. First, it is assumed that the parent owns 100% of the subsidiary. That is often not the case. Secondly, it is assumed that the cost of the investment to the parent is equal to the shareholders' equity of the subsidiary. That is seldom the case. When shares of a subsidiary are purchased in the market, the price reflects the perceived value of the business, not the historical cost data recorded in the accounts. Thirdly, it is assumed that the parent and subsidiary were not doing business with each other. In fact, many parent and subsidiary companies do trade with each other.

A more realistic example can be prepared using data presented for Acme Manufacturing Limited in chapters 2, 3, and 10, and assuming balance sheet and income statement data for Acme Parts Inc., as shown below. (Brackets denote a negative amount.)

Balance Sheets
October 31, 20X
(in thousands of dollars)

	Acme Manufacturing	Acme Parts
Accounts receivable	113	50
Inventories	215	60
	328	110
Investment in Acme Parts	120	—
Property, plant and equipment	105	40
Patents	25	—
	578	150
Accounts payable and accrued	54	30
Other current liabilities	45	—
	99	30
Bonds payable	90	—
	189	30
Shareholders' equity - October 31, 20W	355	100
Income, year ended October 31, 20X	41	20
Cash dividend	(7)	
	389	120
	578	150

Income Statements October 31, 20X (in thousands of dollars)	Acme Manufacturing	Acme Parts
Sales	1,442	400
Cost of goods sold	868	240
Selling and administrative expenses	479	120
Interest	12	—
	1,359	360
	83	40
Income taxes	42	20
Net income	41	20

Note: None of the changes in the shareholders' equity accounts of Acme Manufacturing during the year described in chapter 10 affected the total, except income and the cash dividend.

In addition, assume the following,

1. Manufacturing owns 80% of Parts.

2. Manufacturing paid 120 for its 80% holding at the beginning of the year, when the total ownership equity in Parts was 100. It therefore paid a premium of 40 over its share of the equity of 80. The premium of 40 on 80 was 50%. Manufacturing paid this premium because it believed the company as a whole was worth 150, not the 100 recorded in the accounts. Of this additional value of 50, it attributed 20, or 40%, to productive equipment, which it considered undervalued. The remaining 30, or 60%, it could not allocate specifically but attributed to the earning power of the company, goodwill. The productive equipment had an estimated 8 years of useful life remaining.

3. During the year, Parts sold goods to Manufacturing at selling prices totalling 180. All were included in the sales of Manufacturing during the year; none remained in the year end inventory. At year end, Manufacturing owed 15 to Parts in respect of those sales.

Consolidated statements are prepared using a worksheet to list the accounts of each company, make necessary adjustments, and add the accounts of the companies together. Since the companies are separate legal entities, they retain their own accounting records. Adjustments were made in the consolidation worksheet for Manufacturing and Parts to give effect to the items listed below. The consolidation worksheet is shown on page 150. The consolidated balance sheet and statement of income for Acme Manufacturing Limited are shown on page 151.

(A)   The shareholders' equity of Parts was reduced by 80 to 20. The remaining 20 represents the equity of shareholders other than Manufacturing, described as minority interest. The investment account of Manufacturing was reduced by an equivalent amount, from 120 to 40.

(B)   The remaining 40 of investment was allocated 40%, or 16, to plant and equipment and 60%, or 24, to goodwill, since those were the assets and percentages to which the premium paid over book value was attributed.

(C)   Depreciation and accumulated depreciation were increased by 2, being the annual amount required to write off the added equipment value of 16 over 8 years. (Depreciation is included in cost of goods sold in the statements.)

(D)   Goodwill was not reduced by write off because there was no evidence its value was impaired.

(E)   Sales of Parts were reduced by 180 and cost of goods sold of Manufacturing was reduced by the same amount, since they were transferred within the same economic entity. The cost of those sales is included in the costs of Parts. If any inter-company sales had remained in the year end inventory, a further adjustment would have been required to eliminate from inventory the mark up in the selling price to Manufacturing over the cost to Parts.

(F)   Accounts receivable of Parts and accounts payable of Manufacturing were reduced by 15, the amount owing to one from the other, since the amounts are internal to the combined entity.

(G)   The minority share of the net income of Parts, 20% of 20 or 4, was added to minority interest and deducted from Manufacturing's share of the total income.

Acme Manufacturing Limited
Consolidation Worksheet
October 31, 20X
(in thousands of dollars)

	Acme Manufacturing		Acme Parts		Adjustments for Consolidation		Consolidated	
	Dr.	Cr.	Dr.	Cr.	Dr.	Cr.	Dr.	Cr.
Accounts receivable	113		50			15(F)	148	
Inventories	215		60				275	
Investment in Acme Parts	120					80(A) 40(B)	—	
Property plant and equipment	105		40		16(B)	2(C)	159	
Patents	25						25	
Goodwill					24(B)		24	
Accounts payable and accrued		54		30	15(F)			69
Other current liabilities		45						45
Bonds payable		90						90
Minority interest						4(G)		4 20
Shareholders' equity		355		100	80(A)			355
Cash dividends	7						7	
Sales		1,442		400	180(E)			1,662
Cost of goods sold	868		240		2(C)	180(E)	930	
Selling and administrative expenses	479		120				599	
Interest	12						12	
Income taxes	42		20				62	
Minority interest in income					4(G)		4	
	1,986	1,986	530	530	321	321	2,245	2,245

Acme Manufacturing Limited
Consolidated Balance Sheet
October 31, 20X
(in thousands of dollars)

Accounts receivable		148
Inventories		275
		423
Property, plant and equipment		159
Patents		25
Goodwill		24
		631
Accounts payable and accrued		69
Other current liabilities		45
		114
Bonds payable		90
Minority interest in subsidiary		24
		228
Shareholders' equity, October 31, 20W	355	
Net income for the year	55	
	410	
Less cash dividends	7	
		403
		631

Acme Manufacturing Limited
Consolidated Statement of Income
year ended October 31, 20X
(in thousands of dollars)

Sales	1,662
Cost of goods sold	930
Selling and administrative expenses	599
Interest	12
	1,541
Income before taxes	121
Income taxes	62
	59
Minority interest in income of subsidiary	4
Net income	55

In this illustration, subsidiary assets were revalued to reflect the price effectively paid for them by the acquiring company. In terms of market value however, it was only a partial revaluation. Since only 80% of the subsidiary was acquired, the adjustment to asset values was only 80% of the perceived excess of market value over cost. The equipment was increased in value by 16 and the goodwill recorded at 24, while the price paid indicated increased market values of 20 and 30. A full revaluation would only be made if 100% of the shares were purchased. The lower the percentage acquired, the less significant is the revaluation.

GAAP require consolidated financial statements whenever a company controls one or more other companies. The economic unit, the accounting entity, is the group, not the parent company. Owners and creditors need to know what assets and liabilities comprise the investments in subsidiary companies, to judge the parents' overall financial position. They need to know what the earnings are after eliminating transactions internal to the group.

Statements for the individual companies within a consolidation are often prepared as well. Minority shareholders in a subsidiary need to know the financial position and operating results for their own company. They have no ownership interest in the parent consolidation. Many creditors have a claim against only one company in a combination, while others might have a claim against the group. Individual statements can be required as well for income tax or other special purposes.

Sometimes parent companies revalue the assets and liabilities directly in the accounts of their subsidiaries to reflect the price paid for subsidiary shares. This is described as **push down accounting**. The price paid by the parent is pushed down into the accounts of the subsidiary. This is considered an acceptable practice if the parent holds 90% or more of the subsidiary shares. It is not acceptable when minority interests exceed 10%, because the amounts paid by the parent company are not relevant to minority shareholders.

POOLING OF INTERESTS

A different method of combining accounts has been used at times in the past, when the combination was considered a **pooling of interests**.

A pooling of interests was defined as a combination in which two or more companies got together by exchanging shares, and none could be identified as an acquirer. This usually meant that the shareholders of each combining company received approximately the same number of shares in the new company as the shareholders of each other company. In a pooling of interests, the assets and liabilities of the companies were added together at the values recorded in their respective books. New shares issued were valued at the same amount, recorded net asset value (assets minus liabilities). They were not recorded at their market price. As a result, there was never any excess of payment over book value of net assets acquired, and therefore no adjustment of asset or liability values, and no record of goodwill. No adjustments to income calculations of the combination were required, except to eliminate the effects of inter company transactions. Both financial position and earnings were reported as if the companies had been combined from their inception. If current values were higher than recorded values, as is usually the case, future combined accounts would show lower costs and higher income calculations for a pooling of interests than for a parent subsidiary consolidation. In many cases, the difference in reported income was substantial.

The pooling of interests method of producing consolidated financial statements has rarely been used in Canada. It is no longer acceptable practice in accordance with GAAP.

JOINT VENTURES

A joint venture is a special form of partnership in which two or more entities combine for a specific purpose. Joint ventures are usually formed when businesses have a common interest in a particular project but the anticipated cost of the project is too much for any one to undertake. Examples are aircraft manufacturers combining to develop a new plane and oil companies combining to develop a large oil field.

In a joint venture, control is shared by the venturers, with each one having some control but no one having complete control. If a participant has no control, it is an investment. If a participant has complete control, it is a subsidiary. The law applicable to joint ventures is basically the same as for partnerships, except that each venturer is not automatically an agent for the others and the withdrawal of a venturer does not necessarily dissolve the joint venture.

Joint ventures can take different forms. In some cases the participants use their own assets and incur their own expenses as part of the venture. In others they share ownership of assets and expenses, either directly or by owning shares of a company incorporated for the venture. When participants use their own assets and incur their own expenses, those assets and expenses are recorded automatically in their accounts. When they share ownership of assets, or share liabilities, revenues or expenses, they account for them using **proportionate consolidation**. A company with a 40% stake in another company operated as a joint venture will include 40% of each category of asset, liability, revenue and expense of the venture in its own balance sheet and statement of income. Using the data for Acme Manufacturing and Acme Parts, and assuming Parts was a joint venture 40% owned by Manufacturing and they did not otherwise do business with each other, financial statements for Manufacturing would be prepared as shown on the following page. (The separate accounts of Manufacturing and Parts are shown earlier.)

When the owner of a share in a joint venture does business with the venture, it eliminates its proportionate share of the transaction from its financial statements and includes only the amount applicable to the other owners. For example, if Parts sold goods to Manufacturing, Manufacturing would eliminate 40% of those sales from its combined sales and purchases. It would also eliminate 40% of the mark up on any of the goods remaining in inventory and 40% of any amount owing on the purchase at the year end.

Companies that participate in joint ventures are required by GAAP to disclose the totals and major components of joint venture assets, liabilities, revenues and expenses included in their financial statements.

Acme Manufacturing Limited
Balance Sheet
October 31, 20X
(in thousands of dollars)

Accounts receivable (113 + 40% of 50)	133
Inventories (215 + 40% of 60)	239
	372
Property, plant and equipment (105 + 40% of 40)	121
Patents	25
	518
Accounts payable and accrued (54 + 40% of 30)	66
Other current liabilities	45
	111
Bonds payable	90
	201

Shareholders' equity, October 31, 20W	275	
Net income for the year (41 + 40% of 20)	49	
	324	
Less cash dividends	7	
		317
		518

Note: The investment in Parts at the beginning of the year in this example was 40, 40% of the equity of Parts of 100, not 120 as in the previous example. Shareholder investment in Manufacturing was correspondingly less, 275 not 355.

Acme Manufacturing Limited
Statement of Income
year ended October 31, 20X
(in thousands of dollars)

Sales (1,442 + 40% of 400)	1,602
Cost of goods sold (868 + 40% of 240)	964
Selling and administrative expenses (479 + 40% of 120)	527
Interest	12
	1,503
	99
Income taxes (42 + 40% of 20)	50
Net income	49

SUMMARY

Investments in other businesses are measured and reported in a variety of different ways, depending on the circumstances. The methods used can produce widely different results. It is important for users of accounting data therefore, to know which methods have been used and the significance of those methods for the measurements produced.

Cost or Market

If a company has no significant influence over another, it records the investment at cost. Cost is reduced to market in reporting temporary investments, but not in reporting long term investments if the decline in value is considered temporary. Income consists only of dividends and interest received.

Equity

If a company has significant influence but not control over another, it records the investment initially at cost. Thereafter it adjusts the value upwards and downwards to reflect its proportionate share of the other company's profits, losses and dividends.

Consolidation

When a company controls another, it accounts for the investment as if it had purchased the assets and assumed the liabilities of the other. Consolidated financial statements are prepared in which the assets, liabilities, revenues and expenses are reported in total for the parent and subsidiary. Subsidiary assets and related expenses are included at values based on the cost of the investment to the parent, not costs recorded by the subsidiary. If the parent owns less than 100% of the subsidiary, the minority interest in the subsidiary is shown as an obligation of the consolidation. Transactions and obligations between the companies are eliminated from the statements.

Pooling of Interests

Until recently, when two or more companies combined by exchanging shares and none could be identified as having acquired the other, they could be considered a pooling of interests. In a pooling of interests the companies were treated as if they had been combined from inception. All values were combined at the amounts recorded in the accounts of the individual companies.

Joint Venture

In a joint venture, control is shared by the venturers, with none having complete control. Each venturer combines its proportionate share of the assets, liabilities, revenues and expenses of the venture with its own, in its financial statements.

CHAPTER 12

Business Segments; Foreign Combinations; The National Accounts

Business Segments

Some companies operate two or more significantly different businesses, either as separate subsidiary companies, or as separate divisions of the same company. In some cases, the businesses are different because the products or services are different. A corporation might have both a consumer products division and an industrial products division for example. In others, the businesses are different because they operate in different geographic areas. A corporation might operate in both Canada and Europe. When companies operate in distinctly different businesses, they are said to have "business segments".

Most companies having business segments maintain separate records for each segment for management purposes, regardless of whether they are all part of the same corporation. With few exceptions, it is usually possible to allocate revenues, expenses, assets, and liabilities. Exceptions might include the assets and costs of a corporate head office and general financing liabilities.

When public companies maintain separate segment records, they are required by GAAP to report segment data in their financial statements. This is done in the form of supplementary schedules to the financial statements of the corporation, not as separate financial statements. The segment data required include the following:

1. Revenues, divided into those resulting from sales to outside customers and those to other segments, if any.

2. Profits and losses.

3. Revenues and expenses for the following categories, to the extent they are included in determining segment profits and losses.
   (a) interest revenue
   (b) interest expense
   (c) depreciation and amortization of long term asset costs
   (d) unusual and extraordinary items
   (e) income taxes

4. Total assets.

5. The cost of long term assets purchased during the year.

6. A reconciliation of segment data with the amounts shown in the corporation's statement of income and balance sheet.

Companies that do not keep separate records for different business segments are expected to report as much of the relevant information as it is feasible for them to produce from the records they do maintain.

An example of a schedule reporting segment data is shown on the next page.

The company allocates all its revenues and most of its expenses to the operating segments. Head office incurs some administrative expenses, including depreciation on the head office building. Long term borrowing is done by head office, only the interest costs on short term borrowing are charged to the divisions. Income taxes are not allocated to the divisions.

In addition to the segment data, public companies are required by GAAP to provide information concerning sales to major customers. If 10% or more of a company's sales are made to a single customer, the total amount of sales to that customer, or to each if there is more than one, must be reported. The customers need not be identified.

	Apple Division	**Orange Division**	**Head Office**	**Corporation Totals**
Sales to external customers	2,500	1,500		4,000
Intersegment sales	500	250		
Profit before the following	530	290	(60)	760
Interest expense	20	10	70	100
Depreciation	80	60	10	150
Income taxes			180	180
	100	70	260	430
Segment profit	430	220	(320)	330
Intersegment profit				140
Net profit				190
Assets	1,750	1,000	120	2,870
Plant and equipment purchases	120	80		200

Foreign Combinations

When Canadian companies combine the accounts of foreign companies with their own, they must first translate the foreign currency amounts into Canadian dollars. The methods used to translate foreign currency financial statements depend on the nature of the relationship between the domestic and foreign companies. Foreign enterprises that are **self-sustaining,** that is those that operate essentially independently of the Canadian companies, are treated differently from those that are closely **integrated.** Whether a foreign entity is considered self-sustaining or integrated is a matter of judgment, depending on a variety of factors, including where management decisions are made, where selling prices are determined, where goods and services are purchased and where funds are raised to finance the entity. The judgment is made by those responsible for producing the financial statements.

When a foreign enterprise is self-sustaining, its accounts are translated at current rates of exchange. All assets and liabilities are translated at the rate in effect on the balance sheet date. Revenues and expenses, including depreciation, are translated at rates in effect during the year. As a practical matter, this is usually taken as an average rate for the year.

When a foreign enterprise is integrated with the Canadian company, its accounts are treated as if the underlying transactions had all taken place in Canadian dollars, not in the foreign currency. Intangibles, plant and equipment, inventories and other tangibles are translated at the rates in effect at the time they were acquired. Only monetary items, cash and debts receivable and payable that will be settled in cash, are translated at the current rate. Revenues and expenses are translated at rates in effect during the year, except for depreciation and amortization of intangibles, which are based on the historical rates used to translate the corresponding assets.

Changes in exchange rates result in foreign exchange gains and losses, independent of the operating profits and losses of foreign enterprises. Estimates of these exchange gains and losses are produced by the process of translating the accounts. Since different accounts are translated at different rates of exchange, the accounts will not balance unless something is added to one side or the other. That something is the measure of the exchange gain or loss.

Since the methods used to translate accounts for self-sustaining and integrated foreign entities are different, the estimated gains and losses are also different. The method of reporting them in the financial statements is different as well. For self-sustaining entities, exchange gains and losses are reported in the balance sheet of the Canadian company as a separate component of shareholders' equity. They are not included in the calculation of income. For integrated entities, exchange gains and losses are included in the calculation of income.

The translation of foreign accounts can be illustrated using the data for Acme Manufacturing and Acme Parts, and assuming the following.

1. Parts is an American company, whose accounts are denominated in U.S. dollars.

2. Manufacturing owns 100% of Parts. It invested 120 in Canadian dollars on October 31, 20W to create the U.S. subsidiary. That was equivalent to 100 in U.S. dollars at that time.

3. Parts purchased its property, plant and equipment at the beginning of the year, November 1, 20W. The year end inventory was acquired evenly over the last three months of the year.

4. Cost of goods sold of Parts included depreciation of 10. All other costs and expenses were incurred evenly over the year.

5. The companies do not do business with each other.

6. Exchange rates were as follows:

   (A) November 1, 20W $1.00 U.S.   = $1.20 Canadian
   (B) Average for the year   1.00   =   1.30
   (C) Average for the last
        3 months of the year   1.00   =   1.35
   (D) October 31, 20X   1.00   =   1.40

If Parts is self-sustaining, consolidated financial statements will be prepared as shown on page 164.

Balance Sheet Accounts
October 31, 20X
(in thousands of dollars)

	Manufacturing	Parts U.S.	Parts Canadian	Consolidated
Accounts receivable	113	50	70(D)	183
Inventories	215	60	84(D)	299
	328	110	154	482
Investment in Acme Parts	120	—		~~120~~
Property, plant and equipment	105	40	56(D)	161
Patents	25	—		25
	578	150	210	668
Accounts payable and accrued	54	30	42(D)	96
Other current liabilities	45			45
	99	30	42	141
Bonds payable	90	—		90
	189	30	42	231
Shareholders' equity —				
October 31, 20W	355			355
		100	120(A)	~~120~~
Income, year ended				
October 31, 20X	41	20	26	67
Cash dividends	(7)	—		(7)
Foreign currency translation			22	22
	389	120	168	437
	578	150	210	668

Income Statement Accounts
October 31, 20X
(in thousands of dollars)

	Manufacturing	Parts U.S.	Parts Canadian	Consolidated
Sales	1,442	400	520(B)	1,962
Cost of goods sold	868	240	312(B)	1,180
Selling and administrative expenses	479	120	156(B)	635
Interest	12	—		12
	1,359	360	468	1,827
	83	40	52	135
Income taxes	42	20	26(B)	68
Net income	41	20	26	67

All asset and liability accounts were translated at the year end rate of 1.40 Canadian (D). The revenue and expense accounts were translated at the average rate for the year of 1.30(B). The difference created by using different rates in the two statements requires an adjustment to keep the statements in balance. That adjustment, 22 in the example, is a measure of the exchange gain described as a foreign currency translation adjustment and shown in the balance sheet.

If Parts is an integrated business, consolidated statements will appear as shown below.

Balance Sheet Accounts
October 31, 20X
(in thousands of dollars)

	Manufacturing	Parts U.S.	Parts Canadian	Consolidated
Accounts receivable	113	50	70(D)	183
Inventories	215	60	81(C)	296
	328	110	151	479
Investment in Acme Parts	120	—		~~120~~
Property, plant and equipment	105	40	48(A)	153
Patents	25	—		25
	578	150	199	657
Accounts payable and accrued	54	30	42(D)	96
Other current liabilities	45			45
	99	30	42	141
Bonds payable	90	—		90
	189	30	42	231
Shareholders' equity —				
October 31, 20W	355			355
		100	120(A)	~~120~~
Income, year ended				
October 31, 20X	41	20	37	78
Cash dividends	(7)			(7)
	389	120	157	426
	578	150	199	657

Income Statement Accounts
October 31, 20X
(in thousands of dollars)

	Manufacturing	Parts		Consolidated
		U.S.	Canadian	
Sales	1,442	400	520(B)	1,962
Cost of goods sold	868	240	311	1,179
Depreciation		10	12(A)	
Other		230	299(B)	
Selling and administrative expenses	479	120	156(B)	635
Interest	12			12
	1,359	360	467	1,826
	83	40	53	136
Gain on foreign exchange			10	10
			63	146
Income taxes	42	20	26(B)	68
Net income	41	20	37	78

In this case only the monetary assets and liabilities were translated at the year end rate of 1.40(D). Inventories were translated at the average rate during the period they were acquired of 1.35(C). Property, plant and equipment were translated at the effective rate the date they were acquired of 1.20(A). Revenues and expenses were translated at the average rate for the year of 1.30(B), with the exception of depreciation which was translated at the effective rate the date the assets were acquired of 1.20(A).

As in the previous example, the use of different rates requires an adjustment to keep the statements in balance. In this case, the adjustment is an exchange gain of 10 and is included in the statement of income.

SUMMARY

When the financial statements of foreign businesses are combined with Canadian statements, the accounts must first be translated into Canadian dollars. If the foreign business is self-sustaining, the statements are translated at current rates of exchange. Exchange gains and losses are not included in income. If it is integrated with the Canadian company, its accounts are treated as if the underlying transactions had taken place in Canadian dollars. Tangible and intangible asset values and related expenses are translated at the rates in effect at the time they were acquired. Monetary assets and liabilities and other revenues and expenses are translated at current rates. Exchange gains and losses are included in income.

The National Accounts

The national accounts provide a measure of all goods and services produced in the country during a year, described as **gross domestic product (GDP)**. It is, in effect, a giant consolidation of the income statements of all businesses in the country.

Gross domestic product is reported in two ways, described as **expenditure based** and as **income based**. The expenditure based report shows the goods and services that were produced. It corresponds to consolidated statement revenues. The income based report shows who was paid to produce them. It corresponds to consolidated statement expenses and profit. The two are equal; the total of expenses and profit equals revenues.

GDP, EXPENDITURE BASED

Expenditures (revenues in the income statement) are divided into the following categories.

Personal expenditure on consumer goods and services.
Government current expenditure on goods and services.
Government investment.
    Fixed capital
    Inventories
Business investment.
    Fixed capital
    Inventories
Exports of goods and services.
Deduct: Imports of goods and services.
    Total - Gross Domestic Product

All sales to consumers are described as personal expenditure, with the exception of new housing. This includes cars, furniture and other consumer durables, as well as goods and services for current consumption. Sales of new housing are included in the category business investment, fixed capital. Asset resales are excluded from all categories because they do not represent new production.

Sales to government are divided into two categories. Goods and services for current use (expenses) are described as government current expenditure.

Goods for future use (assets) are described as government investment. These are divided into two further categories, fixed capital (depreciable assets) and inventories.

Sales to businesses include only assets, described as business investment. Sales to other businesses that become expenses for those businesses are eliminated against each other in consolidating the accounts. Inter-business transfers do not add anything to production for the economy as a whole, unless they add to business assets. Business investment, like government investment, is divided into two categories, fixed capital (depreciable assets) and inventories.

Exports of goods and services are shown as a separate category of sales.

Spending on imports of goods and services is deducted because they are not part of domestic production.

GDP, INCOME BASED

Income (expenses and profit in the income statement) is divided into the following categories.

> Wages, salaries and supplementary labor income.
> Corporation profits before taxes.
> Interest and miscellaneous investment income.
> Net income of unincorporated business, including rent.
> > Sub-total - Net Domestic Income.
> Indirect taxes less subsidies.
> Capital consumption allowances.
> > Total - Gross Domestic Product.

Eliminating expense payments to other businesses against business sales in the consolidation of accounts leaves only payments to the factors of production, labor and capital, in the calculation of the sub-total net domestic income. Factor payments are divided into four categories. Wages and salaries are payments for labor. Interest is payment for capital. Corporation profits and income of unincorporated business are partly payments for capital and partly payments for labor and entrepreneurship.

In calculating gross domestic product, income based, two other costs have to be added to those of labor and capital. One is indirect taxes. Some producers are required to collect excise or other indirect taxes in the prices of the things they sell. These taxes become part of the reported value of gross domestic product. Gasoline, liquor and tobacco taxes are examples. If subsidies are paid to producers, they have the opposite effect of reducing prices.

The other cost is depreciation. Depreciation, described as capital consumption allowances in the accounts, is a cost of production but not a payment to labor or capital.

Illustration of GDP Consolidation

Producing the national accounts by consolidating the income statements of all businesses can be illustrated using a highly simplified model of the economy in which there are only three businesses, R, S, and T. R produces goods for current consumption. S produces fixed capital goods, buildings and equipment. T produces services. R and S are corporations. T is unincorporated. A worksheet consolidating their income statements for the year 20X, in billions of dollars, is shown on page 171.

Eliminations:

(1) Sales of services from T to R (290) are offset by purchases of R from T (290). There was no net gain to the economy as a whole.

(2) Sales of consumption goods from R to S (80) are offset by purchases of S from R to the extent they were included in current expenses (73). The difference (7) remained in S's inventory at the year end.

(3) Sales of services from T to S (12) are offset by purchases of S from T (12).

(4) Sales of consumption goods from R to T (258) are offset by purchases of T from R (258).

There are no offsetting amounts for the sales from S to R and T. Those sales were fixed capital goods. They were not expenses of R and T during the year, except to the extent they were included in depreciation.

Consolidated Amounts:

(A) Sales to consumers for current consumption were 298 from R plus 168 from T, a total of 466.

(B) Sales to government for current consumption were 83 from R plus 67 from T, a total of 150.

**Gross Domestic Product
Consolidation Worksheet
for the year 20X**

	R Corp.	S Corp.	T Prop.	Eliminations	Consolidated
Sales					
consumers	298	39	168		466(A)
					39(D)
government	83	17	67		150(B)
					17(C)
export	123	130	36		289(H)
R	—	59	290	290(1)	59(D)
S	80	—		73(2)	7(E)
			12	12(3)	—
T	258	22	—	258(4)	22(D)
	842	267	573	633	1,049
Expenses					
purchases from R (consumption goods)	—	73		73(2)	—
			258	258(4)	—
purchases from S (capital goods)	—	—	—		—
purchases from T (services)	290			290(1)	—
		12		12(3)	—
import	154	55	60		269(I)
wages and salaries	193	51	178		422(J)
interest	26	14	18		58(K)
indirect taxes	81	12	3		96(L)
depreciation	52	33	11		96(M)
	796	250	528	633	941
Profit	46	17	45	—	63(F)
					45(G)
	842	267	573	633	1,049

(C)   Sales to government of fixed capital goods were 17 from S.

(D)   Sales to business of fixed capital goods were 59 from S to R and 22 from S to T, a total of 81. In addition, S sold new housing of 39 to consumers, which is classified in the accounts as business fixed capital, making a grand total of business fixed capital sales of 120.

(E)   Sales to business of inventories were 7, 80 sold by R to S minus 73 included by S in current expenses.

(F)   Corporation profits were 46 for R and 17 for S, a total of 63.

(G) Income of unincorporated business was 45 for T.

The following are totals of the other amounts recorded by each of R, S and T.

(H) Exports, 289.

(I)   Imports, 269.

(J)   Wages and salaries, 422.

(K) Interest, 58.

(L) Indirect taxes, 96.

(M) Capital consumption allowance (depreciation), 96.

Using the consolidated amounts, national accounts are constructed as follows:

Gross Domestic Product, Expenditure Based, 20X
(Income Statement Revenues)
Billions of dollars

Personal expenditure	466(A)
Government current expenditure	150(B)
Government investment	
Fixed capital	17(C)
Inventories	—
Business investment	
Fixed capital	120(D)
Inventories	7(E)
Exports	289(H)
Imports	−269(I)
Gross domestic product	780

Gross Domestic Product, Income Based, 20X
(Income Statement Expenses and Profit)
Billions of dollars

Wages and salaries	422(J)
Interest	58(K)
Corporation profits	63(F)
Income of unincorporated business	45(G)
Net domestic income	588
Indirect taxes	96(L)
Capital consumption allowances	96(M)
Gross domestic product	780

Note: The amounts shown in these accounts are those reported by Statistics Canada for 1995.

ADDITIONS AND ADJUSTMENTS

Although they are based on the same principle, the national accounts go beyond an accounting consolidation of business accounts and are produced using statistical methods. Some significant elements of production are missing from the accounts of business and have to be added. Some business data have to be adjusted.

One element of production added is the value of goods and services produced by government. In the illustration, government was not included as a producer. In fact, all government salary and wage payments are made to provide goods and services, mainly services, although many are not commercial in nature. Government transfer payments, things like pensions and employment insurance payments, are not included, because they are not made for the production of goods and services.

A second element added is the rental value of housing owned by occupants. Owners who occupy their houses or condominiums are regarded as both landlords and tenants. The rental value of their dwellings is added to personal expenditure and to income of unincorporated business. This is consistent with the treatment of rents paid by non-owners.

Much productive work is not included. Work done by people for their own benefit is generally omitted. Work within the home, for example, preparing meals, cleaning, making home improvements and so on, is omitted if performed by the householders. The same work would be included if someone else were paid to do it.

In the Canadian accounts, the income of farmers is shown separately from other unincorporated business income. In calculating farm income, two adjustments are made to the amount received by farmers during the year from the sale of their products. One is an increase in the total by the estimated value of farm production consumed by the farm families themselves. The other is an adjustment to change the estimate of income from one based on sales to one based on production, recognizing that sales of large quatities of some farm products occur at a later date than the value is added in production.

An adjustment for inventory valuation is calculated and reported separately in the calculation of income. As noted in chapter 8, the book values of inventories and cost of sales are calculated in a variety of different ways. The inventory valuation adjustment compensates for the difference between book values and current market values.

If the national accounts were an accounting consolidation, the expenditure and income totals would be exactly equal. Since they are produced using statistical methods and estimates, there is a small difference. The difference is divided in half. One half, described as statistical discrepancy, is added to the smaller total. The other half, also described as statistical discrepancy, is deducted from the larger total. Expenditure and income estimates of gross domestic product are then equal at the average of the two.

STATISTICS CANADA REPORT

The national expenditure and income accounts produced by Statistics Canada for 1995 showed the following. Details of expenditure and income categories are provided by the agency in supplementary reports.

Gross Domestic Product, Expenditure Based, 1995 Millions of dollars	
Personal expenditure on consumer goods and services	466,313
Government current expenditure on goods and services	150,158
Government investment:	
Fixed capital	17,416
Inventories	30
Business investment:	
Fixed capital	120,155
Residential construction	39,148
Non-residential construction	32,809
Machinery and equipment	48,198
Inventories	6,851
Non-farm	5,966
Farm and grain in commercial channels	885
Exports of goods and services	288,543
Merchandise	253,536
Non-merchandise	35,007
Imports of goods and services	−269,223
Merchandise	−225,250
Non-merchandise	−43,973
Statistical discrepancy	−216
Gross Domestic Product at market prices	780,027

Gross Domestic Product, Income Based, 1995
Millions of dollars

Wages, salaries and supplementary labor income	422,346
Corporation profits before taxes	65,850
Interest and miscellaneous investment income	58,033
Accrued net income of farm operators from farm production	3,481
Net income of non-farm unincorporated business, including rent	41,456
Inventory valuation adjustment	−3,446
Net Domestic Income at factor cost	587,720
Indirect taxes less subsidies	96,045
Capital consumption allowances	96,046
Statistical discrepancy	216
Gross Domestic Product at market prices	780,027

CHAPTER 13

Cash Flow

Cash is the lifeblood of business. If a business does not have an adequate, dependable, continuous flow of cash, it will not survive, regardless of how large or profitable it is. The need for cash flow must be balanced against incentives for growth and opportunities for profit. Many a business has failed because it grew too quickly and could not generate enough cash at a comparable pace to meet its short term obligations. Many have failed because they undertook potentially profitable activities without enough cash to see them through. Managers need information about cash flow in addition to income and financial position.

CASH FLOW VERSUS INCOME

For many small businesses, cash flow is virtually synonymous with income. For example, Flora Blumen operates a small flower shop. She rents store space in a strip mall for $1,000 per month. Once or twice a week she goes to the flower auction to make her purchases for sale that week. She employs a part time helper whom she pays out of cash receipts at the end of the day. She does not extend credit to her customers and pays cash for her purchases. At the end of her first year of operation her cash records showed the following.

Cash receipts	$152,000
Cash paid for flowers	83,000
	69,000
Cash paid for other supplies	8,000
Rent paid	12,000
Wages paid	11,000
	31,000
Net cash flow, withdrawn by proprietor	$ 38,000

All of Flora's cash receipts came from sales. All of her payments went for current expenses. The listing of cash receipts and payments is, in effect, a statement of income. Cash flow and income are identical.

Encouraged by her success in the first year, Flora decided to expand her business. She added a line of gift items to sell along with her flowers. She was able to negotiate thirty day credit terms with the supplier. She also purchased a small van to make deliveries, which she financed in part by taking a loan from the bank. At the end of her second year of operation, her cash records showed the following.

Cash received from customers	$209,000
Cash borrowed to purchase van	15,000
	224,000
Cash paid for flowers and gifts	122,000
Cash paid for other supplies	14,000
Rent paid	12,000
Wages paid	16,000
Cash paid for van	22,000
Cash repaid on van loan	5,000
Interest paid on van loan	1,000
	192,000
Net cash flow	$32,000

Flora decided she needed some help. Her business was expanding but her cash flow was diminishing. She called in an accountant. Between them they determined the following as of the end of the year.

1. There was $1,000 in the bank. Flora had withdrawn the remaining $31,000 of cash flow.

2. Flora had an inventory of gifts in the store worth $13,000 at cost.

3. Flora owed $3,000 to her gift supplier.

4. The van had an estimated useful life of 5 years and would be worth approximately $2,000 at the end of that time. Annual depreciation was estimated to be $4,000.

Based on the recorded cash flow and the additional information the accountant prepared the financial statements shown below.

Flora's Flowers
Balance Sheet
at December 31, 20X.

Cash	$ 1,000	Bank loan	$10,000
Inventory	13,000	Account payable	3,000
	14,000		13,000
Van	22,000	Proprietorship	
Less accumulated		Income, 20x	50,000
depreciation	4,000	Less withdrawals	31,000
	18,000		19,000
	$32,000		$32,000

Flora's Flowers
Statement of Income
for the year ended December 31, 20X

Sales	$209,000
Cost of goods sold	112,000
Gross margin	97,000
Supplies	14,000
Rent	12,000
Wages	16,000
Depreciation of van	4,000
	46,000
Operating income	51,000
Interest	1,000
Net income	$ 50,000

The accountant explained the difference between Flora's income and her cash flow as follows:

1. The amount paid to suppliers was different from expenses for two reasons. First, purchases from the gift supplier were made on credit. Purchases were $3,000 more than payments, because $3,000 was owed for purchases at the end of the year. Secondly, not all purchases were expenses of the year. $13,000 of purchases remained in inventory at the end of the year. Cost of sales therefore was purchases paid for (122,000) plus purchases not paid for (3,000) minus purchases left in inventory (13,000), that is, 112,000.

2. Depreciation of the van was an estimated expense of the year but did not involve any payment of cash.

3. Purchase of the van required cash in the amount of $22,000, but the van is an asset, not an expense.

4. Cash flow from operations for the year was supplemented by a loan from the bank of $15,000 less a repayment of $5,000. The loan is a liability, not a revenue.

STATEMENTS OF CASH FLOWS

To illustrate the differences between income and cash flow, the accountant prepared the statement of cash flows shown on the next page.

The statement is prepared using information from the statement of income and the balance sheet. It shows cash flows, positive and negative, in three categories resulting from the following activities.

- Operating
- Investing
- Financing

Operating activities produce income, revenues minus expenses. The cash flows they produce differ from income for two reasons. One is that some expenses, such as depreciation, do not involve the payment of cash. Depreciation, and other non-cash expenses if any, are therefore added back to income in arriving at cash flow. The other reason is that cash receipts and payments do not coincide with revenues and expenses when sales and purchases are made on credit, or when goods are purchased for inventory.

Flora's Flowers
Statement of Cash Flows
for the year ended December 31, 20X

Cash flows from operating activities		
Operating income		$ 51,000
Depreciation		4,000
Interest		(1,000)
Operating cash flow before working capital changes		54,000
Increase in account payable		3,000
Increase in inventory		(13,000)
Net cash from operating activities		44,000
Cash flow from investing activity		
Purchase of van		(22,000)
Cash flows from financing activities		
Bank loan	$ 10,000	
Proprietor's withdrawals	(31,000)	
Net cash from financing activities		(21,000)
Net increase in cash		1,000
Cash at the beginning of the year		—
Cash at the end of the year (bank)		$ 1,000

Income is therefore adjusted for changes in current asset and current liability accounts in calculating cash flow. In this example, income is adjusted to cash flows from operating activities by adding back 4,000 for depreciation, adding 3,000 for purchases not paid for, and deducting 13,000 for goods purchased for inventory.

Investing activities consist of long term asset transactions. In the example, the investment activity consists of the purchase of a van for 22,000.

Financing activities consist of borrowing and ownership transactions. They are reflected in short term borrowings and in the long term debt and ownership sections of the balance sheet. In the example, cash flows from financing activities consist of the bank loan of 10,000 minus the proprietor's withdrawals of 31,000.

Many small businesses keep their accounts on a cash basis, that is, they record only cash receipts and cash payments. There was no difference between

Flora Blumen's income and cash flow in her first year of operation. In the second year, it was easy to adjust from the cash record to produce a conventional balance sheet and statement of income.

For most businesses, a simple record of cash receipts and payments is not adequate. When sales and purchases are made on credit, a record must be kept of amounts owing to and from the business. The books are kept in the manner described and illustrated in chapter 4, Double Entry Bookkeeping, known as accrual accounting. When the books are kept on an accrual basis, statements of cash flows are usually prepared from statements of income and balance sheets using a worksheet, in which revenue and expense data are combined with an analysis of the changes in balance sheet accounts during the period. The procedure is illustrated using the following data for Bucks Limited.

Bucks Limited
Statement of Income
for the year ended December 31, 20X
(in thousands of dollars)

Sales		480
Cost of goods sold		306
Gross margin		174
Selling and administrative expenses		140
		34
Share of income of Nether Inc.		4
Loss on disposal of equipment		(2)
		36
Interest expense		8
Income before taxes		28
Income taxes — current	10	
deferred	3	
		13
Net income		15

Bucks Limited
Balance Sheet
at December 31, 20X and 20W
(in thousands of dollars)

	20X		20W	Changes Dr.	Cr.
Cash		2	1	1	
Accounts receivable		60	52	8	
Inventory		72	67	5	
		134	120		
Investment in Nether Inc.		40	29	11	
Plant and equipment — cost	56		43	13	
Less accumulated depreciation	12		8		4
		44	35		
		218	184		
Short term loan		5	3		2
Accounts payable and accrued		42	49	7	
Accrued income taxes		3	2		1
		50	54		
Lease obligation		20			20
Debenture payable	50		50		
Less debenture discount	2		3		1
		48	47		
Deferred taxes		19	16		3
		137	117		
Capital stock preferred		15	20	5	
common		30	25		5
Retained earnings — beginning	22				
income for the year	15				15
preferred dividends	(1)			1	
ending		36	22		
		81	67		
		218	184	51	51

Additional data:

1. Depreciation expense for the year was 6.
2. Bucks has significant influence in Nether. It recorded its share of the income of Nether for the year of 4 in its income and in the value of its

investment in Nether. It made a further investment in shares of Nether of 7.

3. New equipment costing 20 was acquired by means of a capital lease.
4. Equipment was disposed of during the year which had an original cost of 7 and accumulated depreciation of 2 for a net book value of 5. It was sold for 3 for a loss on disposal of 2.
5. Amortization of bond discount of 1 was included in interest expense.
6. The change in preferred and common stock resulted from the conversion of preferred stock into common.

A worksheet for the preparation of a statement of cash flows is shown on page 185.

A worksheet for the preparation of a statement of cash flows is shown on page 185.

The following adjustments were made.

(A) Cash received from sales was reduced by 8 because an additional 8 remained uncollected in accounts receivable. (If accounts receivable had changed as a result of non-cash adjustments to an allowance for doubtful accounts, a further adjustment would be required.)
(B) Cash paid to suppliers was increased by 5 because goods costing 5 were added to inventory in addition to those sold.
(C) Cash paid to suppliers and employees was increased by 7 because additional payments were made to reduce accounts payable and accrued by 7.
(D) Cash paid in expenses was reduced by 6 for depreciation, a non-cash expense.
(E) The share of income of Nether Inc. was eliminated as a non-cash revenue.
(F) The acquisition of new equipment of 20 was offset against the capital lease obligation because the transaction did not involve cash.
(G) The cost of 7 and accumulated depreciation of 2 written off on disposal of equipment were eliminated as non-cash adjustments. The amounts were applied against the loss on disposal to show the net cash received of 3.
(H) Debenture discount amortized of 1 was a non-cash expense and was applied to reduce interest to the amount of cash paid.
(J) Taxes paid were reduced by 1, the increase in the amount unpaid at the end of the year.

Bucks Limited
Statement of Cash Flows Worksheet
year ended December 31, 20X

	Preliminary Dr.	Preliminary Cr.	Adjustments Dr.	Adjustments Cr.	Cash Flow Dr.	Cash Flow Cr.
Income Statement Amounts						
Sales		480	8(A)			472(M)
Cost of goods sold	306		5(B)			
			7(C)	6(D) }	452(N)	
Selling and administration	140					
Income from Nether Inc.		4	4(E)			
Loss on equipment	2		2(G)	7(G)		3(R)
Interest	8			1(H)	7(P)	
Taxes — current	10			1(J)	9(Q)	
deferred	3			3(K)		
Balance Sheet Changes						
Cash	1					1(V)
Accounts receivable	8			8(A)		
Inventory	5			5(B)		
Investment in Nether Inc.	11			4(E)	7(S)	
Plant and equipment	13		7(G)	20(F)		
Accumulated depreciation		4	6(D)	2(G)		
Loan		2				2(T)
Accounts payable and accrued	7			7(C)		
Accrued taxes		1	1(J)			
Lease obligation		20	20(F)			
Debentures	—	—				
Debenture discount		1	1(H)			
Deferred taxes		3	3(K)			
Capital stock —						
preferred	5			5(L)		
common		5	5(L)			
Retained earnings (*note*)	—	—				
Preferred dividends	1				1(U)	
	520	520	69	69	477	477

Note: No change in retained earnings is recorded because the nominal accounts for the year (revenues, expenses and dividend) have been recorded individually in the worksheet.

(K)   Deferred tax expense of 3 was offset against the increase in deferred tax shown in the balance sheet because there was no cash involved.

(L)   The decrease in preferred stock of 5 was offset against the equivalent increase in common stock because there was no cash involved in the stock conversion.

A statement of cash flows appears as follows:

Bucks Limited
Statement of Cash Flows
for the year ended December 31, 20X
(in thousands of dollars)

Cash flows from operating activities:		
Cash received from customers	472(M)	
Cash paid to suppliers and employees	(452)(N)	
Cash generated by operations	20	
Interest paid	(7)(P)	
Income taxes paid	(9)(Q)	
Net cash from operating activities		4
Cash flows from investing activities:		
Proceeds from sale of equipment	3(R)	
Purchase of shares in Nether Inc.	(7)(S)	
Net cash used in investing activities		(4)
Cash flows from financing activities:		
Increase in short term borrowings	2(T)	
Dividends paid	(1)(U)	
Net cash provided by financing activities		1
Net increase in cash		1(V)
Cash at beginning of the year		1
Cash at end of the year		2

Operating activities produced cash receipts from customers, and cash payments to suppliers and employees and for interest and income taxes. Investing activities consisted of selling equipment and purchasing shares in Nether Inc. Financing activities consisted of short term borrowings and dividend payments to preferred shareholders.

Direct Versus Indirect Method

The statement prepared for Bucks Limited differs from that for Flora's Flowers in the way cash flows from operating activities are described. Bucks Limited shows the amounts of cash received and cash paid directly. Flora's Flowers calculated operating cash flows on the statement, starting with income and adjusting for non-cash items in the income statement and for changes in working capital (current asset and current liability) accounts.

The Bucks Limited method is called the direct method, the Flora's Flowers method is the indirect method. Both methods are acceptable in accordance with GAAP. Accounting authorities favor the direct method, but the indirect method is much more commonly used. When statements of cash flows are prepared using the direct method, a reconciliation with income, similar to the one shown on the face of the Flora's Flowers statement, is usually also provided.

Interest, Dividends and Taxes

Interest, dividends and taxes are reported separately from other sources and uses of cash. Interest and dividends received are classified as operating cash receipts. Interest paid is classified as an operating cash payment. Dividends paid are classified as financing cash payments. Combined payments of principal and interest on debt or on capital leases, are classified as financing to the extent of the principal only and operating to the extent of the interest. Income tax payments are usually classified as operating, unless they can be clearly identified with financing or investing transactions, in which case they are classified as financing or investing.

Non-Cash Exchanges

Financing and investing transactions are omitted from the statement of cash flows if they do not involve a receipt or payment of cash. In the Bucks Limited example, the acquisition of equipment by capital lease and the conversion of preferred stock into common were eliminated. Although they do not involve cash, these transactions are significant to an understanding of the financing and investing activities of a business. They are therefore reported elsewhere in the financial statements, either in notes or in separate schedules.

Short Term Borrowing and Investment

Temporary investments and short term borrowings by their nature often change frequently over the course of a year. When short term borrowings or investments fluctuate, they are reported as the net amount of the change during the year, not as separate receipts and payments. Bucks Limited reported only the net increase in short term borrowings for example, not the various increases and decreases that might have occurred. This practice produces a clearer and simpler view of cash flows.

Cash equivalents, described in chapter 11, are combined with cash balances.

Cash Measurement

Statements of cash flows do not involve any estimates of value, probabilities of collection or payment, or allocations of costs and revenues, unlike statements of income and balance sheets. When they are prepared from statements of income and balance sheets, as in the Bucks Limited example, all accruals, deferments and amortizations are eliminated. They are therefore not subject to assumptions, judgments and opinions. They are statements of fact.

Terminology

The description **statement of cash flows** is used almost universally in the United States, and similar terminology is being used currently by the Accounting Standards Board in Canada. The statement is most often called a **statement of changes in financial position** in Canadian practice however.

CHAPTER 14

Public Accountants and Credibility

Outsiders are almost entirely dependent on management for financial information about a business. In most large businesses, outsiders include most of the shareholders, although shareholders are legally the owners of the business. Outsiders, in particular shareholders and creditors, need assurance that the financial information provided to them by management is reliable. That assurance is provided by independent public accountants.

Public accountants are licensed by the provinces. Each province determines the educational and experience requirements that must be satisfied for someone to practice as a public accountant in that jurisdiction. Most public accountants are Chartered Accountants (CAs). CAs can be licensed to practice in any province. Some public accountants are Certified General Accountants (CGAs). CGAs are restricted in the services they can perform in some provinces. A few public accountants are neither CAs nor CGAs. They are further restricted in the services they can offer.

Public accountants provide assurance to outsiders by reporting independently on the financial information produced by management. Their reports take a variety of forms, depending on the circumstances.

STANDARD AUDITS

Public companies are required to have their annual financial statements audited by public accountants, and to issue the audit reports with the statements. The standard audit report takes the following form.

AUDITOR'S REPORT

To the Shareholders of Client Limited

I have audited the balance sheet of Client Limited as at December 31, 20X and the statements of income, retained earnings and cash flows for the year then ended. These financial statements are the responsibility of the company's management. My responsibility is to express an opinion on these financial statements based on my audit.

I conducted my audit in accordance with generally accepted auditing standards. Those standards require that I plan and perform an audit to obtain reasonable assurance whether the financial statements are free of material misstatement. An audit includes examining, on a test basis, evidence supporting the amounts and disclosures in the financial statements. An audit also includes assessing the accounting principles used and significant estimates made by management, as well as evaluating the overall financial statement presentation.

In my opinion, these financial statements present fairly, in all material respects, the financial position of the company as at December 31, 20X and the results of its operations and its cash flows for the year then ended in accordance with Canadian generally accepted accounting principles.

City ....

Date ....

(signed)   ....

CHARTERED ACCOUNTANT

The report is addressed to the shareholders of the company. Auditors are appointed by vote by shareholders at company annual meetings. They are responsible to the shareholders, not to the management or directors. They are usually nominated or proposed for election by directors or management however, and approval of their remuneration is usually delegated to the directors.

The standard report has three paragraphs: an introductory paragraph, a scope paragraph and an opinion paragraph. The **introductory paragraph** first identifies the financial statements being reported on. It then states that the financial statements are the responsibility of the management, and the auditor's responsibility is for his opinion on those statements. This is an important distinction. Auditors often assist in the preparation of financial statements. In many small businesses they prepare the statements altogether. Nevertheless, the statements remain the responsibility of management. The auditor is responsible only for his opinion on the fairness of those statements.

The **scope paragraph** describes in general terms how the audit was conducted. It begins by stating that the audit was conducted in accordance with generally accepted auditing standards. **Generally accepted auditing standards (GAAS)** are like generally accepted accounting principles (GAAP), except that there is much less diversity in what are considered acceptable auditing practices than in acceptable accounting practices. GAAS, like GAAP, are codified in Canada in the CICA Handbook.

The scope paragraph then explains the objective of an audit conducted in accordance with GAAS. The objective is to obtain reasonable assurance that the statements are free of material misstatement. Reasonable assurance is not absolute assurance. Absolute assurance is not possible and even if it were, the cost of achieving it would be prohibitive. The scope paragraph explains that supporting evidence is examined on a test basis. Tests are based on the probabilities of misstatements and the risks of not detecting them. The paragraph also refers to the auditor's assessment of the accounting principles used and the estimates made, and his evaluation of the overall presentation of the statements.

A material misstatement is one that would affect the judgment or decision of a user of the information. A misstatement can result from misapplying accounting principles, misstating facts, incorrect estimates, omissions, or a combination of factors. A single misstatement by itself might not be material but in combination with others could be. The auditor renders his opinion on the fairness of the statements overall. Whether a misstatement is material is a matter of judgment by the auditor. In making that judgment, he must consider the fact that he might have to defend it in a court of law, if a user of the financial statements is misled and suffers a loss. While auditors are primarily responsible to shareholders, the courts have determined that they are also responsible to some third parties, such as lenders and potential lenders.

A standard audit is not designed to uncover theft, fraud or illegal acts. By the nature of the testing done in an audit these things are sometimes detected, but that is not the purpose of the audit. The purpose is to obtain reasonable assurance that the financial statements are free of material misstatement. If theft, fraud or illegal acts are discovered, the auditor will report them to the appropriate level of authority and will consider their effect on the fairness of the financial statements.

The **opinion paragraph** of the standard report states the auditor's opinion that the statements are presented fairly in accordance with generally accepted accounting principles. Earlier chapters showed that accounting results can vary significantly within generally accepted accounting principles, depending on the measurement methods chosen. The auditor does not comment on the appropriateness of the methods chosen by the business in question, so long as they are acceptable. The user of the statements must make his or her own judgments, based on the description of accounting policies and measurement methods included in the notes to the financial statements.

The standard report concludes with the signature of the auditor and the date. The date of the report is usually the date the audit work was completed. The auditor is responsible to ensure that any events occurring up to that date that have a material effect on the finances of the company are reported. After that date, he or she is not responsible.

It was noted earlier (chapter 5), that public corporations often include other, sometimes extensive, information in their annual reports, in addition to their financial statements and the auditor's report. The auditor does not provide assurance on that information as part of a standard audit. The auditor does however, review the information included to ensure that none of it is inconsistent with the financial statements, and to ensure that so far as he or she is aware, it does not contain a material misstatement.

It was noted earlier that many corporations also issue quarterly financial statements. Quarterly statements are not required to be audited.

While most private companies and unincorporated businesses are not required by law to have an audit, some do. Potential lenders and investors sometimes require audited statements as a condition of their loan or investment.

REPORT RESERVATIONS

Occasionally an auditor is unable to issue a standard audit report. This can happen for two reasons, either because the auditor is not able to get all the information he requires to render an opinion, or because the statements are not presented fairly in accordance with generally accepted accounting principles. Failure to obtain information can result from restrictions imposed on the auditor by management, or from circumstances beyond the control of management and the auditor. Management might refuse to disclose the minutes of directors' meetings for example, or the minutes could have been lost in a fire.

If statements as originally presented are not in accordance with GAAP, the auditor will request that changes be made, but in some cases the management are adamant that things be reported in a certain way. Management might refuse to record deferred taxes for example, on the grounds the taxes have not been levied.

If he is not able to obtain the information he needs or the statements are not presented fairly in accordance with GAAP, the auditor will do one of three things; he will either deny an opinion, he will issue a qualified opinion, or he will issue an adverse opinion, If the lack of information is such that the auditor cannot reasonably form an opinion on the financial statements as a whole, he will deny an opinion. If he lacks information only on particular items in the statements, but is able to describe those items and the possible effect of a misstatement of those items, he will qualify his opinion.

If departures from GAAP and their effects on the statements can be explained and do not otherwise invalidate the statements as a whole, the auditor will qualify his opinion. If they make the statements as a whole misleading or virtually useless, he will render an adverse opinion.

When reservations are made in audit reports, an **explanatory paragraph** is included between the scope and opinion paragraphs. If the auditor has not been able to obtain information, a reference to the explanation is included in the scope paragraph. In all cases, the opinion paragraph is modified. In a denial, the auditor states that he is unable to express an opinion. For a qualification, the opinion states that "except for" the item described in the explanatory paragraph, the statements are presented fairly in accordance with GAAP. An adverse opinion states that the statements are not presented fairly in accordance with GAAP.

REVIEWS AND COMPILATIONS

Many small businesses want some assurance from a public accountant concerning their financial statements, but do not want to incur the cost of a full audit. For them, the accountant can perform what is known as a review engagement. In a review engagement, the accountant makes enquiries about the business and its accounting practices, applies analytical procedures such as comparing current statements with previous statements and budgets, and questions management about matters affecting the financial statements. If his queries and analysis raise doubts about the veracity of the data, he will expand the scope of his investigation, but otherwise he will not seek independent verification as he would in an audit. If the accountant is satisfied with the results of his review, he will issue a review report. A review report takes the form shown on the next page.

The report provides what is described as **negative assurance**. It does not say the statements are in accordance with GAAP, it says nothing causes the accountant to believe that they are not in accordance with GAAP. If the accountant has reservations, he reports them as he would in an audit report. When a review report is issued, every page of the statements is clearly marked "unaudited".

Sometimes public accountants are asked to prepare or help prepare financial statements from information provided by business managers,

---

REVIEW ENGAGEMENT REPORT

To Client

I have reviewed the balance sheet of Client as at December 31, 20X and the statements of income, retained earnings and cash flows for the year then ended. My review was made in accordance with Canadian generally accepted standards for review engagements and accordingly consisted primarily of enquiry, analytical procedures and discussion related to information supplied to me by the company.

A review does not constitute an audit and consequently I do not express an audit opinion on these financial statements.

Based on my review, nothing has come to my attention that causes me to believe that these financial statements are not, in all material respects, in accordance with Canadian generally accepted accounting principles.

City ....
Date ....

(signed)   ....
CHARTERED ACCOUNTANT

---

without any assurance concerning the validity of the information, positive or negative. So long as he has no reason to believe the data provided are false or misleading, an accountant will perform the work and append a notice to reader such as that on the next page.

NOTICE TO READER

I have compiled the balance sheet of Client as at December 31, 20X and the statements of income, retained earnings and cash flows for the year then ended from information provided by management. I have not audited, reviewed or otherwise attempted to verify the accuracy or completeness of such information. Readers are cautioned that these statements may not be appropriate for their purposes.

City ....

(signed)   ....

Date ....   CHARTERED ACCOUNTANT

Each page of the statements will be marked "Unaudited - see Notice to Reader".

PROSPECTUSES AND PRO-FORMAS

Companies issuing securities to or acquiring them from the public are required to publish certain information in offering documents described as prospectuses and circulars. The information includes audited financial statements and in some cases unaudited interim statements and pro-forma statements giving effect to proposed transactions.

When audited financial statements are included in a document, it must be with the auditor's consent. If he is aware of any happening since the date of his audit report that would have changed the statements, he will require the appropriate changes to be made.

If the audited statements are not sufficiently current, interim statements are required as well. When interim statements are required, they are accompanied by a negative assurance from the auditor, similar to that of a review engagement.

In some instances, for example when the proceeds of a securities issue are to be used to purchase another business, pro-forma statements are included to show how past financial statements would have appeared if the contemplated transaction had already occurred. When pro-forma statements are included, the auditor will ensure that the transactions and assumptions on which they are based are clearly disclosed, and that the statements are properly compiled to give effect to those transactions and assumptions. He will include a report confirming his opinion that they are properly compiled.

In addition to his work in reviewing and updating the financial statement data in an offering document, an auditor must read the document in its entirety to ensure that to the best of his knowledge it does not contain any misrepresentations. He does not however, report on the document as a whole.

FORECASTS AND PROJECTIONS

Sometimes public accountants are asked to report on forecasts or projections of what financial results will look like in the future. A forecast reflects management's best guess of the future, based on what exists and what they plan to do. A projection is based on other hypotheses or suppositions as well. For example, a projection might be based on the supposition that a company merges with one of its competitors.

When reporting on a forecast or projection, the accountant must ensure that assumptions and hypotheses are clearly disclosed and distinguished. He reports that they are reasonable and that the forecast or projection reflects those assumptions and hypotheses, if any. He also states that he has no responsibility to report the effect of events and circumstances happening after the date of his report, and that actual results will vary from the information presented, possibly significantly. He disclaims any opinion on whether the results will be achieved.

OTHER REPORTS AND SERVICES

Public accountants are occasionally requested to report on matters other than financial statements. For example, they might be asked to audit the amount of a company's gross sales in connection with a lease agreement, or the amount of royalties payable under a royalty agreement. Sometimes they are asked to report on whether a company has complied with the terms of an agreement, for example a loan agreement, or with a government regulation. The form and content of these reports varies, depending on the needs of the client and the degree of assurance provided.

In addition to reporting, public accountants provide many other services to business, including advice on taxes, finance, insolvency, business valuation and business management.

PART

III

—

ANALYSIS
AND
CONTROL

CHAPTER 15

Financial Statement Analysis

Much useful information about a business can be learned by analyzing its financial statements, using ratios and percentages. The ratio of current assets to current liabilities for example, known as the **current ratio**, gives an indication of how easy or difficult it will be to make payments promptly to creditors. The percentage of profit on shareholders' investment is a measure of how well a business is managed.

Absolute amounts are much less meaningful. Working capital, current assets minus current liabilities, of $10,000 would indicate a very strong position if current liabilities were $5,000, but a weak position if they were $50,000. A profit of $100,000 would be an excellent return on shareholder investment of $200,000 but a poor return on $2,000,000.

A single ratio or percentage by itself is often not much better than a single dollar amount. A current ratio of 2 to 1 is strong if the current assets are mainly in the form of cash and accounts receivable, but weak if they consist of slow moving inventory. An increase to 2 to 1 from 1 to 1 would likely be a positive development, a further increase to 3 to 1 might not be positive. It could indicate a slowdown in the rate of collection of accounts receivable or a buildup of idle cash balances. There are no absolute standards. Ratios and percentages have to be analyzed and compared with other ratios and percentages.

Two kinds of comparisons can be made. Data can be compared with other data for the same business, and they can be compared with similar data for other businesses. Within the same business, comparisons are made with the same data for other time periods, and with other data for the same time period. Total working capital for example, can be compared with the same amount in the previous year, and with the percentage represented by cash and accounts receivable in the same year. Comparisons with other businesses are made with those in similar lines of business. A retailer who sells for cash will not have a current ratio comparable to a manufacturer who sells on 30 day credit terms.

For outsiders, the main sources of information are company reports to shareholders, annual and interim. Management have access to additional internal data as well. Other sources of data, for both individual companies and industries, are reports issued by business publishers, credit rating agencies and stock brokers.

METHODS OF ASSESSMENT

The economic performance of a business is judged by the income it generates for the owners. The more income it generates per dollar of owner investment, the better the economic performance. Income per dollar of owner investment is the fraction:

$$\frac{\text{Income}}{\text{Owner Investment}}$$

This fraction can be expanded as follows:

$$\frac{\text{Income}}{\text{Revenue}} \times \frac{\text{Revenue}}{\text{Assets}} \times \frac{\text{Assets}}{\text{Ownership}}$$

In other words, income on ownership is the result of three factors:

1. The amount of income generated per dollar of revenue, described as profitability.
2. The amount of revenue generated per dollar of investment in assets, described as asset turnover.
3. The amount of assets employed per dollar of ownership investment, described as financial leverage.

Return on investment can be increased by increasing any of these factors. They are not completely independent of each other however, an attempt to increase one can have the effect of reducing another. For example, it might be possible to increase asset turnover by increasing sales, but doing so could require reducing prices and consequently operating margin.

Each factor can be assessed in different ways.

Profitability

Profitability is profit on sales. It is determined by the relationship between sales and expenses. This relationship is reflected in the statement of income.

Assessing the data shown in statements of income requires some adjustments. To begin with, it is usually better for comparative purposes, to eliminate income taxes. Income taxes are a form of profit distribution, normally outside the influence of management. Unless operating methods affect the amount of taxes levied, they are not relevant to the measurement of performance.

Extraordinary items should be eliminated. Depending on the purpose of the analysis, it is probably appropriate to eliminate unusual items and the results of discontinued operations as well.

In assessing operating margin, the profit should be calculated before interest and other financing costs. Financing costs are an element of financial leverage, to be taken into account in assessing that factor.

In most cases, charges for intangibles should be eliminated. Intangibles are not treated consistently by different companies. Within the same company, the amounts reported for intangibles are often not consistent and not reliable measures of value.

Adjustments to depreciation expense are sometimes needed. Different companies calculate depreciation in different ways. Over time, historical cost data become less and less relevant. Cost of goods sold can also need adjustment, depending on the valuation methods used.

Profitability is analyzed by calculating expenses and margins as percentages of sales. **Common size statements of income**, in which sales are shown at 100% and expenses and margins at corresponding percentages, are prepared to compare with other time periods and with other companies.

Rates of change in sales and margins are calculated by taking the earliest year at 100 and calculating the percentage change from that amount each year thereafter. These data are adjusted for inflation by using an appropriate price index to deflate them.

Asset Turnover

Asset turnover is analyzed by measuring various asset amounts against related revenue and expense amounts. As in measuring profitability, some adjustments are needed in analyzing asset turnover. Non-operating assets, such as investments in other companies, should be eliminated. Plant and equipment costs should be adjusted to current values, if that is feasible. Inventory values should also be adjusted to market to the extent it is feasible to do so. Inventory values based on the LIFO method of valuation are usually of no use in measuring asset turnover, because they are so much lower than current market. When asset amounts change significantly during a period, an average should be used.

Fixed asset turnover is calculated as

$$\frac{\text{Sales}}{\text{Net fixed assets}}$$

Fixed asset turnover is a measure of how effectively the productive capacity of a business is being used. The greater the volume of sales generated from the investment in capacity, the more productive it is. Comparisons of fixed asset turnover are limited in value when they are based on historical cost data or on differing methods of calculating depreciation. They can sometimes be improved by using cost data before the deduction for accumulated depreciation. Comparisons can also be misleading if production levels vary significantly from sales from one period to another.

Inventory turnover is calculated as

$$\frac{\text{Sales}}{\text{Inventory}} \qquad \text{or as} \qquad \frac{\text{Cost of Goods Sold}}{\text{Inventory}}$$

Calculations using cost of goods sold are better, because they use consistent cost data for goods sold and inventory. Calculations based on sales overstate the turnover ratio, since sales exceed costs by the gross margin. The sales calculation method is often used by outside analysts who lack adequate information about cost.

Inventory turnover is a measure of how many times on average a business sells and restocks its products over a period of time, usually a year. The more often the inventory turns over, the more effective the inventory management. Fast inventory turnover is required in businesses with low profit margins on sales, if they are to remain viable. Slow turnover relative to other companies in the same business can indicate inventory problems, such as obsolescence.

In manufacturing businesses, a separate calculation of inventory turnover is sometimes made for raw materials and for finished goods. In seasonal businesses, when inventories fluctuate significantly, an average of month end inventories should be used if possible.

Inventory turnover can be expressed in terms of how many days it takes on average from purchase to sale, by dividing the annual rate of turnover into 365. If inventory turns over 4 times a year for example, it takes $365 \div 4 = 91^1/4$ days from purchase to sale.

Receivable turnover is calculated as

$$\frac{\text{Sales}}{\text{Receivables}}$$

This ratio is usually translated into the number of days it takes on average to collect accounts receivable. This is calculated as

$$\frac{\text{Receivables}}{\text{Sales per day}}$$

Calculated on an annual basis, this is

$$\frac{\text{Receivables}}{\text{Annual sales}/365}$$

On a monthly basis, it is

$$\frac{\text{Receivables}}{\text{Monthly sales}/30}$$

Receivables turnover is a measure of how effective the credit and collection practices of a business are. The faster the collections, the more effective are the practices. In calculating receivables turnover, only credit sales should be used. Outside analysts seldom have access to data for cash and credit sales however, so they use total sales.

The **operating cycle** of a business is the time it takes from the purchase of inventory through sale and collection of receivables to cash. It is the sum of the inventory turnover and receivables turnover expressed in average numbers of days.

The **cash cycle** is the time required from the payment of cash to the collection of cash. It is the operating cycle reduced by the average time taken to pay suppliers. The length of the cash cycle determines the amount of current financing needed from owners and lenders to support a given level of activity. If the cash cycle is 60 days for example, a business can support the current requirements of annual sales with financing equal to approximately 1/6 (365 ÷ 60) of those sales.

The relationship between various kinds of assets and liabilities can be assessed by preparing **common size balance sheets**. In a common size balance sheet, total assets and total equities are each shown as 100%, and each of the individual asset and equity categories is shown as a percentage of the total. This simplifies the comparison of asset and equity relationships between different balance sheets.

Financial Leverage

Financial leverage, the relationship between total assets and ownership, is a reflection of the relationship between debt and ownership. The more debt used to finance the investment in assets, the less ownership equity required.

So long as the cost of debt is less than the return that can be earned on assets, the return on shareholder investment can be increased by borrowing. This can be illustrated with a simple example. Assume a company has an investment in assets of 100 and earns 20% on those assets before tax. Assume further that it can replace equity with borrowings to the extent of 50, at an interest rate of 10%. Depending on whether it borrows, it will show the following returns on ownership equity.

	Without Borrowing	**With Borrowing**
Return on assets	20	20
Interest expense	—	5
Return before taxes	20	15
Ownership equity	100	50
Return on ownership	20%	30%

If the cost of borrowing is higher than the return on assets, the effect is reversed. If the return on assets in the example is 5%, the results are the following.

	Without Borrowing	**With Borrowing**
Return on assets	5	5
Interest expense	—	5
Return before taxes	5	—
Ownership equity	100	50
Return on ownership	5%	—

If the return on assets falls below 5%, the interest expense is not covered and the shareholders suffer a loss.

Most businesses have a variety of sources of debt and equity financing available to them, with different characteristics. Loans carry interest at different rates, depending on the degree of risk, and usually require asset security and impose some restrictions on management. Trade credit does not normally involve interest, provided payment terms are observed. Preferred shares have many variations in dividends, security and restrictions, as described in chapter 10. Interest expense is deductible in calculating taxable income, preferred dividends are not.

For any business, the management must decide what is the best mix of financing sources and attempt to maintain that mix. In general, the best mix is the one that produces the highest return to the common shareholders at an acceptable level of risk. The level of risk to common shareholders is a function of two factors: the stability of profits and the rights of creditors and preferred shareholders. Companies that have consistent profits from year to year can safely assume greater obligations to creditors and preferred shareholders than those whose profits fluctuate.

In measuring financial leverage, both assets and the corresponding equities need to be adjusted to current values. If historical values for fixed assets are significantly below current values, ownership equity will also be undervalued and the relationship between equity and debt will be distorted. Obligations omitted from the balance sheet, such as those under long term operating leases, should be taken into account. Deferred taxes should be excluded from leverage calculations. They are provisions for expected future payments, but they are not legal obligations until taxable income is earned.

Financial leverage is assessed in two ways: in terms of the profit available to cover financing payments, and in terms of the ratios between debt, ownership and assets.

Fixed charge coverage is calculated as

$$\frac{\text{Profit before financing payments}}{\text{Financing payments}}$$

Financing payments include interest, sinking fund requirements, if any, and payments required in respect of obligations such as long term leases, regardless of whether they are recorded in the balance sheet.

The fixed charge coverage ratio is a measure of the number of times the required financing payments are covered by the profit available to pay them. The greater the ratio, the less risk there is of non-payment.

Coverage ratios for specific forms of debt and for preferred dividends are also calculated, in particular by the holders of the debt or shares in question. Holders of bonds, for example, calculate the number of times their interest is covered as

$$\frac{\text{Profit before interest}}{\text{Interest payments}}$$

Holders of preferred shares calculate their coverage as

$$\frac{\text{Profit after taxes}}{\text{Preferred dividends}}$$

The **debt/equity ratio** is calculated as

$$\frac{\text{Debt}}{\text{Ownership}}$$

The debt/equity ratio shows the relative reliance on debt and ownership equity in financing a business. The greater the reliance on debt, the greater is the risk to both creditors and shareholders. The relative reliance on debt and ownership equity can also be assessed by relating ownership and debt to assets, as shown in the following ratios.

$$\frac{\text{Assets}}{\text{Ownership}} \qquad\qquad \frac{\text{Assets}}{\text{Debt}}$$

Short term creditors, both lenders and trade creditors, are particularly interested in the current position of a business, that is, the relationship between current assets and current liabilities.

The **current ratio**, referred to earlier, is calculated as

$$\frac{\text{Current assets}}{\text{Current liabilities}}$$

The current ratio is a measure of a company's ability to pay its short term creditors. The more current assets, relative to current liabilities, the less likely it will be forced to default on payments.

The **quick ratio**, sometimes called the **acid test ratio**, is calculated as

$$\frac{\text{Current assets less inventory and prepayments}}{\text{Current liabilities}}$$

The quick ratio is a stricter measure of ability to pay, because it relates current liabilities to highly liquid current assets only, cash, temporary investments and receivables.

Illustration of Financial Statement Analysis

The analysis of financial statements using ratios and percentages is illustrated with the statements for Growth Industry Inc. shown below.

Growth Industry Inc.
Balance Sheet
at December 31
(in thousands of dollars)

	20X	20W	20V
Cash	1	2	5
Receivables	52	43	35
Inventory	32	26	22
Current assets	85	71	62
Fixed assets	33	32	30
Total assets	118	103	92
Accounts payable and accrued	53	37	25
Taxes payable	3	3	2
Current liabilities	56	40	27
Debentures payable	10	20	30
Total liabilities	66	60	57
Shareholders' equity	52	43	35
Total equities	118	103	92

Growth Industry Inc.
Statement of Income
for the year ended December 31
(in thousands of dollars)

	20X	20W	20V
Sales	480	436	400
Cost of goods sold	362	324	295
Gross margin	118	112	105
Selling expenses	69	65	60
Administrative expenses	30	29	28
	99	94	88
Operating margin	19	18	17
Interest expense	1	2	3
Profit before taxes	18	16	14
Income taxes	9	8	7
Net profit	9	8	7

Rate of return on investment (net profit divided by average shareholders' equity)

$$20X - \frac{9}{\frac{52+43}{2}} = 18.9\% \qquad\qquad 20W - \frac{8}{\frac{43+35}{2}} = 20.5\%$$

The product of

Profitability (net profit divided by sales)

$$20X - \frac{9}{480} = 1.87 \qquad\qquad 20W - \frac{8}{436} = 1.83$$

Asset turnover (sales divided by average assets)

$$20X - \frac{480}{\frac{118+103}{2}} = 4.34 \qquad\qquad 20W - \frac{436}{\frac{103+92}{2}} = 4.47$$

Financial leverage (average assets divided by average shareholders' equity)

$$20X - \frac{\frac{118+103}{2}}{\frac{52+43}{2}} = 2.33 \qquad\qquad 20W - \frac{\frac{103+92}{2}}{\frac{43+35}{2}} = 2.50$$

20X – 1.87 × 4.34 × 2.33 = 18.9
20W – 1.83 × 4.47 × 2.50 = 20.5

Although net profit increased in 20X, the rate of return on investment declined. Profitability improved slightly, but asset turnover slowed and less financial leverage was employed.

Common Size Statements of Income

	20X	20W	20V
Sales	100.00%	100.00%	100.00%
Cost of goods sold	75.42	74.31	73.75
Gross margin	24.58	25.69	26.25
Selling expenses	14.37	14.91	15.00
Administrative expenses	6.25	6.65	7.00
	20.62	21.56	22.00
Operating margin	3.96%	4.13%	4.25%

Sales have been increasing, but the gross margin on sales has decreased, probably because prices have been lowered to achieve the volume increase. Selling and administrative expenses have declined per dollar of sales as a result of the increased volume, but not enough to compensate for the reduced margins. The data show that the operating margin declined in 20X. The slight increase in the rate of net profit on sales resulted from the reduction in interest expense, financial leverage.

Growth Rate

	20X	20W	20V
Sales	120.0%	109.0%	100.0%
Operating margin	111.8	105.9	100.0

Sales increased 9% over 20V in 20W and a further 11% in 20X. Operating margin did not keep pace, increasing only 5.9% in each year. If the rate of inflation was 4% in each year, the adjusted data would be the following.

	20X	20W	20V
Sales	112.0%	105.0%	100.0%
Operating margin	103.8	101.9	100.0

The adjusted data indicate modest growth in sales and very slow growth in profitability.

Asset Turnover Ratios

	20X		20W	
Fixed asset turnover (sales divided by average net fixed assets)	$\dfrac{480}{\frac{33+32}{2}}$	= 14.8	$\dfrac{436}{\frac{32+30}{2}}$	= 14.1
Inventory turnover (cost of goods sold divided by average inventory)	$\dfrac{362}{\frac{32+26}{2}}$	= 12.5	$\dfrac{324}{\frac{32+30}{2}}$	= 10.5
Days sales in receivables (average receivables divided by average sales per day)	$\dfrac{\frac{52+43}{2}}{\frac{480}{365}}$	= 36.1	$\dfrac{\frac{43+35}{2}}{\frac{436}{365}}$	= 32.6

Fixed asset and inventory turnover have improved. The increased sales volume has been achieved without a proportionate increase in fixed assets and inventory. Collection of accounts receivable has slowed however, probably as a result of accepting greater credit risks to expand sales.

Common Size Balance Sheets

	20X	20W	20V
Cash	0.8%	1.9%	5.4%
Receivables	44.1	41.8	38.1
Inventory	27.1	25.2	23.9
Current assets	72.0	68.9	67.4
Fixed assets	28.0	31.1	32.6
Total assets	100.0%	100.0%	100.0%
Accounts payable and accrued	44.9	35.9	27.2
Taxes payable	2.5	2.9	2.2
Current liabilities	47.4	38.8	29.4
Debentures payable	8.5	19.4	32.6
Total liabilities	55.9	58.2	62.0
Shareholders' equity	44.1	41.8	38.0
Total equities	100.0%	100.0%	100.0%

The increase in sales volume has resulted in a larger investment in current assets relative to fixed assets. Receivables and inventory have both expanded. Increased volume and the repayment of debentures has also required much greater reliance on supplier credit in the form of accounts payable and accrued.

Fixed Charge Coverage

	20X	20W	20V
Fixed charge (interest) coverage (operating margin divided by interest expense)	$\frac{19}{1} = 19$	$\frac{18}{2} = 9$	$\frac{17}{3} = 5.7$

Interest coverage increased from 5.7 times in 20V to 9 times in 20W to 19 times in 20X, mainly as a result of paying down the debentures.

Debt/Equity Ratio

	20X	20W	20V
Debt/equity ratio (total debt divided by shareholders' equity)	$\frac{66}{52} = 1.27$	$\frac{60}{43} = 1.40$	$\frac{57}{35} = 1.63$

Reliance on debt financing is decreasing. The retention of earnings and repayment of debentures have more than offset the increasing use of supplier credit.

Current and Quick Ratios

	20X	20W	20V
Current ratio (current assets divided by current liabilities)	$\frac{85}{56} = 1.79$	$\frac{71}{40} = 1.78$	$\frac{62}{27} = 2.30$
Quick ratio ("quick" assets divided by current liabilities)	$\frac{53}{56} = .95$	$\frac{45}{40} = 1.13$	$\frac{40}{27} = 1.48$

The current ratio declined in 20W but remained relatively constant in 20X as increases in receivables and inventory closely matched the increase in supplier credit. The quick ratio declined significantly in both years as the investment in inventory grew.

LIMITATIONS

Ratios and percentages must be assessed with caution for a variety of reasons.

A ratio calculated for the current year might be an improvement over the previous year but still not be satisfactory.

Annual ratios involving balance sheet amounts can be very different depending on the time of year they are calculated, if the business is seasonal.

Ratios can be changed by management to appear better, by making temporary changes in the operation of a business. For example, a business with current assets of $10,000 and current liabilities of $6,000 would have a current ratio of 1.67 to 1. If purchases were decreased temporarily so that inventory and accounts payable were both reduced by $2,000, current assets would be $8,000 and current liabilities $4,000 for a current ratio of 2 to 1.

When companies operate in more than one line of business or issue consolidated financial statements, ratios calculated for the whole are often not representative of any of the components.

Ratios calculated over extended periods of time can be distorted by the effects of inflation. They can also be affected by cyclical factors such as significant changes in interest rates.

Comparisons with other companies will not be valid if their operating methods differ significantly. A company that leased its building under an operating lease for example, would show some very different ratios from one that owned it. A company could show less income in the short term as a result of higher maintenance costs, but have better preserved assets than another for the long term.

Comparisons with other companies will be distorted if they follow significantly different accounting practices. A company that calculated depreciation using a decreasing charge method could show very different results from one that used the straight line method.

Constant growth in absolute terms is declining growth in percentage terms. A retailer that grows by adding one store a year shows 100% growth the first year, when it adds one store to one. It shows 50% growth the second year, when it adds one store to two. It shows 33% growth when it adds one to three, and so on.

The same amount is smaller as a percentage decrease than as a percentage increase. A decline in profit from $100,000 to $50,000 is a drop of 50%. A recovery from the $50,000 to $100,000 is an increase of 100%.

Changes from small amounts can appear as very large percentages. An increase in profit from $50,000 to $100,000 is 100%, from $10,000 to $100,000 it is 900%, from zero to any amount it is infinite.

CHAPTER 16

Share and Bond Values; Corporate Acquisitions

Share and Bond Values

The market values of shares and bonds vary with changes in interest rates and in the expectations of investors. A decrease in interest rates reflects an expansion of credit and the money supply, and stimulates an increase in demand, including the demand for shares and bonds. Share and bond prices in general increase. An increase in interest rates reflects a tightening of credit, restricting demand and decreasing share and bond prices in general.

The value of individual shares and bonds depends on the expectations of investors concerning the issuing corporations. If investors expect a company to prosper and generate relatively high profits, they will bid up the price of its stock. They will also consider its bonds to be a relatively safe investment and be willing to pay more for them. If they expect a company to encounter difficulties and suffer depressed profits or losses, they will offer less for its shares and bonds.

BONDS

The relative values of bonds are reflected in **bond yields**. The yield on a bond is the effective rate of interest that will be earned by an investor who buys the bond at the current market price. It is the rate of interest that equates the market price with the bond's interest and principal repayment terms. For example, if an investor buys a bond for $928, which has a maturity value after five years of $1,000, and which pays $100 per year in interest, he receives an effective interest rate of 12%. $928 today is equivalent to $100 a year for five years plus $1,000 at the end of five years, at 12% interest. The bond yield is 12%. If he bought the bond for $1,080, the yield would be 8%. Higher yields reflect higher perceived risks and lower bond values. Lower yields indicate lower risks and higher values.

PREFERRED SHARES

Preferred share values and yields depend in part on the terms of the share issues. A preferred share having no conversion or redemption rights, paying a $6 annual dividend and purchased for $50, has a 12% yield (6/50). If it is redeemable, the value and yield will be affected by the terms of redemption. A redeemable preferred share is similar to a bond in that a lump sum repayment of a fixed amount at some point in the future affects the calculation of present value. Preferred shares that are convertible into common shares acquire the value of common shares as and when that value exceeds their value as preferreds. Preferred shares that are cumulative have higher values than comparable non-cumulative shares, because there is more assurance the dividends will be paid.

COMMON SHARES

The market values of common shares bear little relation to their dividend yields. The equity of common shares in a corporation is increased by all of its residual income, after the payment of interest and preferred dividends, regardless of how much is paid in common dividends. Some investors prefer shares that pay regular dividends, but for many it is not important. Common shareholders are more concerned with corporate earnings per common share.

EARNINGS PER SHARE

In accordance with GAAP, corporations are required to report earnings per common share in their financial statements. They are reported on the face of the income statement. If there are discontinued operations or extraordinary items reported in the statement of income, earnings per common share are calculated and reported both before and after taking those items into account.

Earnings per share are calculated and reported in two ways, depending on the circumstances, as basic earnings per share and as diluted earnings per share.

Basic Earnings Per Share

If there is only one class of shares outstanding and the number of shares issued has not changed during the year, basic earnings per share are calculated simply as net income divided by the number of shares. If there is more than one class of shares, or if the number outstanding has changed, the calculation is different.

When there are preferred shares outstanding, the income available to common shareholders is reduced by the amount of preferred dividends. The calculation is then net income less preferred dividends, divided by the number of common shares. Preferred dividends are the amounts declared by the directors on non-cumulative preferred stock, plus any cumulative dividends, declared or not.

For purposes of earnings per share calculations, preferred shares are those whose rights to participate in income are limited. Common shares are those not restricted in the right to share in residual income, after the claims of other equity holders are satisfied. There can be more than one class of shares with that right, as noted in chapter 10. If so, a separate earnings per share calculation is reported for each.

The number of common shares outstanding can change either because shares are sold or purchased by the corporation, because stock is split or stock dividends are declared, or because preferred stock or debt with conversion rights is converted to common stock.

When new shares are sold or shares are repurchased, earnings per share are calculated based on the weighted average number of shares outstanding during the year. For example, if there were 1,000 shares outstanding at the beginning of the year and a further 200 were issued at the end of the first quarter, earnings per share would be calculated on the weighted average of 1,150 ($1,000 \times {}^1/_4 + 1,200 \times {}^3/_4$).

When stock is split or stock dividends are declared, all earnings per share calculations are based on the number of shares outstanding after the split or dividend. This includes earnings per share reported for periods preceding the split or dividend. This practice recognizes the fact that the position and interests of common shareholders are unchanged, except that they are represented by a larger number of shares. An exception is the issue of a common stock dividend to preferred shareholders. This does affect the position of common shareholders. In this case, the dividend shares are recognized as a new share issue, and earnings per share are calculated on the weighted average number outstanding.

When common shares are issued on conversion of preferred shares or debt, a weighted average number outstanding is calculated based on the effective date of the conversion. The effective date is the date on which the obligation for preferred dividends or interest on the converted securities ended. If the obligation to pay interest on converted bonds ended June 30, for example, that would be the effective date of conversion.

If the conversion of preferred shares or debt will have a significant effect on future earnings per share, a supplementary calculation is reported as well, showing what earnings per share would have been if the conversion had been made at the beginning of the period. Whether future earnings per share will be significantly affected can be determined by comparing earnings per share calculated for the full year with and without conversion.

Diluted Earnings Per Share

Diluted earnings per share are calculated to show what earnings per share would have been, if outstanding rights and options to purchase common shares and rights to convert other securities into common shares, were exercised as of the beginning of the period, or as of the date they were granted if they were granted during the period.

When rights or options to purchase common shares are exercised, they increase the number of shares outstanding and they increase the corporation's cash. The effect on earnings per share is calculated by assuming the cash received would be used to purchase shares previously issued, at the average market price during the period. For example, assume there are 10,000 rights outstanding to purchase shares for $8 each and the average market price of the shares during the year was $10. If the rights were exercised, they would generate cash of $80,000 (10,000 × $8), which would purchase 8,000 shares in the market ($80,000 ÷ $10). The net effect would be to increase the number of shares by 2,000, 10,000 issued less 8,000 purchased. In calculating diluted earnings per share, the number of shares is increased by 2,000.

When other securities, bonds and preferred shares are converted into common shares, the number of common shares is increased and the income available to common shareholders is also increased as a result of reduced interest and preferred dividends. In calculating diluted earnings per share, shares outstanding are increased by the number that would be issued on conversion, and earnings are increased by the net saving in interest (after tax) and the preferred dividends that would not have been declared or accumulated. For example, if 100,000 preferred shares with a cumulative annual dividend in total of $80,000 were convertible into an equal number of common shares, diluted earnings per share would be calculated increasing the number of shares outstanding by 100,000 and increasing the earnings available to common shareholders by $80,000.

All rights, options and potential conversions are taken into account in calculating diluted earnings per share, unless they have the effect of increasing earnings per share, in which case they are not. Rights to purchase shares at prices above current market for example, if included in the calculation would reduce not increase the number of shares and increase earnings per share. Similarly if earnings are small, the elimination of interest on bonds or preferred dividends could increase the earnings per share calculation, in spite of increasing the number of shares. If losses are incurred, the per share amounts will always be reduced by increasing the number of shares.

Subsequent Events

If a transaction occurs that significantly changes the number of common shares outstanding or potentially outstanding after the period covered by a corporation's financial statements but before the statements are issued, a description of the transaction is included in the statements. Examples are issues of common shares, convertible securities, warrants and options.

PRICE/EARNINGS RATIOS

The relationship between market price and earnings per common share is measured by the price/earnings ratio or price earnings multiple, market price divided by earnings per share. If investors believe a corporation will outperform the average, its shares will have a relatively high price/earnings ratio. If they believe it will underperform, the shares will have a low price/earnings ratio. Price/earnings ratios vary widely between different industries and between different companies within the same industry. Slow growth industries such as steel making have relatively low price earnings multiples. Rapid growth industries like computer software have high multiples. Within an industry, those companies perceived to be well managed have relatively high multiples; those perceived to be poorly managed have low multiples. Multiples are also affected by changes in credit and the money supply. They are higher when the monetary system is expansionist and lower when it is tightening.

Corporate Acquisitions

Many corporations and some individuals expand their business interests by acquiring other corporations, buying most or all of their common voting shares. The purchase is usually financed by issuing shares of the acquiring company or of a new company incorporated for the purpose. The shares can be issued for cash and the cash used to make the purchase, or they can be issued directly to the shareholders of the acquired company in a share exchange.

SHARE VALUE ACQUISITIONS

Corporations with high price earnings multiples are often able to grow rapidly and cheaply by acquiring other companies with lower multiples. The following is an example.

Hare and Tortoise are two corporations in similar lines of business. Comparative data for the two companies are as follows:

	Hare	Tortoise
Total assets	$300,000	$300,000
Shareholders' equity	$ 90,000	$ 90,000
Current annual income	$ 20,000	$ 10,000
Number of shares outstanding	100,000	100,000
Shareholders' equity per share	$\frac{\$90{,}000}{100{,}000} = \$\ .90$	$\frac{\$90{,}000}{100{,}000} = \$\ .90$
Earnings per share	$\frac{\$20{,}000}{100{,}000} = \$\ .20$	$\frac{\$10{,}000}{100{,}000} = \$\ .10$
Share market price	$4.00	$1.00
Price earnings multiple	$\frac{\$4.00}{\$0.20} = 20\times$	$\frac{\$1.00}{\$0.10} = 10\times$

The companies are the same size in terms of assets and shareholders' equity, but Hare is better managed, generating twice as much annual income. As a result, its stock has a market value of $4.00 per share, a price earnings multiple of 20 times, while Tortoise's stock has a market value of only $1, a price earnings multiple of 10 times.

With a market value of $1 per share and 100,000 shares outstanding, the total market value of Tortoise's shares is $100,000. At that price, Hare could purchase all of the Tortoise shares by issuing 25,000 of its own shares at $4. In fact, it would probably have to pay more than $1 per Tortoise share, because purchasing a controlling interest usually requires paying a premium. It might have to pay $1.20 per share. which would require issuing 30,000 shares at $4, for $120,000.

If Hare issues 30,000 shares to purchase all the shares of Tortoise, it will then have 130,000 shares outstanding. Assuming no change in the profitability of the two units, it will have combined annual income of $20,000 plus $10,000, or $30,000. The income per share will be $.231, $30,000 divided by 130,000 shares. By acquiring Tortoise, Hare increases its earnings per share from $.20 to $.231 and doubles its tangible assets from $300,000 to $600,000. If it continues to enjoy the same price earnings multiple of 20 times, its stock increases in value from $4 per share to $4.62 (20 × $.231). If it brings better management to the assets of Tortoise, the improvement in earnings and share value is better still. So long as it can find other companies with low price earnings multiples and acquire them, without paying excessive premiums over book value for goodwill or other assets and without sacrificing profitability, it can continue to increase its earnings per share and its share value.

If Hare paid too much for goodwill, that is if a subsequent estimate of its value determined that it was worth less than the $30,000 paid for it, the excess would have to be charged as an expense. This would affect the combined earnings and therefore the market value of the stock based on a price earnings multiple. If for example, the value of the goodwill was estimated to be only $25,000 at the end of a year of combined operations, the excess of $5,000 would have to be charged to expense for that year, reducing the combined income to $25,000. That would reduce the earnings per share to $.192 ($25,000 ÷ 130,000) from the previous $.20 and the value of a share from $4 to $3.84, assuming the same price earnings multiple of 20 times. In fact, the price earnings multiple would likely drop as well with lower earnings, reducing the share value further. On the positive side, the reduction in earnings would only be a one time event, unless further write downs of goodwill become necessary.

The pooling of interests method of combining accounts avoided the possibility of having to charge goodwill to expense, because goodwill was never recorded. For that reason, it was favored by many managers and investors. Depending on how much was paid for goodwill, the effect of never having to expense it could have a sigificant positive effect on reported earnings per share and share market value.

LEVERAGED BUY-OUTS

Corporations can sometimes be acquired with relatively little investment in common shares by changing the structure of their long term financing. The following is an example.

Rock Solid Inc. has the following balance sheet, in thousands of dollars.

Current assets	100	Current liabilities	50
Fixed assets	200	Shareholders' equity	250
	300		300

It has had consistent earnings for many years, ranging between $40 thousand and $50 thousand and averaging $46 thousand before taxes, $23 thousand after taxes. Its shares have a market value of 12 times its average earnings, $276 thousand.

A group of entrepreneurs who believe Rock Solid has the potential to be more profitable, decides to buy it. They incorporate a new company, LBO Inc., for the purpose and invest $50 thousand of their own money in LBO common shares. They negotiate with lenders to issue $200 thousand in LBO debentures at 10% interest and with other investors to issue $50 thousand in 12% cumulative preferred shares, contingent on the acquisition of Rock Solid. They offer $300 thousand for the shares of Rock Solid, a premium of $24 thousand over market, and acquire the company. After completing the transactions, the balance sheet of LBO Inc. appears as follows, in thousands of dollars.

Current assets	100	Current liabilities	50
Fixed assets	200	Debentures payable	200
Goodwill	50	Preferred shares	50
		Common shares	50
	350		350

Based on experience, it can anticipate returns to the investors in the range shown below, if nothing else is changed, in thousands of dollars.

	Low	Average	High
Earnings before the following	40	46	50
Debenture interest	20	20	20
	20	26	30
Income taxes	10	13	15
	10	13	15
Preferred dividends	6	6	6
Return to common shareholders	4	7	9

This type of acquisition is described as a leveraged buy-out. It is accomplished with little equity financing by employing a high level of financial leverage. It can be used effectively to acquire a company that has relatively consistent and dependable earnings from year to year.

In the example, earnings before interest are twice the interest payable in a low profit year. That fact, plus payment of a relatively high interest rate of 10% to compensate risk, allows the company to borrow heavily in relation to its assets and equity. The company is able to raise additional financing from the issue of preferred shares, by offering a high rate of 12% cumulative dividends, that is well covered by earnings after taxes in a low profit year. Sometimes debt and preferred share investors are offered a further inducement in the form of common share purchase rights or conversion privileges.

If the company continues to operate as it has in the past, the common shareholders will earn an average return of 14% on their investment (7/50). Any increase in profitability they can achieve will be magnified by the high degree of financial leverage.

Leveraged buy-outs are often used by senior management personnel to acquire their corporations. When that is the case, other investors have added assurance that the business will be competently managed. Some leveraged buy-outs are undertaken only for the advantage of greater financial leverage.

ASSET PLAYS

Corporations are sometimes acquired in large part by, in effect, using their own assets to purchase them. Land, buildings and many kinds of equipment can be sold and leased back. The cash raised from the sale can then be used to repay money borrowed to buy the company. Companies with two or more segments or divisions are sometimes acquired and one or more divisions is subsequently sold to help pay for the acquisition. Occasionally a company is acquired having assets surplus to its needs that can be sold.

Selling assets to help pay for an acquisition is a method often used in conjunction with a leveraged buy-out. Excess debt is incurred temporarily until the assets are sold.

CHAPTER 17

Cost and Revenue Analysis

Making business decisions is a process of choosing between alternatives. Is it better to hire more employees for example, or to invest in new labor saving equipment?. Other things being equal, the best alternative is the one that will produce the maximum profit or minimum loss. To assess alternatives, managers must have information concerning relative costs and revenues.

Cost and revenue data for decision making purposes are different from those used in measuring business income in three important respects. First, they are estimates of future costs and revenues, not past. Decisions are made to affect the future. Past experience is relevant only to the extent that it provides a basis for predicting the future. Secondly, they include opportunity costs. The opportunity cost of a choice is the income sacrificed by not choosing the best alternative. Opportunity costs never appear in accounting records. Thirdly, they omit cost and revenue data that are common to all of the alternatives being considered. The only costs and revenues relevant to a decision are those that will be different depending on which alternative is chosen. For example, if a decision to hire more staff would increase the cost of supervision but new labor saving equipment would not, the cost of supervision is relevant. If supervision cost is not affected by the decision, it is not relevant.

Many business decisions are concerned with the use of assets. These can be divided into two categories, those that involve significant new investment or disinvestment and those that do not. A decision to purchase equipment to produce a product is an investment decision. A decision to switch existing equipment from the production of one product to another is not. Decisions involving investment are the subject of capital budgeting. They are discussed in the next chapter. Decisions concerning the use of existing assets are discussed in the remainder of this chapter.

OPTIMUM USE OF ASSETS

When a business has idle assets, any use of those assets is better than none, provided the incremental revenues exceed incremental costs. The following is an example.

Hy Seeling owns a rental condominium that is currently vacant. He is paying property taxes at the rate of $300 per month and operating costs of $200 per month. A prospective tenant has offered to rent the apartment for six months at $250 per month. If he accepts the offer, Hy's operating costs will increase to $250 per month. Should he accept the offer?.

If it is a choice between accepting that offer or having the apartment remain vacant for the next six months, he should accept it. He will receive rent of $250 less increased operating costs of $50, or incremental income of $200, per month. He will still be losing money but not as much as he would by having the apartment vacant, as shown by the following monthly comparison.

	Apartment Rented	Apartment Vacant	Differential
Revenue	$250	$ —	$250
Operating costs	250	200	50
Property taxes	300	300	—
	550	500	50
Net loss	$300	$500	$200

Only the differential costs and revenues are relevant.

Before accepting the offer, Hy should consider whether there are other alternatives. It might be possible for him to save money by moving out of his present accommodation and into the apartment himself for example. If he could save $250 per month by moving, that is the opportunity cost of continuing to rent. In that case, renting is not the best economic alternative. The incremental income from renting, $200, is less than the opportunity cost of not moving, $250.

He should also consider whether there are other implications for costs and revenues in a decision to rent. If he owned other rental apartments in the same building for example, it might be difficult to maintain other rent levels if he accepted less for one. The potential loss of revenue from other units would be a cost of accepting the offer.

In summary, before making his decision, Hy should ensure that he has considered all of the feasible alternatives (opportunity costs) and all of the cost and revenue implications (relevant costs and revenues).

This example reflects an all or nothing situation. Either the apartment is rented or it is not. In most businesses, there is a range of possibilities for the use of assets between shut down and full utilization. The same principle applies however. Whenever there is available capacity, any use of that capacity that generates incremental income is better than none.

When the assets of a business are fully employed, that is, when it is operating at capacity, the optimum use of assets is the use or combination of uses that produces the maximum **contribution**. The contribution of a use is the difference between the revenues and the costs that can be attributed directly to that use and would not be incurred without that use. Costs incurred regardless of that use are not relevant.

For example, Gufi Gadgets Inc. has a choice of producing one or more of three products: widgets, gizmos, and gimmicks. The following are the potential revenues, directly attributable costs and contributions per unit of each.

	Widgets	**Gizmos**	**Gimmicks**
Revenue	$ 50	$ 30	$ 20
Attributable costs	30	15	10
Contribution	$ 20	$ 15	$ 10

With available capacity and current market conditions, Gufi can make and sell the following quantities.

	Widgets	Gizmos	Gimmicks
Possible production	2,000	3,000	6,000
Possible sales	2,000	2,000	3,000

Widgets have the highest contribution per unit but fewer of them can be produced with available capacity. The best use of capacity is to produce gimmicks. Twice as many can be produced as gizmos and three times as many as widgets. If everything produced could be sold, the contributions from producing each would be the following.

Widgets	2,000	×	$20	=	$40,000
Gizmos	3,000	×	15	=	45,000
Gimmicks	6,000	×	10	=	60,000

Gimmicks produce the biggest contribution per unit of capacity used, gizmos the second biggest, and widgets the smallest. Since only 3,000 gimmicks can be sold, only that quantity will be produced, using only half the productive capacity (3,000 of a possible 6,000). The remaining capacity will be used to produce gizmos. Half the productive capacity will permit production of 1,500 gizmos. In total, contributions will be the following.

Gimmicks	3,000	×	$10	$30,000
Gizmos	1,500	×	15	22,500
Total				$52,500

This is the optimum use of capacity.

The example illustrates the use of incremental cost and revenue analysis to select the most profitable products to produce. The same kind of analysis can be applied to non-manufacturing businesses, retailing, wholesaling, and services, in deciding the most profitable goods and services to offer.

APPLICATIONS

The concepts of incremental revenues and costs and contributions can be applied to a variety of business decisions, but the results often need to be tempered by other considerations. The following are some examples.

Choice of Products

In choosing goods and services to produce and sell, managers must be careful to consider all of the potential consequences of their decisions. If a company discontinued offering a product because it was not as profitable as some others, that might have a negative effect on the sales of other products. A manufacturer of razors and blades who stopped selling razors for example, would probably soon suffer a significant loss of blade sales.

When capacity is not being fully used, differential income analysis can be used to decide whether a special order should be accepted, for example an order from a retail chain to produce some of its house brand merchandise. When deciding whether to accept special orders, managers must also consider the potential effect on other sales. If the products will be sold in the same markets as the company's regular products, they will likely reduce the regular sales. If they will be sold in other markets, for example export, they will not.

Make or Buy

Incremental cost and revenue analysis can be used to decide whether to make or buy a part or a product. If a manufacturer has unused capacity, the incremental cost of producing a part might be less than the cost to buy it.

If a company can generate more incremental income by devoting all of its capacity to the production of one product, it might be better to purchase a complementary product from another supplier. The producer of razors and blades might find it more profitable to buy its razors from another manufacturer for example, and devote all of its capacity to making blades.

Another consideration in make or buy decisions is the security and dependability of supply from an outside source.

Sell or Process Further

In some situations, companies have the option of selling inventory in its existing state or processing it further to sell at a higher price. Some joint products for example, can be sold at the point of split-off or processed further. Sometimes damaged or obsolete goods can be reworked to sell at higher prices or sold as scrap or seconds. In each case, if the additional costs are less than the additional revenues, the products should be processed further or reworked, provided there are no better uses for the productive capacity required.

Sales Promotion

Contribution analysis can be used in relation to advertising and other sales promotion costs such as sales commissions and bonuses. If additional contribution exceeds the cost of promotion, the cost is worth incurring.

THE NATURE OF COSTS

For analysis purposes, costs can be divided into three categories: fixed, variable, and semi-variable. Fixed costs are those that do not change with the level of activity of a business. The cost of employing a factory manager and the cost of property taxes on the factory are fixed costs. They are the same regardless of how much is produced. Fixed costs are not fixed in any absolute sense, only in the context of existing operations. The cost of the factory manager could be eliminated by shutting down the factory. The cost of property taxes could be eliminated by selling it. Fixed costs result from management commitments to operate in a given way. Management could commit to an advertising campaign for example, making it a fixed cost in the context of its current operations.

Most costs vary with some factor. Most factory costs, direct material, direct labor, and overhead, vary with the volume of production, measured either in units produced, or direct labor hours worked, or machine hours worked. Selling costs can vary with sales volumes measured in units or dollars. Many administrative costs vary with the overall level of company activity, production and sales. Some costs vary with more than one factor. Electric power costs, for example, can vary with the amount used and the maximum demand.

Some costs are completely variable, others are only semi-variable. Direct material costs can be expected to vary in direct proportion to units produced. Power costs can be expected to vary with production, but not in direct proportion.

Many semi-variable costs increase in proportion over most levels of activity but out of proportion at very low and high levels. The labor costs of warehousing and shipping in many businesses could be expected to follow this pattern. They would increase in close parallel with most increases in activity. At very low levels they would be disproportionately high, because a minimum staff would be required regardless of the volume. At very high levels they would be disproportionately high, because of overcrowding. Other semi-variable costs increase in steps, as increased levels of activity are reached. Supervision costs for example, can be expected to increase each time a new work shift is added but remain constant between additions.

The behaviour of semi-variable costs is illustrated in the following graphs.

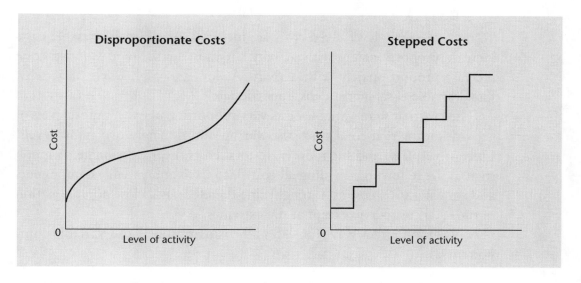

While some individual categories of cost follow a stepped pattern, semi-variable costs as a whole for most businesses approximate a smooth curve similar to the graph for disproportionate costs. Different stepped costs increase at different levels of activity, most steps are usually small relative to total cost, and increases are often offset by changes in other costs. For example, the cost of hiring an additional employee could be largely offset by the saving in overtime paid to existing employees.

For most businesses, total short run costs follow the pattern shown in the following graph.

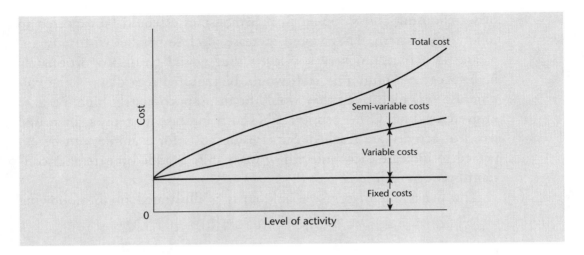

To operate at any level, fixed costs are incurred. At all levels, variable costs increase proportionately with activity. At most levels, semi-variable costs increase proportionately with activity. At low and high levels of activity, semi-variable costs increase disproportionately.

The fact that semi-variable costs vary proportionately over most levels of activity means that total costs also vary proportionately over most levels. Only at very low and high levels are total costs disproportionate. A graph such as the following, dividing all costs into fixed and variable components and showing total cost as a straight line therefore, is a close approximation of the total cost curve, except at the extremes.

This graph effectively translates all costs into fixed and variable components.

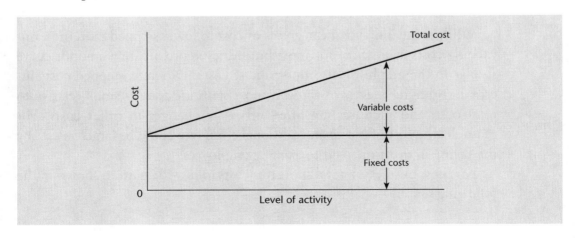

COSTS, VOLUME, AND PROFIT

The relationship between costs, level of activity or volume, and profit can be shown by plotting revenues on a graph of fixed and variable costs, as shown in the following example.

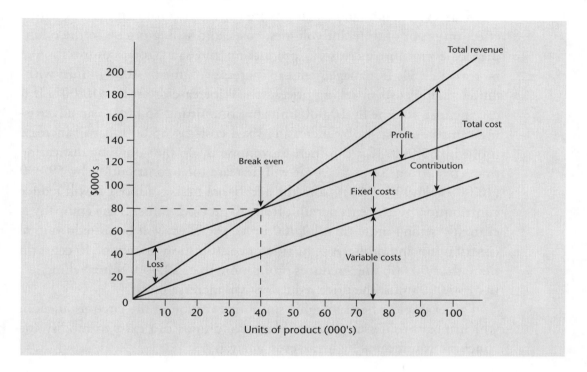

In this example, fixed costs have been plotted above variable to make clearer the profit relationship between costs, revenue, and volume. The company sells its product for $2 per unit. It has variable costs of $1 per unit and fixed costs of $40,000 in total. It has a contribution margin of $1 per unit ($2 revenue minus $1 variable cost) or 50%. Since fixed costs are $40,000, it will therefore break even, that is show neither profit nor loss, at a level of 40,000 units, or $80,000 in revenue. Below 40,000 units, it will show a loss, because total contribution, the excess of revenues over variable costs, will not cover fixed costs. Above 40,000 units, it will show a profit.

This type of graph is commonly described as a break-even graph or chart, and the corresponding analysis as **break-even analysis**.

The information shown by the graph can also be stated as a simple algebraic equation.

$$\text{Profit} = \text{contribution margin per unit} \times \text{units} - \text{fixed costs}$$

Break-even graphs and equations are useful for considering the potential effect on profit of different volumes, costs, and selling prices. In the example, for every unit increase in production and sales, total contribution is increased by $1. If management can increase volume by 10,000 units without changing costs or selling prices, it will increase profit by $10,000. If it can increase volume by 10,000 units by committing $5,000 to an advertising campaign, that is, by increasing fixed costs by $5,000, it will increase profit by $5,000. If it can increase volume by 10,000 units by decreasing prices 5%, from $2 to $1.90, it will increase total contribution by $9,000 (10,000 × [1.90 − 1.00]) from the additional units sold, but it will reduce contribution by 10 cents per unit from all previous units. If the company is currently selling more than 90,000 units, the effect will be to reduce total contribution and profit. A reduction of contribution margin of 10 cents on more than 90,000 units reduces profit more than $9,000. If it is selling less than 90,000 units, the price reduction will increase profit.

This example reflects a highly simplified version of the circumstances in which most businesses operate. Many conditions can exist to modify the conclusions indicated by break-even analysis.

Extremes of Capacity

Break-even analysis is valid only over the middle range of available capacity. As noted earlier, at low and high levels of capacity usage, a straight line does not approximate the reality of total costs.

Multiple Products

Most companies produce and sell more than one product, each with its own selling price, variable costs, contribution margin and productive capacity requirements. Break-even analysis can only be applied in these circumstances by assuming products are made and sold in a fixed mix or proportion to each other at all levels of capacity. If the proportions are changed, the revenue and cost lines have to be redrawn on the graph or restated in the equation.

Cost Variability

Costs usually described as variable are not always as variable as they might appear. The direct labor cost per unit of product for example, can change as experience is gained in producing that product and production becomes more efficient. Some costs described as fixed can change with changes in management commitments. The change in the advertising commitment described in the previous example is an illustration.

Some costs are fixed only in relation to the production of specific products and can be eliminated by discontinuing those products.

Costs can vary with different measures of volume. Most manufacturing costs vary with the volume of production, but selling costs vary more directly with the volume of sales. If production and sales volumes are significantly different during a period of time, no general measure can be applied.

Some costs vary with factors independent of volume. Costs of setting up to produce products for example, will vary with the number of different products made, not with the total number of units produced.

Demand

The quantity of product a company can sell is usually related to price. As volume increases, price decreases. The total revenue line on a break-even graph should therefore be described by a curve, not a straight line, as shown here.

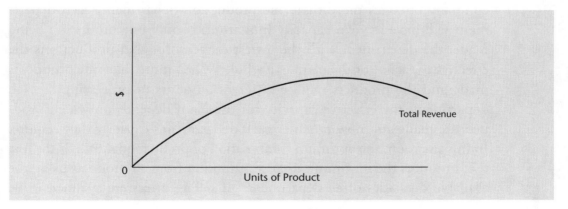

Total revenue increases with volume but at a decreasing rate up to a certain point, as additional units sold increase revenue but declining price reduces revenue from previous units. At some point, the effect of decreasing price begins to exceed the effect of increasing volume and total revenue begins to decline. This was illustrated in the last example.

In practice, few companies attempt to define their demand curves. When there are multiple products and a variable sales mix, it is virtually impossible.

The demand for products changes over time, sometimes over a relatively short space of time. Some companies develop products, bring them to market for a few years and then replace them with other products. Computer and electronic products are examples. The demand for these products can change dramatically over a period of two or three years. In making pricing decisions for these products, managers must consider potential changes in demand over that period.

Pricing decisions are also influenced by considerations of how competitors will react. It might be better for the long run to charge a lower than optimum price in the short run, and discourage potential new competitors from entering the market.

Capacity

Available capacity can change. The capacity of a plant can be doubled for example, by working two shifts instead of one. A change of this kind will cause costs to change as well.

Available capacity can depend on the products being made. When a company operates more than one production department, each department will have its own capacity limitation. If only one product is being made, the department with the lowest capacity for that product sets the effective capacity for the plant as a whole. When more than one product is made and the products require different amounts of processing in each department, the effective capacity for the plant depends on which products are made and how much of each department's capacity they require. In this situation, the optimum combination of product quantities is the one that produces the maximum total contribution from all products using the available capacities of all departments. If selling prices are assumed to be constant over the relevant range of potential sales volumes, the optimum combination can be calculated using the mathematical technique linear programming. When demand curves are introduced, attempting to solve the problem becomes impractical.

VARIABLE COSTING

Some accountants advocate valuing inventories at variable cost only and treating all fixed costs as period costs. This is described as **variable costing** or **direct costing**. The conventional practice of allocating fixed manufacturing costs to inventory is described as **absorption costing** or **full costing**.

Advocates of variable costing argue that absorption costing leads managers to make bad decisions. They can be induced to produce at full capacity when the effective demand does not warrant full production, because fixed costs are being absorbed in inventory instead of being written off, and the income statement looks better. On the other hand, they can be persuaded to reject production of a product because the selling price does not exceed full costs, although it might cover variable costs and produce a contribution.

While variable costing is useful for decision making purposes, it is not generally accepted for income and asset measurement.

CHAPTER 18

Capital Budgeting

Capital budgeting is the process of allocating funds to investment in assets. A decision to build and equip a new plant for example, is a capital budgeting decision. Capital budgeting pertains to investments in all types of assets not just productive equipment. A decision to add a new product to the product line is a capital budgeting decision if it means increasing the investment in inventory. A decision to extend more liberal credit terms to customers is a capital budgeting decision if it means increasing the investment in accounts receivable. Investments also include spending to acquire intangible value, although intangible value is not always recorded as an asset in conventional accounting statements. The decision to research and develop a new product for example, is an investment decision, although much of the cost might be written off as current expenditure.

There are many opportunities for investment available to a business. Some are potentially profitable, others are not. Some are potentially more profitable than others. Managers must choose among alternative opportunities.

EVALUATING INVESTMENTS

There are four methods in common use for evaluating investment opportunities: payback, internal rate of return, net present value, and accounting rate of return. These are illustrated assuming the following data for a potential investment.

Initial cash outlay	$12,000
Lifetime of investment	10 years
Residual value	0
Annual incremental cash flow	$ 2,300

Payback

Using the payback method, potential investments are evaluated by reference to the length of time it will take to recover the investment. Using the assumed data,

$$\frac{\$12,000}{\$ 2,300} \; = \; 5.2$$

It will take 5.2 years to recover the investment. If that is considered acceptable, the investment is acceptable. Otherwise, it is not.

Payback is not a satisfactory method of evaluating investments for two reasons. First, it does not take into account the lifetime of the investment. The investment with a lifetime of 10 years is not shown to be any better than it would be if it had a lifetime of 20 years. Secondly, it ignores the time value of money. A dollar to be recovered six years from now is not worth a dollar today. The payback calculation does have some merit in assessing risk. If an investment can be recovered in three years, it is less subject to future uncertainties than if recovery takes six years.

Internal Rate of Return (IRR)

The internal rate of return is the effective rate of interest that equates the cash returns to be received with the cash outlay of an investment. Using the data in the example, what rate of return is earned, when $2,300 is received every year for 10 years, from an investment of $12,000? The answer is 14%. This can be calculated by trial and error using interest tables and different interest rates, or by using a sophisticated financial calculator. If 14% is an acceptable rate of return, the investment is acceptable.

The internal rate of return calculation incorporates both the lifetime of the investment and the time value of money.

Net Present Value (NPV)

Using the net present value method, a minimum required rate of return is decided before making the calculation. Using that rate, the present value of the cash return is calculated. If the present value of the return is greater than the cash outlay of the investment, the investment is acceptable. The excess of present value over cost is the net present value.

Assume the required rate of return is 12%. At that rate, a return of $2,300 per year for 10 years has a present value of $12,995. The cash outlay of the investment is $12,000. The present value of the return exceeds the initial outlay of the investment by $995, the net present value. Therefore, the investment is acceptable.

The present value of a return can be calculated directly from interest tables or by using a financial calculator.

The net present value method, like the internal rate of return method, incorporates both the lifetime of the investment and the time value of money in the calculation.

Accounting Rate of Return (ARR)

The accounting rate of return is usually calculated as the annual incremental net income divided by the average investment, expressed as a percentage.

Assume that the incremental income before depreciation in the example is the same as the incremental cash flow, $2,300, and that the investment is written off to depreciation at the rate of $1,200 per year for 10 years. The incremental income is $1,100, $2,300 minus $1,200 depreciation.

The average investment is calculated from the net asset value shown in the accounts each year. That value starts at $12,000 and decreases by $1,200 yearly as depreciation accumulates, until it reaches zero at the end of ten years. The average over the 10 year period is $6,000, half of $12,000.

The accounting rate of return is

$$\frac{\$1,100}{\$6,000} \times 100\% = 18.3\%$$

Sometimes the ARR is calculated based on the initial investment instead of the average. In that case the ARR would be half that calculated above, or 9.2% ($1,100 ÷ $12,000 × 100%).

The ARR differs from the IRR in two respects. First, the return used is accounting income, not cash flow. Secondly, the calculation ignores the time value of money.

Accounting income differs from cash flow because revenues and expenses are recognized on an accrual basis not as cash is received and paid, and because the cost of long term assets is amortized over their lifetimes. In most cases, the difference between income and cash flow resulting from accruals is not enough to affect rate of return calculations significantly. The difference between recording the cost of long terms assets at the time they are paid for and the time they are charged to expense however, is significant. Combined with the failure to discount future cash flows, it has the effect of overstating the rate of return. The ARR rate of return was calculated at 18.3%, the IRR at 14%.

The difference between ARR and IRR calculations is greater, the longer the time period of the investment. If the investment in the example had a lifetime of 20 years instead of 10 years, the annual depreciation would be $600 instead of $1,200 and the annual income would be $1,700, not $1,100. The accounting rate of return would then be

$$\frac{\$1,700}{\$6,000} \times 100\% = 28.3\%$$

Using the same data, the IRR is 18.5%.

The ARR is not a satisfactory method of assessing potential investments.

IRR Versus NPV

Both the IRR and the NPV methods show whether a particular investment has an acceptable rate of return. The IRR method shows it as a rate of return, the NPV method as a dollar value.

In comparing alternative investments, the NPV method will indicate a higher value for larger investments. In the example, an investment of $24,000 producing returns of $4,600 would produce a present value of

$25,990, and a net present value of $1,990, double those for an investment of $12,000 and returns of $2,300. The IRR method shows the same rate of return regardless of the size of the investment.

The effect of size on the apparent attractiveness of alternatives using NPV can be eliminated by calculating a **present value index** for investments. The present value index is the ratio of the present value of the return to the cost of the investment. In the example it is ($12,995 ÷ $12,000) × 100% = 108.3%. If the amounts are doubled, it is still the same, ($25,990 ÷ $24,000) × 100% = 108.3%.

Both the NPV and the present value index calculations indicate higher values for longer term investments. If the investment had a lifetime of 20 years, an annual cash flow of $1,812 would produce an IRR of 14%, the same as an annual cash flow of $2,300 for 10 years. At the required rate of return of 12%, the 20 year investment produces a present value of $13,535 and a net present value of $1,535 ($13,535 − 12,000). The 10 year investment produces a present value of $12,995 and a net present value of $995 ($12,995 − 12,000). The present value index for the 20 year investment is,

$$\frac{\$13,535}{\$12,000} \times 100\% = 112.8\%$$

The present value index for the 10 year investment is,

$$\frac{\$12,995}{\$12,000} \times 100\% = 108.3\%$$

In comparing alternatives, a difference in terms might or might not be significant. An investment yielding 14% over ten years is better than one yielding 16% for one year, if the cash cannot be reinvested at the end of the year to yield more than 12%.

Both the NPV and the IRR calculations are useful guides, provided their limitations are recognized and understood. The NPV makes investments look better, the larger they are and the longer their lifetimes. The effect of size can be eliminated by using the present value index but not the effect of longer lifetimes. The IRR makes investments with the same rate of return look equal, regardless of their lifetimes. In choosing alternatives, managers must consider not only the returns on those investments but their terms and the prospective opportunities for reinvesting their cash flows.

CALCULATING RETURNS

The data assumed for illustration purposes are highly simplified. A variety of factors can complicate rate of return calculations.

Investment

The total cost of an investment is often underestimated because essential elements of the investment are overlooked. The investment in a plant expansion for example, is not just the cost of additional building and equipment. Expansion is intended to increase the volume of production and sales, which usually requires additional investment in inventories and receivables as well.

Investment in a project is not always made all at once. Product development for example, can extend over a period of years and cash outlays can be irregular in both amounts and timing.

Investments usually involve a cash recovery at the end of their lifetime. Productive assets have a salvage or resale value. Complementary investments in inventories and receivables can sometimes be recovered. The initial cost of an investment is often reduced by the salvage value of assets replaced.

Cash Return

Cash flows from investments are seldom uniform over their lifetime. Like the investments, they can be irregular in both amounts and timing.

The lifetime of many investments is difficult to predict. In some cases, the lifetime is indefinite. An investment adding intangible value to a product trade mark for example, can have a virtually unlimited lifetime. Investments in inventories and receivables accompanying plant expansions often have virtually unlimited lifetimes.

The longer an investment is expected to last, the more difficult it is to predict future cash flows.

Taxes

Taxes can affect both the cash outlays and the cash returns.

Tax credits are sometimes available to companies that invest in certain kinds of assets, reducing the effective cost of those investments.

Capital cost allowances (depreciation expense) reduce income and taxes on income, and therefore affect net cash inflows. Sometimes accelerated allowances are permitted on certain kinds of assets, reducing taxes and affecting cash flows sooner.

If assets are leased instead of purchased, cash outlays are spread over their lifetimes, capital cost allowances are not available to the lessee, and lease payments incorporate the cost of depreciation and the capital cost allowances available to the lessor.

Inflation

Future cash flows will increase with inflation but not necessarily at the same rate. Not all prices rise proportionately. Taxes will be based in part on future revenues and expenses and in part on current costs such as depreciation.

Making Predictions

Predictions of the timing and amounts of cash flow can usually be improved by applying probabilities to different possible outcomes. In the example, the investment was predicted to last 10 years. If the probabilities were judged to be 40% that it would last 9 years, 50% for 10 years and 10% for 11 years, a better estimate would be produced by a weighted average calculated as follows:

.40	×	9 years	=	3.6 years
.50	×	10	=	5.0
.10	×	11	=	1.1
1.00				9.7 years

The calculated IRR is then 13.6%, not 14%. The same kind of analysis can be applied to cash flows and investment outlays. Depending on the distribution of probabilities, the effect on rate of return can be significant.

Predictions are based on the experience and information available to management. They can often be improved by buying more information. Knowledge concerning the demand for new products can be improved by doing market research for example. In deciding whether to buy more information, management will be guided by the cost relative to the potential loss from making a bad decision in the absence of that information. In general, the larger the investment, the more potentially costly is a bad decision, and the more valuable is additional information.

CHOOSING ALTERNATIVES

Cash for investment comes from two sources, from the operations of a business and from new debt and equity. Depending on the opportunities available, the cash flow from operations can be adequate, inadequate, or excessive. If cash flow is excessive, it should be returned to investors in the form of debt repayments, extra dividends, and equity repurchases. If it is inadequate, management can attempt to raise new cash from lenders and owners. Sometimes it is possible to raise all the cash desired, but often it is not. When it is not, management must choose between alternative investment opportunities. Often management will opt not to raise new cash regardless of opportunities, either because they do not want the business to grow too quickly or because they do not want to expand the ownership. Again, they must choose between alternatives.

The best choice from a group of alternatives is not always the investment or combination of investments with the highest potential returns, for several reasons.

"No Return" Investments

Some investments have no return, or at least no measurable return, but are nevertheless important to a business. Investments in pollution control and accident prevention are examples.

Future Investments

A high return investment might be rejected in anticipation of a higher return investment in the future. This is often the case when technology and costs are changing rapidly. Acquisition or replacement of computer equipment for example, could be deferred in anticipation of better or cheaper equipment. Some companies hold reserves of relatively low return marketable securities so they can take advantage of future opportunities.

Related Investments

Some potentially high return investments are rejected because they are complementary to low return investments. A purchase of some new equipment to service a railway line could promise substantial cost savings, but if the line itself is basically unprofitable it could be better to shut it down and sell all of the existing equipment.

Full Investment

Sometimes it is better to accept a lower return on some investments in order to use all or most of the funds available for investment. For example, if a company has $100,000 available and has three investment opportunities, two at $50,000 each yielding 12% and one at $80,000 yielding 14%, it is better to earn $12,000 on the two at $50,000 each than to earn $11,200 on the one at $80,000 and leave $20,000 unused.

Risk

Different investments involve different degrees of risk. An investment in research and development for example, involves more risk than an investment to replace a machine, but it might produce a much higher return. The rate of return required from a potential investment is usually related to the risk of that investment. The lowest risk investments must meet the minimum required return. As the level of risk increases, the margin required in excess of the minimum increases. Very high risk investments may be rejected regardless of the potential return.

Two measures can be applied in assessing risk: the distribution of probable outcomes and the sensitivity of the calculations to changes in predictions.

Probability Distribution   The effect of a difference in the distribution of probable outcomes can be illustrated using the original investment example and assuming two different sets of probabilities concerning its lifetime as follows:

Assumption A					Assumption B				
Probability		**Lifetime**			**Probability**		**Lifetime**		
0.00	×	8 years	=	0.0 years	0.15	×	8 years	=	1.2 years
0.40	×	9	=	3.6	0.20	×	9	=	1.8
0.50	×	10	=	5.0	0.50	×	10	=	5.0
0.10	×	11	=	1.1	0.10	×	11	=	1.1
0.00	×	12	=	0.0	0.05	×	12	=	0.6
1.00				9.7 years	1.00				9.7 years

The predicted lifetime is the same with both sets of assumptions and the IRR is the same at 13.6%, as calculated earlier. The dispersion of the probabilities (the standard deviation in statistical terms) is greater in B than in A however, indicating it is more likely the lifetime will be different from that predicted. Standard deviations can be calculated to quantify comparisons.

Sensitivity Analysis   The sensitivity of the calculations to changes in the predictions can be tested in a variety of ways. Management might want to know what the rate of return would be if the investment lasted only 9 years for example, or if the annual cash flow was only $2,000. They might want to know what amount of cash flow would produce a return of 15%. Answers to any of these questions can be provided by making calculations based on the new criteria. If the investment lasted only 9 years, the IRR would be 12.6%. If the cash flow was only $2,000, the IRR would be 10.6%. A return of 15% would be produced by a cash flow of $2,391.

THE COST OF CAPITAL

Calculating Cost

Investment in assets is financed by owners and creditors. The cost of that financing is the weighted average of the cost from each source. For example, assume a company is financed as follows:

CHAPTER 18   Capital Budgeting   **253**

	Amount		Cost	
	$000's	%	%	$000's
Bonds	300	30	4	12
Preferred shares	150	15	10	15
Common share equity	550	55	12	66
	1,000	100		93

The weighted average cost of capital for the company is

$$\frac{(30 \times 4) + (15 \times 10) + (55 \times 12)}{100} = 9.3\%$$

30% of the money costs 4%, 15% costs 10% and 55% costs 12%.

The effective cost of bond financing is the after tax cost because bond interest is a deductible expense for tax purposes. The effective cost of share financing is the before tax cost because dividends are not.

The cost of debt financing is the stated interest rate payable, adjusted to amortize issuing costs and any issue discount or premium. Non interest bearing trade debt has no cost. In making rate of return calculations, any anticipated increase in trade debt can be treated as a reduction of the cost of the investment.

If preferred shares are issued for an unlimited period of time, there is no basis for amortizing issue costs, discounts, and premiums. The cost of preferred share financing is the annual dividend payable on the net amount received from the issue after issue costs, discounts, and premiums.

The cost of common share equity is difficult to define. There is not a simple, direct relationship between the return on shareholder equity and the market price of a share, as there is between the interest rate and the market price of a bond. Share market values fluctuate constantly and often widely. They reflect the expectations of investors. They are influenced not only by reported earnings but by anticipated changes in the business, the economy, interest rates, inflation rates and so on. In general, corporate managers attempt to impute a return to common share equity that will sustain or increase the market value of the shares, allowing for factors they cannot control such as interest and inflation rates.

The cost of capital changes in response to changes in the economy and in the business. A change in the general level of interest rates changes the cost of new debt. Increased borrowing by a company can cause an increase in the cost of debt, as lenders demand a higher rate to compensate for increased risk. The cost of equity capital changes as the market values of stocks change with the state of the economy and with the fortunes of the business.

Optimum Mix

For any business there is an optimum mix of debt and equity financing from various sources. The optimum mix is the one that produces the highest return to the owners, the common shareholders in a corporation, at an acceptable level of risk.

The optimum mix is determined by managers and investors. It varies. Different managers and investors have different opinions about acceptable risk. Some favor more debt and financial leverage for a higher rate of return, others favor less debt and a lower return in exchange for more security.

The optimum mix changes with changes in the cost of capital from different sources. It can also change with changes in the economy and in the business itself.

The actual mix varies from the optimum as debt is incurred and repaid, and as equity is increased by issuing shares and earning income and decreased by paying dividends.

A common mistake in assessing investments is to mix financing decisions with the investment decision. An investment might look attractive because it can be made with apparently cheap money by leasing or by assuming a mortgage for example. If by doing that the company must use equity financing to make other investments, in order to keep a satisfactory financing mix, the other investments will have to produce a higher return to maintain the average. All investments must be judged by the same cost standard to produce the best combination of investments.

Return to Owners

If the return on an investment does not equal or exceed the cost of capital, the rate of return to the owners is reduced. The cost of debt and preferred stock is fixed, so any shortfall must be absorbed by the owners. This can be illustrated using the capital mix and costs assumed earlier, and assuming three potential investments of $1,000 each, returning 10%, 8%, and 9.3%.

Investment	$1,000	$1,000	$1,000
Return on investment	10% = $100	8% = $ 80	9.3% = $ 93
Cost of debt	12	12	12
Cost of preferred stock	15	15	15
	27	27	27
Return to common shareholders	$ 73	$ 53	$ 66
Rate of return to shareholders	$\frac{73}{550}$ = 13.3%	$\frac{53}{550}$ = 9.6%	$\frac{66}{550}$ = 12%

The 10% investment increases the return to shareholders because it exceeds the weighted average cost of capital. The 8% investment decreases the return because it is less than the weighted average cost. The 9.3% investment maintains the return at 12% because it equals the weighted average.

Minimum Required Rate of Return

To maintain the rate of return to shareholders, the minimum rate of return earned on investments must equal or exceed the weighted average cost of capital. As a practical matter, it is difficult to define that cost. The cost of common share equity is difficult to determine. The cost of capital from different sources changes. The optimum mix of financing from different sources changes and the actual mix varies from the optimum. Because of the many uncertainties and the fact that all investments involve some element of risk, the minimum required rate of return is usually set somewhat above the estimated cost of capital.

CHAPTER 19

Responsibility Accounting

In business, the authority to make decisions and responsibility for the consequences of those decisions are delegated to various levels of management. The chief executive, usually the president in a corporation, has the ultimate responsibility for the success or failure of a business. He or she delegates portions of that responsibility to subordinates, production to a production manager, sales to a sales manager and so on. Each of those managers in turn delegates portions of his or her responsibility to further subordinates, the production manager to plant foremen and supervisors for example. The process of delegation flows from the highest to the lowest level of management. Depending on the size and complexity of a business, the number of levels can be few or many.

Lines of authority and responsibility are commonly described in the form of an organization chart. A sample organization chart for the Consumer Products Division of Mega Corporation is shown at the top of page 258.

The general manager has delegated authority and responsibility for sales to a sales manager, for production to a manufacturing manager, and for finance and administration to a financial manager. Each of these three has in turn delegated authority and responsibility to further subordinates, the sales manager to three regional managers, the manufacturing manager to three production and two service department managers, and the financial manager to an accounting, a treasury, and a credit manager.

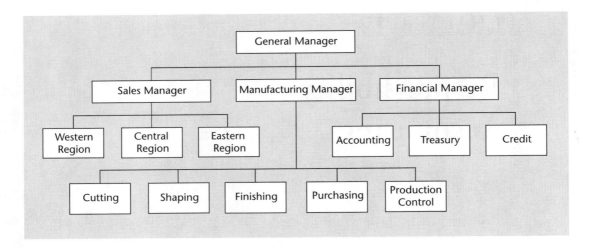

This organization is used as the basis for illustrating responsibility accounting in the remainder of this chapter.

COST, PROFIT AND INVESTMENT CENTERS

Management accounting systems are designed to measure and report the performance of managers at all levels in terms of revenues and costs. Each manager's area of responsibility (division, department, section) is a separate accounting unit. Those revenues and costs that can be controlled by a manager are assigned to his or her accounting unit. Some managers, such as production foremen, can control certain costs but have no influence on revenues. Their accounting units are described as **cost centers**. The costs they are able to control are assigned to their cost centers. Some managers, for example retail store managers, are responsible for revenues as well as costs. Their accounting units are described as **profit centers**. Both revenues and costs are assigned to their profit centers. Some senior managers, such as operating division managers in large corporations, are responsible for capital investment decisions as well as for revenues and current costs. Their accounting units are described as **investment centers**. Revenues, costs, and return on investment are all measured for their investment centers.

Delegating responsibility does not relieve a manager of that responsibility. The chief executive remains ultimately responsible for the entire business, regardless of the fact that he or she has delegated responsibilities to subordinates. The production manager remains fully responsible for what has been delegated to him, regardless of the fact that he may have delegated further. The accounting unit for every manager therefore, incorporates the accounting units for all of his or her subordinates.

Profit and investment centers can be created within an accounting system for other purposes, as well as for measuring the performance of managers. A product line for example, could be made a profit center to measure the contribution of that product to the profitability of the business. Revenues and costs attributable to the product would be assigned to that profit center.

COST CENTERS

The performance of cost centers is reported to managers in the form of statements of the costs they can control, usually comparing actual costs incurred with predetermined budgets or standards. Reports are usually prepared monthly but some are prepared more frequently, weekly, or even daily, when quick action to correct possible problems is required.

The following is an example of a cost control report for the Cutting Department of the Consumer Products Division.

Cutting Department
Cost Control Report
for the month —

	Incurred	Budgeted
Direct material	$41,500	$40,000
Direct labor	14,500	15,000
Supplies	1,800	2,000
Indirect labor	4,300	4,000
Maintenance	600	500
Total	$62,700	$61,500

The Cutting Department manager is responsible for a very limited range of costs, only those directly incurred in his department. They consist of materials and supplies used, labor applied directly to product, departmental indirect labor for such things as make ready and clean up, and maintenance.

The manufacturing manager's report appears as follows:

	Manufacturing Cost Control Report for the month—	
	Incurred	**Budgeted**
Cutting department	$ 62,700	$ 61,500
Shaping department	73,300	74,000
Finishing department	16,200	15,000
Purchasing	2,900	3,000
Production control	5,200	5,000
Supervision	15,000	15,000
Power	3,200	3,000
Heat and water	900	1,000
	$179,400	$177,500

The totals from the Cutting Department report are shown in this report. Similarly, the totals for the other manufacturing departments are included. If the manufacturing manager wants to pursue the details of a department's costs, he can refer to the departmental report. Also included in this report are the other costs the manufacturing manager is directly responsible for, the cost of his departmental managers and the costs of power, heat and water used in the factory. In some instances, costs such as power, heat and water are metered or traced to departments for control. In this case, the cost of that refinement is not justified by the potential improvement it would provide in cost control.

Not included in the manufacturing manager's report are the costs he cannot control, such as depreciation, property taxes, and insurance. Depreciation and property taxes are the result of decisions made by more senior managers. Insurance coverage is the responsibility of the financial manager.

A cost control report prepared for the general manager follows the same pattern as that for the manufacturing manager. Totals are shown from the reports of manufacturing, sales and finance, together with those costs for which the general manager is directly responsible.

Cost control reports can be presented in a variety of different formats, depending on the preferences of managers. Many show year to date as well as current month amounts. Some show the difference between incurred and budgeted amounts, either in dollar amounts or percentages or both.

PROFIT CENTERS

The performance of profit centers is reported in a form of income statement. Each of the three sales regions of the Consumer Products Division is treated as a profit center. The following is a profit center report for the manager of Eastern Region sales.

	Actual	Budget
Eastern Region		
Profit Contribution		
for the month —		
Sales	$144,000	$150,000
Cost of goods sold	96,000	100,000
Gross margin	48,000	50,000
Salaries and commissions	9,500	10,000
Travel and entertainment	4,200	4,000
Office expenses	3,100	3,000
Communications	1,900	2,000
Total controllable costs	18,700	19,000
Controllable contribution	$ 29,300	$ 31,000

Costs controllable by the regional sales manager are deducted from the revenues generated in the region, to show his controllable profit contribution. As in the case of cost center reports, only controllable costs are included. Advertising and office space rental are not included because they are controlled by the senior sales manager. Standard costs are used both in valuing inventory and cost of goods sold and in preparing budgets, so the gross margin generated from sales is not affected by any variations in production costs.

Sometimes a profit center report is extended by deducting other direct operating costs, rent for example, not controllable by the center manager, to show the net contribution of the center. The only costs omitted are those that are common to all centers and cannot be identified with or allocated to individual centers, except arbitrarily; for example the general manager's salary. The net amount is the contribution of the center towards covering those common costs and producing a profit.

INVESTMENT CENTERS

The Consumer Products Division is an investment center. The general manager is responsible for asset investment in the division. His performance is measured in terms of the profit contribution of the division to Mega Corporation and in terms of the rate of return on division assets.

Return on investment is usually calculated as the accounting rate of return, that is, using current revenue and expense measurements and historical asset costs and depreciation. It was shown in the last chapter on capital budgeting that the accounting rate of return is not a satisfactory measure for making investment decisions. Similarly, it is less than satisfactory for measuring the performance of managers and divisions. The common use of accounting rates of return appears to be due to the fact that income is measured and reported in general in accounting terms.

In addition to the conceptual deficiencies of the accounting rate of return, there are problems in measuring it. Some valuable elements of investment can be left out of the calculation. Investment in intangibles for example, is usually recorded as a current expense at the time it is made, regardless of whether it has ongoing value. Leased assets are often omitted from the investment base, although they represent a significant investment commitment.

Inflation can cause substantial distortions in rate of return calculations. Historical costs of investment and depreciation expense are shown at lower than current dollar amounts, both of which have the effect of increasing the calculated rate of return. Adjustments to compensate for inflation are almost never made.

The process of recording depreciation itself distorts rate of return calculations, by systematically reducing the recorded value of investments. This can be illustrated with the investment example used in the previous chapter. The investment had a cost of $12,000, income before depreciation of

$2,300, and depreciation of $1,200 per year for 10 years. Over the 10 year period, it would show increasing rates of return as illustrated below.

Year	Net Asset Value	Income after Depreciation	Accounting Return on Investment
1	$12,000	1,100	9.2%
2	10,800	1,100	10.2
3	9,600	1,100	11.5
4	8,400	1,100	13.1
5	7,200	1,100	15.3
6	6,000	1,100	18.3
7	4,800	1,100	22.9
8	3,600	1,100	30.6
9	2,400	1,100	45.8
10	1,200	1,100	91.7

The dollar value of the return remained constant but the calculated rate of return increased by ten times, as the net asset value declined with accumulated depreciation.

To avoid the effect of a decreasing investment amount, a few companies base the calculations on original cost. In the example, that would produce the same rate of return, 9.2%, in each of the 10 years. The disadvantage of this, as described in the previous chapter, is that it significantly understates the rate of return. The IRR calculated for the investment was 14%.

Reporting accounting rates of return for investment centers can result in faulty business decisions, as managers attempt to maximize returns.

Investment centers that spend more on intangible value show lower returns when those costs are incurred and expensed, and higher returns when results are reflected in higher revenues with no intangible expense. Management is influenced to direct less effort to expanding those centers in the earlier period and more in the later.

When leased assets are omitted from the investment base, the center that leases shows a higher return than a comparable center that purchases its assets. Management is influenced to direct more effort to expanding the center that leases.

Inflation makes the return on older assets bought at lower price levels, appear higher than that on new assets. The older the asset becomes, the higher the return. Managers are discouraged from replacing older assets and from making new investments, because the rate of return on comparable current dollar investments will be lower and will reduce the overall investment center return.

Return on investment calculations can lead managers to make investment decisions that appear to be good for their investment centers but are bad for the company as a whole. For example, a manager whose investment center is producing a 16% rate of return will be influenced to reject an investment with a potential 14% return, because it would reduce his overall return. If the company in total is showing a 12% return however, the 14% investment would increase its overall return.

To overcome this problem, some companies assess the performance of investment centers by reference to what is called "residual income". Residual income calculations are similar in concept to the net present value calculations used in capital budgeting. The residual income of an investment center is its contribution or income less a charge for the cost of capital invested in its assets. For example, if a division is earning $16,000 on an investment of $100,000 and is charged 12% for capital, it has residual income of $4,000, $16,000 minus $12,000 (12% of $100,000).

The residual income of the investment center is increased by any additional investment that exceeds its cost of capital. An additional investment of $10,000 promising $1,400 income, 14%, would increase total income to $17,400 ($16,000 + $1,400), cost of capital to $13,200 (12% of $100,000 + $10,000) and residual income to $4,200 ($17,400 − $13,200) from $4,000 ($16,000 − $12,000).

TRANSFER PRICING

In some companies, one or more profit centers or investment centers sell goods or services to other profit or investment centers, as well as to outsiders. These transfer sales are priced in one of three ways: by reference to market prices, by negotiation, or by reference to costs.

Market

For many goods and services there is an active market in which the producing profit center can sell to a variety of purchasers and the consuming center can purchase from a variety of sellers. In this situation there should be little difference in prices charged by suppliers, and the transfer price can be based on market. The price is discounted from market, recognizing that selling costs are less for an internal sale and sharing the saving between the selling and buying divisions.

Negotiation

Some goods and services are not generally available but can be produced by other suppliers. Automotive parts for example, can be made to specification by independent contractors as well as by other divisions of car manufacturers. In this situation the transfer price can be set by negotiation. The selling division makes a bid to supply the goods or services, or the buying division makes an offer to purchase. If the selling division is willing to accept a lower price than the buying division can get from an outside supplier, it will get the order. If not, the buying division will purchase from the outside supplier. This process usually maximizes the profit result for the company. The buying division gets the lowest available price. The selling division will accept the order at that price only if it cannot earn a higher return by producing for someone else.

For this arrangement to work, there must be outside suppliers who are willing to bid. They will only continue to do so if outside bids are accepted with reasonable frequency.

Cost

Many companies base transfer prices on costs. Some use variable costs only, some use full costs and some use full costs plus a profit mark-up. Transfer prices based on costs generally have negative effects on management performance and profitability. Managers are not motivated to minimize their operating costs if they can pass them on in their prices to other divisions. When full costs are used, managers of buying divisions often buy from outside sources when selling divisions have unused capacity and would have generated profit from a lower negotiated price. When variable costs are used, there is no incentive to sell to other divisions because the sales generate no contribution to the selling division, although interdivision sales could be good for the company overall.

Other Considerations

Companies that operate divisions in more than one country are sometimes motivated to set transfer prices for purposes other than management responsibility. Within limits, different transfer prices can be used to shift taxable income from countries with higher tax rates to those with lower rates, or to minimize import duties. They can also be used as a means of transferring money between countries, if more conventional methods are restricted.

Service Departments

For responsibility accounting purposes, transfer prices are used to charge other departments for the use of service departments. Managers are held responsible for the cost of internally provided services just as they would be if the services were purchased from outsiders.

Service department charges can be based on market prices or negotiated, but are usually based on cost. The cost per unit of service provided is calculated and user departments are charged for the number of units used.

The appropriate unit of measure depends on the nature of the service provided. The unit chosen should be the factor most closely related to the service department's costs. Purchasing might be charged on the basis of number of purchase orders issued for example, and data processing on the basis of computer time used.

The actual cost per unit will vary depending on the efficiency of a service department. It will also vary with changes in the level of activity of a service department, as fixed costs are distributed over differing numbers of units. User departments cannot be held responsible for inefficiencies in service departments, nor for fluctuations in their overall levels of activity. To avoid charging them for these variations, standard costs per unit are calculated for services.

LIMITATIONS

Responsibility accounting has some practical limitations. Responsibility for revenues and costs is sometimes difficult to assign. Revenues of one unit in a group can be affected by the activity of another. Advertising by one division of a corporation for example, could generate increased sales for other divisions.

In some cases it is not feasible or practical to allocate a cost between managers, for example the cost of water used by different departments in a factory.

Some costs are controlled jointly by two or more managers. Salary and benefit costs for example, are the result of numbers of people, wage rates, and benefit packages, each of which could be controlled by a different manager.

Sometimes divisions of a company are required to buy from or sell to other divisions, for reasons such as product quality or reliability of supply. Managers are usually prevented from buying services from outsiders, when the services are provided by service departments. If the authority of a manager to buy or sell is restricted, he cannot be held responsible for excess costs incurred as a result. Both buyers and sellers are less motivated to minimize the costs of goods or services transferred.

CHAPTER 20

Standard Costs

Standard costs are predetermined estimates of what the direct material, direct labor, and manufacturing overhead costs should be to produce a unit of product. Standards are employed by many manufacturers. They are helpful in forecasting and planning, they are valuable for comparison with incurred costs as a method of cost control, and they provide consistent valuations for inventory and simplify the valuation process.

SETTING STANDARDS

Standards are usually based on what are considered attainable costs under reasonably efficient operating conditions. They include allowances for normal levels of wastage, spoilage, production delays and so on. Standards based on ideal performance are not useful for management purposes. They are misleading if used for forecasting, disregarded by managers as unrealistic if used for cost control, and produce unduly low valuations if used for inventory valuation.

Direct Material

Direct material standards are calculated as the quantity of each type of material required, multiplied by the price. Quantities are usually based on engineered specifications, adjusted for normal wastage. Prices are based on expected market conditions and efficient purchasing practices.

Direct Labor

Direct labor standards are calculated as the time required for each procedure, multiplied by the labor rate. Some companies have engineered times for labor, calculated using work methods and time study measurements. Others base their time estimates on past experience. Times based on methods and time studies are adjusted to allow for normal delays, work interruptions and so on. Rates are based on employee agreements and can include allowances for normal overtime, shift bonus, or other wage premiums.

In process cost systems, labor and manufacturing overhead are combined in conversion cost standards.

Manufacturing Overhead

Overhead standards are calculated as the normal overhead rate per hour multiplied by the standard number of hours required to produce a unit of product. Normal overhead was described in chapter 7. The normal overhead rate per hour is total estimated production overhead at reasonable efficiency divided by total production hours, both at the normal level of production. If the normal level of production is 5,000 direct labor hours and it is estimated that total production overhead at that level should be $60,000, the normal overhead rate per hour is $12 ($60,000 ÷ 5,000). If the standard number of direct labor hours required to produce a unit of product is 2, the standard overhead per unit is $24 (2 × $12).

Overhead costs are either fixed costs or semi-variable costs. Fixed costs are known. Semi-variable costs are usually estimated, and divided into fixed and variable components, using either a **high-low** or a **scattergraph** method. With the high-low method, the amount of a semi-variable cost is estimated at a high level of activity and at a low level, and the two amounts are plotted on a cost-activity graph. A straight line is drawn through the two points and extended to the vertical, cost axis. The distance between the origin and the point where the line intersects the axis represents the fixed component of cost. The slope of the line represents the variable component. This method is illustrated in the following diagram.

At a level of 2,000 hours, the cost was estimated to be $3,000. At 6,000 hours, it was estimated at $5,000. The connecting line intersects the cost

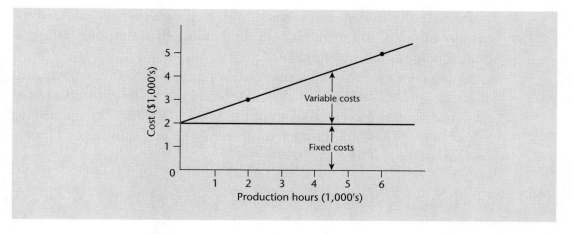

axis at $2,000. The fixed cost component is therefore estimated to be $2,000. The variable cost component is $1,000 for 2,000 hours, or 50 cents per hour.

Using the high-low method, care must be taken not to select estimating points too high or too low in the range of activity, to avoid areas of disproportionate change.

Using the scattergraph method, the amounts of a semi-variable cost experienced in several past periods are plotted on the graph. A straight line of best fit to all the points is then drawn and extended to the vertical axis. The line can be drawn by visual observation or more precisely by using the mathematical technique, regression analysis.

The scattergraph method is illustrated in the following diagram.

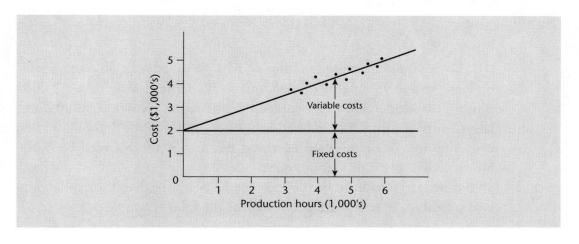

In using the scattergraph method, historical data must be adjusted for changes in prices and methods, and those that reflect abnormal or inefficient conditions must be eliminated.

Combining all fixed and semi-variable production cost estimates produces a graph such as the one below. The business has a fixed component of total manufacturing overhead costs of $25,000 and a variable component of $7 per hour. (These are the data assumed for this and subsequent illustrations of overhead in this chapter.)

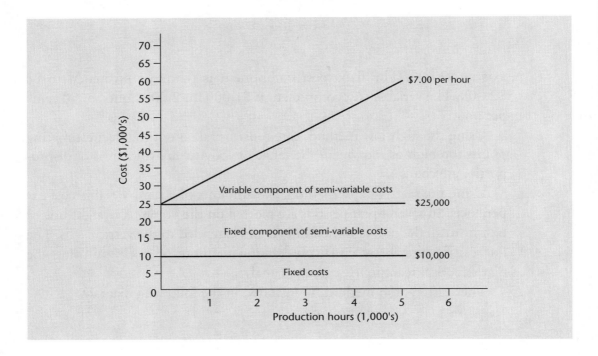

This is a graphic representation of what is called a flexible or variable budget. At any volume of production, total overhead should be $25,000 plus $7 per production hour worked. If the normal volume is 5,000 direct labor hours, the total should be $25,000 + $5,000 × $7, or $60,000. In that case, the normal or standard overhead rate is $60,000 divided by 5,000 hours, or $12 per direct labor hour.

Normal overhead can be plotted together with fixed and variable budgeted overhead, to produce a graph such as the following.

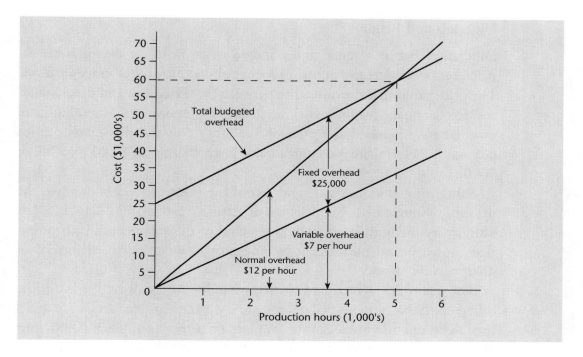

In this graph, fixed overhead is plotted above variable overhead. As the graph shows, at production volumes below normal, budgeted overhead exceeds normal overhead; at volumes above normal, budgeted overhead is less than normal overhead.

Revisions

Standard costs for material, labor, and overhead are the product of standard quantities multiplied by standard prices or rates. Whenever quantities or prices change therefore, standards need to be revised. Quantities seldom change. Prices and rates often change. Most companies review and revise standards annually, and in response to significant operating changes such as new labor contracts.

VARIANCES

Differences between standard costs and costs actually incurred are described as variances. If costs incurred are more than standard, a variance is unfavorable; if they are less than standard, a variance is favorable. Variances are written off in the period they are incurred.

Materials and Labor

Differences between actual and standard costs for direct materials are divided into two variances: a price variance and a quantity or usage variance. The price variance is the difference between the actual cost and the standard cost for the quantity of material purchased. For example, if 10,000 units of material are purchased at a price of $4.06 per unit and the standard price per unit is $4.00, there is an unfavorable price variance of 10,000 × $.06, or $600.

Some companies calculate and record the price variance, not when the material is purchased, but when it is used in production. This is a less satisfactory method. It separates the record of the variance from the event that caused it and measures it by reference to quantities used instead of quantities purchased.

The quantity variance is calculated when the materials are used. It is the difference between the actual quantity and the standard quantity of material used in production, valued at the standard price. For example, if 7,800 units of material are used in production and the standard quantity required for the volume of production is 8,000, there is a favorable quantity variance of 200 × $4.00, or $800.

Differences between actual and standard costs for direct labor are also divided into two variances, similar to those for direct material: a rate variance and an efficiency or usage variance. Both are calculated as the labor is applied. The rate variance is the difference between the actual cost and the standard cost for the number of hours worked. For example if 4,100 hours are worked at a cost of $41,410, an average of $10.10 per hour, and the standard is $10 per hour, for a total of $41,000, there is an unfavorable rate variance of $410.

The efficiency variance is the difference between the actual number of hours worked and the standard number required for the volume of production, valued at the standard rate. If 4,100 hours are worked and the standard calls for 4,000, there is an unfavorable efficiency variance of 100 hours × $10 per hour, or $1,000.

In calculating variances for both materials and labor, the conventional practice is to calculate the price or rate variance first, using actual quantities purchased or hours worked. The quantity and efficiency variances are then calculated using standard prices and rates. These calculations result in assigning to price and rate variances, that portion of the total material and labor variances attributable to the combined effect of price and quantity variations taken together. This is illustrated in the following table, using the actual and standard labor data from the example.

Actual hours (4,100) at actual rate ($10.10)	$41,410
Standard hours (4,000) at standard rate ($10.00)	40,000
Total variance	$ 1,410
Calculated rate variance	
Standard hours (4,000) at excess rate ($0.10) (the effect of rate only)	$ 400
Excess hours (100) at excess rate ($0.10) (the combined effect of rate and hours)	10
	410
Calculated efficiency variance	
Excess hours (100) at standard rate ($10.00) (the effect of hours only)	1,000
Total variance	$ 1,410

In summary, differences between costs incurred and standard costs for direct material and direct labor are allocated to variances as follows:

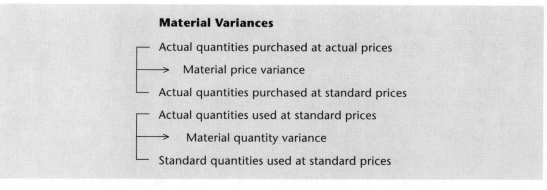

Material Variances

Actual quantities purchased at actual prices

→ Material price variance

Actual quantities purchased at standard prices

Actual quantities used at standard prices

→ Material quantity variance

Standard quantities used at standard prices

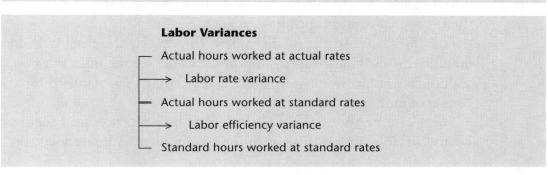

Labor Variances

Actual hours worked at actual rates

→ Labor rate variance

Actual hours worked at standard rates

→ Labor efficiency variance

Standard hours worked at standard rates

Overhead

Differences between actual overhead and standard overhead are divided into two variances, a volume variance and a controllable or budget variance.

The volume variance is the difference between the flexible budget and the standard overhead for the number of units produced. It is described as overhead under or overapplied, and results from producing less or more than the normal quantity of product.

The controllable variance is the difference between the overhead actually incurred and the overhead that should have been incurred in accordance with the flexible budget for the quantity of product produced. It results from variations in spending and efficiency.

Assume actual overhead in total is $54,200 and that 2,000 units are produced at a standard labor requirement of 2 direct labor hours per unit, or 4,000 hours. The flexible budget for 4,000 hours is $25,000 + 4,000 × $7 ($28,000), or $53,000. The overhead applied at standard is $24 per unit multiplied by 2,000 units, or $48,000. The overhead variances are the following.

Flexible budget overhead	$53,000	
Standard overhead applied	48,000	
Volume variance		$5,000
Actual overhead incurred	54,200	
Flexible budget overhead	53,000	
Controllable variance		1,200
Total variance		$6,200

Many manufacturers divide the controllable variance into two parts, an efficiency variance and a spending variance.

The efficiency variance is the difference between the flexible budget allowance for the hours worked and the allowance for the number of units produced. It results from using more or less hours than standard for the number of units produced.

The spending variance is the difference between overhead incurred and the flexible budget allowance for the number of hours worked. It results from over or underspending on overhead for the number of hours actually worked.

If the number of hours worked in the example is 4,100 and the standard number for the units produced is 4,000, the spending and efficiency variances are the following.

Flexible budget for 4,100 hours ($25,000 + 4,100 × $7)	$53,700	
Flexible budget for 4,000 hours ($25,000 + 4,000 × $7)	53,000	
Efficiency variance		$ 700
Actual overhead incurred	54,200	
Flexible budget for 4,100 hours	53,700	
Spending variance		500
Total variance		$1,200

Calculation of the overhead variances is illustrated in the following graph.

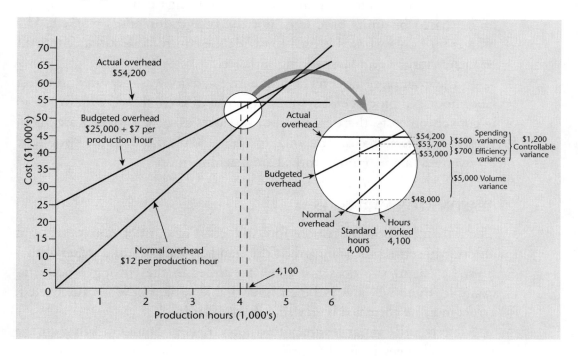

In summary, differences between overhead costs incurred and standard overhead costs are allocated to variances as follows:

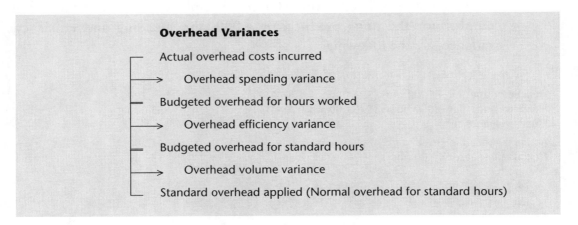

Overhead Variances

— Actual overhead costs incurred

  → Overhead spending variance

— Budgeted overhead for hours worked

  → Overhead efficiency variance

— Budgeted overhead for standard hours

  → Overhead volume variance

— Standard overhead applied (Normal overhead for standard hours)

The spending variance and the efficiency variance taken together are the overhead controllable variance.

Note that the volume variance is calculated using the budget for standard hours, based on units produced, not the budget for hours worked. The budget for hours worked is used to divide the controllable variance into an efficiency variance and a spending variance.

In the examples, the level of productive activity was measured in direct labor hours. In process cost systems, when labor is combined with overhead in conversion costs, there are no labor variances as such. Variances are calculated for conversion costs, the total of labor and overhead, as they would be for overhead alone. Hours worked are machine hours.

REASONS FOR VARIANCES

There are many possible reasons for variances. The most obvious perhaps, is an error in setting the standard. If the standard quantity of a material that must be cut to size does not allow for losses in the cutting process for example, there will always be an unfavorable variance. When discovered, errors must be corrected by revising the standards.

Material price variances are purchasing variances. Sometimes they are the result of changes in market prices and beyond the control of managers. Often they are the result of purchasing practices. A purchasing agent might buy in large quantities to obtain lower prices or in small quantities and incur higher prices, for example. He might fail to consider alternative sources of supply. He might use more or less expensive means of transportation to obtain delivery. The purchasing agent is usually responsible for controllable purchasing variances but not always. If sales are low, it may not be possible to buy in economical lot sizes. If production schedules are changed, it may be necessary to pay more for quick delivery.

Material quantity variances are production variances. They are produced by more or less efficient use of materials and more or less spoilage in the production process. They are usually the responsibility of production managers but can in some cases be attributable to others. Excessive waste for example, could result from the use of substandard material purchased to obtain a lower price.

Labor rate variances result from using higher or lower paid employees to perform work and from incurring more or less overtime or other wage cost premiums. Rate variances are often the responsibility of production managers but can be caused by uncontrollable factors or by other managers. The absence of an employee due to sickness for example, can require a higher paid employee to do a job. A rush order from the sales department might require extra overtime work.

Labor efficiency variances can be caused in several ways, most of them production related. The relative skill of employees can affect the amount of time required for a job. The reliability of machinery and equipment can affect it. Substandard material resulting in spoilage and rework will produce unfavorable variances. New employees and new products require a learning period and produce unfavorable variances.

When employees are paid only in accordance with piecework rates, there are no labor variances.

The overhead spending variance is a combination of differences of actual prices and quantities from the flexible budget allowances, for the complete range of semi-variable and fixed overhead costs including indirect materials and indirect labor. As such, it has many possible causes. To ascertain the causes, the actual and budgeted costs must be compared by individual cost category. For most fixed costs there are no differences, or only small differences arising from errors in the budget estimates.

The overhead efficiency variance is the difference in total overhead incurred attributable to the fact that more or less than the standard production hours were worked for the number of units of product produced. It includes only the variable component of semi-variable overhead; the fixed elements of overhead are not affected by differences in hours worked. The overhead efficiency variance corresponds to the labor efficiency variance, except that an overhead efficiency variance can exist when employees are paid on a piecework basis but a labor efficiency variance cannot. The overhead cost is affected by production hours, the piecework labor cost is not.

The overhead volume variance results entirely from producing a quantity of product more or less than normal. It is made up of only fixed elements of overhead costs, since only fixed costs per unit change with numbers of units produced. Variable costs per unit are not affected by the number of units produced. When companies use variable costing for internal reporting purposes, there is no volume variance. All fixed costs are period costs.

REPORTING VARIANCES

Standard cost variances are reported to managers following the principles described in the preceding chapter, Responsibility Accounting. Reports are provided monthly or more often to the managers primarily responsible for the costs, with summaries to their superiors.

Material price variances are reported to the purchasing agent. Material quantity and both labor variances are reported to production supervisors, usually plant foremen. Variances in overhead spending costs can be the responsibility of several managers and are reported in accordance with responsibility by cost categories. Overhead efficiency variances, like labor efficiency variances, are the responsibility of production supervisors and should be reported to those supervisors. When overhead spending and efficiency variances are combined in an overhead controllable variance, responsibilities become mixed and sometimes difficult to allocate. Overhead volume variances usually result from conditions beyond management control, more or less demand for the company's products than normal. They are reported to senior management.

While variances are reported initially to the managers primarily responsible for the costs, the causes of unfavorable variances are sometimes outside their control. For example, an unfavorable labor efficiency variance reported to a foreman might be the result of excessive rework due to substandard material; or an unfavorable rate variance might result from having to assign another employee to a job because someone was ill. When this happens, the manager explains the reason for the variance to his superior, and in due course responsibility, if any, is attributed to the right party.

Not all variances are reported. Most companies follow the practice of management by exception, that is, they concern themselves only with results that are significantly different from those expected. Those matters that call for management action are not obscured by reporting many things that do not. Most companies set minimum levels in terms of percentage and absolute amounts of cost, below which they do not report variances.

NON MANUFACTURING COSTS

Standard costing methods were developed for manufacturing costs and are most commonly used for those costs, but the methodology can be applied to many other costs as well. The use of standards for charging service department costs to user departments was referred to in the previous chapter. Standards can be developed for almost any routine, repetitive activity. Examples are materials handling and shipping, sales order and invoice processing, purchase order and invoice processing and data recording and processing.

CHAPTER 21

Budgets

A budget is a plan, expressed in numerical terms. It is a plan for the use of resources, assets or time or both. Almost all businesses make use of budgets in some form. In small businesses, a budget is often no more than an estimated statement of income for the coming year. In well managed large businesses, it is a comprehensive set of financial plans, encompassing every aspect of the business and center of responsibility.

The preparation and use of budgets assists management in planning, coordinating, and controlling the operations of a business. Managers at all levels are required to plan their activities and to translate those plans into dollar estimates. Combining the plans of all managers to produce a comprehensive financial plan for the business as a whole requires coordination of all aspects of the business. The final plans of all managers must come together in an integrated whole. Future requirements are identified well in advance so appropriate action can be taken. For example, advance planning could indicate a need to acquire new equipment to meet production requirements, or a need to negotiate future bank financing to meet cash requirements. When completed, the budget is a basis for comparison with, and control of, actual performance. Reports of actual versus budgeted results are prepared daily, weekly, or monthly as appropriate, for all levels of responsibility.

BUDGETING BASICS

Budget Period

Most businesses prepare their budgets on a yearly basis, corresponding with their financial year, and divided into quarterly and monthly periods. Some businesses budget continuously, adding a month at the end as each month passes, so that the budget always covers the coming twelve months.

For some activities, budgets are prepared for longer time periods. Plant and equipment acquisitions for example, are often budgeted for several years, because they require much advance planning.

Budget Estimates

Budget estimates should be made initially by each manager for those things that are his or her responsibility. This is important for two reasons. First, the manager responsible for an activity usually has the most complete knowledge of that activity. Secondly, the performance of managers is measured against their budgets. Unless they have an important part in setting their budgets, it is difficult to hold them responsible for meeting budget targets.

Each manager has his estimates reviewed and discussed with his immediate superior, starting at the lowest level of management and proceeding up to the chief executive. Managers naturally want their budget targets to be easily attainable, so their initial estimates are usually generous. Their superiors challenge questionable estimates and collectively they arrive at acceptable targets.

Budget estimates can be made in different ways. Perhaps the most common method is to base them on prior experience. In many cases this consists of taking last year's figures and adjusting them upwards for inflation. Estimates based on past experience have the disadvantage that they can relate to different circumstances and they can build in past inefficiencies.

Some costs are discretionary, for example the costs of advertising and product research. For discretionary costs, a procedure described as zero-based budgeting can be used. Managers are required to make the case for every dollar of cost they propose to incur, starting at zero. This avoids the disadvantages of past based estimates, and the incentive for managers to spend to the limit of each year's budgeted allowances so that the following year's allowance will not be reduced.

Most kinds of cost, production and selling wages, materials and supplies, power, telephone and so on, are unavoidable in the operation of a business. These costs change to varying extents with levels of activity. Methods of estimating these costs were described in the previous chapter in connection with standard costs. The same techniques can be applied to selling and administrative costs, except that the measures of activity are not production hours, but sales units or dollars or something else.

Budgets are often revised during the course of a budget period. Circumstances can change to render projections made several months earlier unrealistic. The farther an event is in the future, the more difficult it is to estimate.

Budget Management

The budgeting process is usually coordinated by a budget director, a financial manager such as the controller. He and his staff provide technical help and advice to other managers as required, and bring all of the estimates together in final budget form. They should not make the estimates, however. That is the responsibility of the operating managers.

Many companies have a budget committee as well, usually consisting of the budget director, the president, and the senior production, sales and financial executives. The committee reviews, coordinates, and approves proposed budgets.

PROCEDURE

Before beginning the budgeting process, management at all levels should be informed of the objectives and expectations for the business for the coming period, and how they relate to each manager's area of responsibility. This should start from the chief executive and be communicated down through the organization to the lowest level of management.

The starting point for the budgeting process is a budget of forecast sales. This is prepared by the sales manager and his staff based on their knowledge and research of the economy, the industry, customers, competition and so on. The sales budget must be prepared in detail, showing the number of units and selling prices for each product in each territory each month, as a basis for the preparation of production schedules and cost and expense budgets.

Based on the sales budget, the production manager and his staff prepare a production schedule. From this they produce budgets of materials and labor requirements, and of overhead expenses.

Based on the sales forecast and the production schedule, budgets of selling and administrative expenses are produced by the managers of those areas.

Purchases of plant and equipment are budgeted separately in a capital expenditures budget.

When all of the operating budgets have been completed, the budget director and his staff prepare a cash budget, combining the operating data with planned capital expenditures and incorporating any budgeted changes in debt and equity financing. Finally, they combine all of the data to produce budgeted statements of income and balance sheets.

Budgeting Illustration

Following is an illustration of the development of a comprehensive budget for Pricey Product Inc., a company that produces and sells whatzits.

The standard manufacturing cost of a whatzit is that described in the previous chapter, consisting of the following.

Direct material, 4 units @ $4 per unit	$16
Direct labor, 2 hours @ $10 per hour	20
Production overhead, 2 hours @ $12 per hour	24
Total standard cost per unit of product	$60

The flexible budget for manufacturing overhead consists of $25,000 fixed cost plus $7 variable cost per production hour. The normal volume of production is 2,500 units requiring 5,000 direct labor hours per month.

For the year 20X the sales manager produced the following sales budget.

The company budgets monthly for the first quarter and quarterly for the remainder of the year. As each quarter passes, the budget for the following quarter is refined and restated by months.

Pricey Product Inc.
Sales Budget
for the year 20X

	Units (000's)	Price per unit	Total (000's)
January	1	$90	$90
February	2	90	180
March	3	95	285
First quarter	6		555
Second quarter	8	100	800
Third quarter	9	110	990
Fourth quarter	7	95	665
	30		$3,010

The business is seasonal. Demand is high in the summer months and low in winter. This is reflected in the estimates of quantities that can be sold and prices that can be charged throughout the year.

Based on the sales budget, the production manager scheduled his production as follows:

Pricey Product Inc.
Production Schedule
for the year 20X
(in thousands of units)

	Inventory Beginning	Sales	Production	Inventory Ending
January	2	1	2	3
February	3	2	2	3
March	3	3	3	3
First quarter		6	7	
Second quarter	3	8	8	3
Third quarter	3	9	8	2
Fourth quarter	2	7	7	2
		30	30	

Management agree that the company should have a minimum of 2,000 units of product on hand at all times to avoid being out of stock. The production manager scheduled to meet that requirement. At the same time he spread production over the year as evenly as possible, to utilize available capacity efficiently and to minimize costs, including the carrying costs of the inventory.

Next, the production manager directed the purchasing department to prepare a budget of raw material purchases and the production control department to prepare a budget of direct labor costs, based on the production schedule. They produced the following.

Pricey Product Inc.
Material Purchase Budget
for the year 20X

	Inventory Beginning (000 units)	Production Usage (000 units)	Purchases Quantity (000 units)	Purchases Cost (000's)	Inventory Ending (000 units)
January	4	8	8	$ 32	4
February	4	8	10	40	6
March	6	12	13	52	7
First quarter		28	31	124	
Second quarter	7	32	32	128	7
Third quarter	7	32	31	124	6
Fourth quarter	6	28	26	104	4
		120	120	$480	

Material is purchased to meet scheduled production requirements. Approximately two weeks' supply of raw material is maintained in inventory as an optimum balance between the risk of a shortage and the costs of carrying more. Purchases are therefore scheduled approximately two weeks before production.

Pricey Product Inc.
Direct Labor Budget
for the year 20X

	Hours (000's)	Cost (000's)
January	4	$ 40
February	4	40
March	6	60
First quarter	14	140
Second quarter	16	160
Third quarter	16	160
Fourth quarter	14	140
	60	$600

Direct labor costs are incurred as the labor is applied in production.

Monthly and quarterly estimates of manufacturing overhead costs are taken from the flexible overhead budget, based on the planned volume of production. In summary, the budget of manufacturing overhead appeared as follows:

Pricey Product Inc.
Budget of Manufacturing Overhead
for the year 20X

	Production (000 hours)	Cost (000's) ($25,000 per month + $7 per hour)
January	4	$ 53
February	4	53
March	6	67
First quarter	14	173
Second quarter	16	187
Third quarter	16	187
Fourth quarter	14	173
	60	$720

The company employs flexible budgets to plan and control selling and administrative expenses as well as manufacturing overhead. The following is a combined summary budget of these expenses.

Pricey Product Inc.
Combined Budget of Selling and Administrative Expenses
for the year 20X

	Selling (000's)	Administration (000's)
January	$ 39	$ 18
February	51	20
March	63	24
First quarter	153	62
Second quarter	177	68
Third quarter	189	70
Fourth quarter	165	64
	$684	$264

Selling and administrative expenses are mainly fixed. Selling expenses vary to a limited extent with the number of units of product sold. Administrative expenses vary to a more limited extent, with a combination of units sold and units produced.

Using the foregoing budgets, and incorporating planned capital expenditures, the budget director produced a cash budget. The cash budget is based on the operating budgets, but adjusted for differences in timing between cash flows, and sales and purchases. Cash receipts from sales are expected, on average, one month after sale. Cash payments for materials, supplies, utilities, and most other purchased services are made on average one month after purchase. Payments for some capital additions are made at the time they are acquired, others a month later. Depreciation expense does not involve a payment.

When operating and capital expenditure budgets indicate a need for additional cash or a surplus of cash, a source or use of cash is included.

The cash budget by quarters appeared as follows: (Details of differences between sales and purchases and cash flows are not enumerated.)

Pricey Product Inc.
Cash Budget
for the year 20X, by quarters
(in thousands of dollars)

	First Quarter	Second Quarter	Third Quarter	Fourth Quarter
Collections from sales	550	790	975	690
Direct material purchases	100	127	126	123
Direct wages	140	160	160	140
Other materials and supplies	35	40	45	35
Other salaries and wages	240	280	290	230
Utilities and other	115	90	105	110
Capital expenditures	40	10	—	30
Interest	3	2	—	(4)
	673	709	726	664
Cash flow	(123)	81	249	26
Cash beginning	16	3	4	3
Borrowing (repayment/investment)	110	(80)	(250)	(25)
Cash ending	3	4	3	4

The cash budget by months for the first quarter, not illustrated, followed the same format.

The cash budget indicates a need for short term borrowing in the first quarter, when sales and collections are low. As business quickens in the second and third quarters, a strong positive cash flow develops and the debt can be repaid with a surplus for short term investment. Provision is made for interest to be paid on the debt and earned from investment.

Using the operating and cash budgets, the budget director then produced budgeted statements of income. The quarterly statement appeared as follows:

Pricey Product Inc.
Budgeted Statement of Income
for the year 20X, by quarters
(in thousands of dollars)

	First Quarter	Second Quarter	Third Quarter	Fourth Quarter	Total
Sales	555	800	990	665	3,010
Cost of sales (standard, $60 per unit)	360	480	540	420	1,800
Gross margin	195	320	450	245	1,210
Selling expenses	153	177	189	165	684
Administration	62	68	70	64	264
Interest	3	2	—	(4)	1
	218	247	259	225	949
Profit (loss) before tax	(23)	73	191	20	261
Taxes on income	—	25	95	10	130
Net profit (loss)	(23)	48	96	10	131

The budgeted income statement indicates a loss in the first quarter with profits in the following three quarters. Based on this projection, the budget director estimated the taxes payable and calculated the net profit or loss.

Finally, the budget director produced budgeted balance sheets for the end of each quarter. He did this by starting with the balance sheet at the end of 20W and calculating the quarterly changes indicated by the operating and cash budgets. The budgeted balance sheets appeared as shown on page 292. (Assumed data at December 31, 20W have been added to help illustrate the procedure.)

Pricey Product Inc.
Budgeted Balance Sheet
for the year 20X, by quarters
(in thousands of dollars)

	Dec 31, 20W	March 31	June 30	Sept 30	Dec 31
Cash	16	3	4	3	4
Short term investments	—	—	—	220	245
Receivables	220	225	235	250	225
Raw materials	16	28	28	24	16
Finished goods	120	180	180	120	120
	372	436	447	617	610
Plant and equipment	715	755	765	765	795
Less accumulated depreciation	112	124	137	150	165
	603	631	628	615	630
Total assets	975	1,067	1,075	1,232	1,240
Loan payable	—	110	30	—	—
Accounts payable	164	169	184	180	168
Taxes payable	—	—	25	120	130
	164	279	239	300	298
Shareholders' equity	811	788	836	932	942
	975	1,067	1,075	1,232	1,240

Cash, borrowing, and investment came directly from the cash budget. Changes in receivables were calculated from sales and cash collections. Changes in raw materials and finished goods inventories were taken from the material purchase budget and calculated from the production schedule. Changes in plant and equipment came from the cash budget and from depreciation expense in the operating budgets. Changes in accounts payable were calculated from purchases, expenses, and cash payments. Changes in taxes payable and shareholders' equity came from the budgeted statement of income. (Details of the calculated changes are not provided. It is not necessary to trace through the details to understand the procedure.)

The illustration, like earlier examples, is highly simplified. There is only one product, one raw material and one productive process. Amounts have been rounded to thousands. Budgets of manufacturing overhead, selling, and administrative expenses are shown in summary form only; details of expense categories are not given. Taxes payable are accumulated, not paid in instalments as is usually the case. The balance sheet does not include any prepayments, accruals or long term debt. The illustration is simplified so that the basic principles and procedures involved are not obscured by detail. Regardless of the size or complexity of a business, the basic budgeting process is the same.

FIXED AND FLEXIBLE BUDGETS

The budgets developed in this chapter for Pricey Product are fixed budgets, often described as planning budgets. They are useful for planning and coordinating business activity but are less valuable for control purposes. All of the amounts are based on the initial budget estimates of sales quantities, prices, and timing. If the actual results prove to be different, as they invariably do to some extent, the other budget estimates will be incorrect as well. Depending on the size of the differences, the budgets will become less and less relevant for comparison with actual results, as a measure of management performance. Costs incurred to make and sell eight thousand units of product for example, cannot be compared with costs budgeted for six thousand units. For cost control purposes, flexible budgets should be used. They provide valid comparisons for costs incurred at actual levels of activity.

Many, but not all, manufacturers employ flexible budgets for production cost control. Some use fixed budgets only. Relatively few companies apply flexible budgets to selling and administrative expenses, probably because those expenses tend to vary much less with changing levels of activity.

BUDGET VARIANCES

Differences between actual and budgeted results can be analyzed in the form of variances, in the same manner as differences between actual and standard costs.

Sales Variances

There are three variances commonly calculated for sales: a price variance, a quantity variance, and a product mix variance. The price variance is a measure of the effect on profit of selling at prices different from budget. The quantity variance measures the effect of selling quantities different from budget. The mix variance measures the effect of selling products in different proportions from budget.

A difference in prices has an equal effect on profit. A difference in quantities or mix does not, because different quantities and mixes involve different costs. The effect on profit of differences in quantities and mixes is the difference in contribution margins, that is, the selling prices of the products less their variable costs. Fixed costs are not relevant because they do not change with quantity or mix. Sales variances are therefore calculated by reference to contribution margins.

The difference between total actual contribution margin and total budget contribution margin is allocated to sales variances as follows:

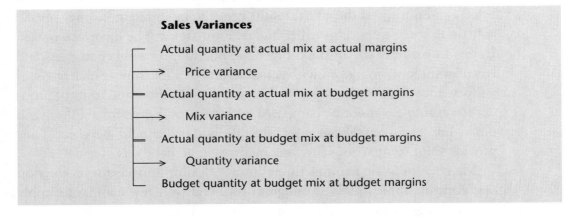

Sales Variances

Actual quantity at actual mix at actual margins

→ Price variance

Actual quantity at actual mix at budget margins

→ Mix variance

Actual quantity at budget mix at budget margins

→ Quantity variance

Budget quantity at budget mix at budget margins

Starting with actual results, the price variance is calculated first, keeping actual quantity and mix constant. The mix variance is calculated next, keeping actual quantity and budget margins constant. The quantity variance is calculated last, keeping budget mix and margins constant.

The price variance, as an alternative, can be calculated from actual and budget prices, since the difference in price has an equal effect on margin.

Positive sales variances are favorable, because they result from higher actual than budget revenues, unlike cost variances for which higher actuals are unfavorable.

Calculation of sales variances can be illustrated using data for Pricey Product Inc. Assume the company sells two kinds of whatzits, a deluxe model and an economy model. For the second quarter the company budgeted sales of 8,000 units totalling $800,000 as follows:

Budgeted					
	Deluxe		**Economy**		**Total**
Sales in units	2,000 (25%)		6,000 (75%)		8,000 (100%)
	Per Unit	**Total**	**Per Unit**	**Total**	**Total**
Sales in dollars	130	260,000	90	540,000	800,000
Variable costs	65	130,000	45	270,000	400,000
Margin	65	130,000	45	270,000	400,000

Actual sales, costs and margins were the following.

Actual					
	Deluxe		**Economy**		**Total**
Sales in units	3,000 (30%)		7,000 (70%)		10,000 (100%)
	Per Unit	**Total**	**Per Unit**	**Total**	**Total**
Sales in dollars	120	360,000	95	665,000	1,025,000
Variable costs	65	195,000	45	315,000	510,000
Margin	55	165,000	50	350,000	515,000

A. Actual quantity at actual mix at actual margins

Deluxe	3,000	(30%) × 55	165,000
Economy	7,000	(70%) × 50	350,000
	10,000		515,000

B. Actual quantity at actual mix at budget margins

Deluxe	3,000	(30%) × 65	195,000
Economy	7,000	(70%) × 45	315,000
	10,000		510,000

C. Actual quantity at budget mix at budget margins

Deluxe	2,500	(25%) × 65	162,500
Economy	7,500	(75%) × 45	337,500
	10,000		500,000

D. Budget quantity at budget mix at budget margins

Deluxe	2,000	(25%) × 65	130,000
Economy	6,000	(75%) × 45	270,000
	8,000		400,000

Price variance, (A–B)	515,000 – 510,000 =	5,000
Mix variance, (B–C)	510,000 – 500,000 =	10,000
Quantity variance, (C–D)	500,000 – 400,000 =	100,000
Total (A–D)	515,000 – 400,000 =	115,000

All variances are favorable.

The price variance could have been calculated on sales as follows:

Actual sales at actual prices

Deluxe	3,000 × 120	360,000	
Economy	7,000 × 95	665,000	
			1,025,000

Actual sales at budget prices

Deluxe	3,000 × 130	390,000	
Economy	7,000 × 90	630,000	
			1,020,000
Price variance			5,000

Cost Variances

The calculation of production cost variances using standard costs and flexible budgets was described in the previous chapter. For selling and administration expenses, the usual practice is to calculate differences between actual and budget amounts as budget or spending variances only, regardless of whether flexible or fixed budgets are used for cost control. Sometimes the budget variances are divided into price and quantity components but volume variances are not calculated.

CHAPTER 22

Internal Control

Businesses design their administrative and accounting systems to minimize the chance of errors and omissions and the risk of theft, fraud, and other illegal acts. They do this through what is called internal control. Internal control consists of maintaining adequate records and of following procedures that provide checks on the work of employees and limit the opportunities to commit improper acts by employees who might be inclined to do so. It is applied throughout the operations of a business but it has particular relevance to accounting.

An adequate system of records requires that all transactions are recorded and no fictitious transactions are included. This is accomplished in a variety of ways. Cash registers are used to ensure that all cash sales and collections are recorded, for example. Employee time cards are used to ensure that work times are valid. Documents such as cheques and purchase orders are preprinted with consecutive numbers so that none will be missed and to protect against misuse. Subsidiary ledger accounts are totalled and compared to control account balances. Accounts are reconciled with independent outside records, cash with bank statements for example, and accounts payable with monthly supplier statements. Assets, for example investment securities, inventories and equipment, are counted periodically and the amounts compared with book records.

When records are processed by computer, special checks are applied to ensure that the data input is correct. Examples are checks that the totals entered are correct, that the number of characters per entry is correct, and that the type of characters is correct, for example numeric only.

In designing procedures, responsibilities must be clearly defined and specific to individual employees or their positions. A specific individual must be responsible for a cash fund or an inventory supply room, for example.

Duties should be assigned so that different employees **authorize** or approve transactions, **record** those transactions, and **retain custody** of the related assets. For example, the purchasing department approves material purchases, the accounting department records purchases, a storekeeper retains custody of goods received, and the treasury department makes payments. No single employee controls the process of purchasing and payment, so none is in a position to misappropriate assets without it being revealed by the work of the others.

For computer systems, duties should be assigned so that different employees are responsible for **programming**, for **data processing**, and for **custody** of the data files and programs, to minimize the risk of unauthorized changes.

Employees must be qualified for their positions in terms of their competence and their reliability. In sensitive areas of asset control such as handling cash, employees are frequently bonded. A bonding company investigates the employees and provides insurance against their dishonesty.

Employees must be required to take vacations and during those times other employees are assigned to do their work. If feasible, employees should be moved between jobs periodically. An accounts receivable clerk might be moved to accounts payable for instance, or vice versa. No one person should have complete control of an activity at all times, preventing improprieties, if any, from being discovered.

In large companies it is common practice to have procedures manuals detailing the records to be maintained and the methods and procedures to be followed in the process. Many large companies also employ internal auditors, who perform independent reviews to ensure that specified procedures are being followed and the data being recorded are correct.

A well designed system of internal control can minimize the risks of fraud and error but it cannot eliminate them. If employees do not follow the procedures specified, the system will not be effective. Two or more employees acting in collusion can defeat the purpose of dividing responsibilities.

Some senior managers are in a position to override system requirements. In many small businesses there are not enough employees to permit an effective division of responsibilities. Systems and employee performance need to be monitored to ensure their effectiveness.

TRANSACTION CONTROLS

The basic transactions of a business, as described in chapter 4, Double Entry Bookkeeping, are sales, purchases, collections, payments, and payroll. Internal control systems are designed to ensure the integrity of the following groups of related transactions.

- Sales and collections
- Purchases and payments
- Payroll and payments

Sales and Collections

Control systems for credit sales are more extensive than those for cash sales because they involve creating and monitoring accounts receivable. A typical sequence of events for credit sales is the following.

Order received $\rightarrow$ credit approved $\rightarrow$ goods shipped $\rightarrow$
customer invoiced $\rightarrow$ sale and receivable recorded $\rightarrow$
cash received and recorded $\rightarrow$ cash deposited in bank

Each activity is performed by an employee independent of the others, with the exception that the accounts receivable clerk can record both the amount invoiced and the amount received, but from information provided by different sources.

The order is received and recorded on a prenumbered sales order form in the sales department and initialled by the order taker. It is sent to the credit department for approval. Approval is indicated by initial and the order is sent to the warehouse for shipment. Shipment is indicated by a further initial or by preparing a separate prenumbered shipping document and the documents are sent to invoicing. Invoicing prepares a prenumbered sales invoice and mails it to the customer. A copy of the invoice is attached to the order and shipping document and sent to accounting. Accounting records the sale and account receivable.

A mail clerk opens the incoming mail and prepares and initials a list of the cheques received. Cheques are stamped for deposit only to the account of the business. A copy of the list, together with the cheques, is sent to treasury for deposit in the bank. A second copy is sent to accounting to be recorded in the cash and accounts receivable accounts.

When sales are made for cash, the control requirement is to ensure that some form of record is made each time a sale is made, and to agree the total recorded with the cash collected, usually at the end of each day. Most cash businesses use cash registers for this purpose. In addition to producing customer receipts, the registers record and accumulate the sales data internally on tape. Many businesses employ register systems that price sales and produce sales and inventory statistics as well, from product codes.

Purchases and Payments

Purchases and payments follow a sequence such as the following.

Purchase requisition $\rightarrow$ purchase order issued $\rightarrow$ goods and invoice received $\rightarrow$ purchase and payable recorded $\rightarrow$ cash paid and recorded

As in the case of sales and collections, each activity is performed by a different employee, except that the payables clerk records both the purchase and the payment in the supplier's account.

The purchase requisition is prepared by the manager or employee authorized to incur the cost, and sent to the purchasing department. Managers have authority as described in chapter 19, Responsibility Accounting. Authority to requisition raw materials and supplies is often delegated to inventory control employees or storekeepers. The purchasing department prepares a prenumbered purchase order, specifying the description, quantity, and price of the item to be purchased, and sends it to the supplier. A copy of the purchase order is sent to accounting and a copy to receiving. Sometimes data such as prices are omitted from the receiver's copy.

When the goods are received, the receiver inspects them and records the quantity and description on a prenumbered receiving report. A copy of the report is sent to each of purchasing and accounting. If the receiving report indicates anything different from the purchase order, the purchasing department will undertake to have it corrected by the supplier.

The supplier's invoice is sent to accounting. Accounting match the invoice with the purchase order and receiving report to confirm that quantities and prices are the same. They also check the calculations. If all documents are in order, the purchase and account payable are recorded.

When payment is due, a prenumbered cheque is prepared by treasury. The cheque and supporting documents, invoice, purchase order, and receiving report, are presented to the authorized signing officer of the company. The signing officer reviews the documents, signs the cheque and stamps the invoice paid. Treasury retains the cheques for mailing and returns the documents to accounting to be recorded in payments and accounts payable. In many companies, a cheque copy is prepared along with the cheque and attached to the invoice and other documents.

Payroll and Payments

For internal control of payroll, hiring and dismissing employees, and setting wage rates, must be independent of payroll preparation, distribution, and accounting. In most medium sized and large companies, hiring and wage rates are administered by a personnel department. The personnel department authorizes the payroll department to add and delete employees and advises of changes in wage rates.

Wages are calculated in one of three ways: either as a fixed amount per week or month, as an amount per hour, the total varying with the number of hours worked, or as a rate per unit of product produced. When wages are based on hours or units, the sequence of events is as follows:

Time or production cards → wages calculated →
cheques prepared and recorded → cheques distributed

Time worked is recorded by employees on time cards, usually by means of time clocks. When wages are based on production, production cards or tickets with quantities prerecorded are issued with the material to be worked on and returned by employees with the completed work. Time and production cards are initialled by supervisors and sent to the payroll department. The payroll department calculates gross wages from time and production cards and from authorized wage rates. It then calculates tax, insurance, and other deductions, and net wages. A copy of the payroll data is sent to accounting to record wages, deductions, and payments. A second copy is sent to treasury for the preparation of cheques. Cheques accompanied by the payroll summary are presented to the authorized signing officer. When there are many employees, cheques are usually signed under the supervision of the signing officer by an employee using a mechanical cheque signer. Treasury supervises the distribution of cheques to employees. Any unclaimed cheques are retained by treasury. If they remain unclaimed for more than a short time, the reason is investigated.

For wages that are fixed in amount per week or month, the same procedures are followed, except that time or production cards are not required.

ASSET CONTROLS

In addition to transaction controls, methods and procedures are applied directly to control the assets of a business. The following are illustrations for various asset categories.

Cash

All cash receipts are deposited in bank accounts and all payments are made by cheque from those accounts, with the exception of very small payments that may be made in cash from petty cash funds. Different bank accounts are used when payments are made for special purposes such as payroll or dividends. Lump sum transfers equal to the total payroll or dividend payment are made to these accounts as required. Receipts for special purposes can be deposited to different accounts as well.

Receipts are deposited daily in full. Deposits are delivered to the bank by employees different from those who prepare the deposits. Regular comparisons are made between the original records of cash received, the deposit records, and the deposits recorded in the accounts.

Cheques are prenumbered. Unused cheques are kept in the custody of a treasury officer who has no access to cash receipts or accounting records. If cheques are spoiled, they are mutilated to make them unusable and retained so that all numbers are accounted for.

A cheque protector is used to imprint the amounts on cheques so they cannot be altered. Large cheques must be signed by two officers. Many companies require all cheques to have two signatures. If a cheque signing machine is used, it is in the custody of the authorized signing officers. Cheques are never signed by an officer in advance.

Bank reconciliations are prepared monthly by an employee independent of cash handling and recording. Bank statements with paid cheques are received directly from the bank by the employee doing the reconciliations. Paid cheques are examined for dates, signatures, and suppliers' endorsements. Cheques outstanding for extended periods of time are investigated.

Petty cash funds are used only for very small payments. Both the size of the funds and the maximum authorized payments from them are small. Funds are kept in the custody of employees having no other responsibilities for cash, and surprise counts of the funds are made from time to time.

Petty cash funds are kept by the imprest method. They are started by entrusting a fixed amount of cash to the custodian. As payments are made, the custodian obtains receipts. The total of receipts and cash remaining must always equal the original amount of cash. When the cash is almost exhausted, the custodian is issued a cheque in return for the accumulated receipts, to replace them with cash.

Employees who handle cash are bonded and have no access to other liquid assets such as investment securities.

Investments

Investment securities are either deposited with an independent custodian, such as a trust company, or are kept in a bank safe deposit box. When a safe deposit box is used, two authorized employees must together sign for access. Whenever possible, securities are registered in the name of the company.

Authority to buy and sell securities is restricted to one or two senior company officers. In most companies, approval of the board of directors is required for all but temporary investments of surplus cash.

Detailed accounting records are kept of all securities, showing certificate numbers and particulars of interest or dividend income. Periodically, securities are inspected, or confirmed with an independent custodian, and compared with accounting records. Income received is compared with accounting records.

Custody, authority to buy and sell, and accounting records are the responsibilities of different employees. Employees who handle securities are bonded.

Receivables

At the end of each month, accounts receivable are listed and the total of the subsidiary ledger is agreed with the amount shown in the general ledger control account. The list is aged to show amounts current, over 30 days, over 60 days, and over 90 days. The credit manager reviews the list to determine what action needs to be taken regarding collections. Monthly statements of account corresponding to the list are mailed to customers by the credit department and disputes, if any, are investigated.

All adjustments to accounts receivable for bad debt write-offs must be approved by the credit manager. Credits for sales returns and allowances are recorded on prenumbered credit notes and must also be approved by the credit manager. Credits for returns must be supported by receiving reports.

Inventories

Raw materials inventories are kept in locked storerooms in the custody of storekeepers. They are issued only to authorized production personnel, who must sign written requisitions. Finished goods are kept in storerooms or in warehouses in the custody of warehouse managers. They are issued or shipped only on receipt of approved sales orders.

Perpetual inventory records are kept independently of storekeepers and warehouse managers, based on purchases, production records, and sales. Perpetual records are kept for all items of significant value. Small items are controlled by periodic comparisons of quantities purchased with standard or budget estimates of normal usage.

Inventories are counted, weighed, or measured at least once per year, sometimes more frequently when close control is required. Most companies count all items at the same time but some spread the task over the year by counting approximately one twelfth of the inventory categories at the end of each month. Stocktaking is done by personnel other than custodians. Inventory counts are compared with perpetual records and significant differences are investigated.

Plant and Equipment

Plant and equipment purchases and disposals must be authorized in the capital expenditures budget. Large items are approved by the board of directors. Smaller items are approved by managers, based on their levels of authority and responsibility.

Supplies of small tools and equipment are kept in storerooms and issued to authorized personnel by requisition. Larger items of equipment are identified by numbering.

Detailed records of plant assets are maintained. Periodically an inventory of plant assets is taken and compared with the records. The total value of each category is agreed with the control accounts in the general ledger.

EQUITY CONTROLS

The obligations assumed by a business are controlled by applying procedures such as the following.

Payables

At the end of each month, the total of the individual accounts payable is agreed with the general ledger control account. Month end statements of account received from suppliers are compared with amounts shown as payable and any differences are investigated.

Short Term Debt

Authority to borrow short term is restricted to one or two senior officers, and subject to an upper limit. Notes payable and other borrowing documents require two signatures. Repaid notes are voided.

Long Term Debt and Equity

All long term debt and equity financing must be authorized and approved by the board of directors.

Large companies usually appoint an independent agent, such as a trust company, to act as registrar and transfer agent of their securities. Companies that maintain their own registers control security certificates as they would cash and investment securities. Certificates are prenumbered. Unissued certificates are kept in locked storage under the joint control of two employees. When signatures are required on certificates, there must be two signatures. Cancelled certificates are voided.

Many companies appoint independent agents to act as interest and dividend payment agents. When companies process their own interest and dividend payments, they open separate bank accounts and employ the same controls as they do for other cash payments.

Index